CROSS WALK

AN AMAZING JOURNEY OF FAITH

BY
CAROL CRUISE

Shirley ~
I hope you
are blessed by
reading how God carried
me 10,867 miles ~ God Bless you ☨
Hugs ~
Carol C

Dedicated to
Wendi Love Miller
and
Walker T.

Thank you both for your loyal companionship and steadfast service. I could not imagine the journey or this book without the two of you on my team!

ACKNOWLEDGMENTS

I would like to extend a special thanks to

Jenny Shaw, for editing the manuscript and

Molly Vignos, for the cover design.

CONTENTS

CONTENTS

CONTENTS

INTRODUCTION

THE MOST FREQUENTLY ASKED QUESTION in the past nine years of my life was: "Will there be a book?" Yes, there will be a book! This is the book—a true story about a nine-year journey of 10,467 miles on foot, literally on foot! I only have one! I begin with a story of a bridge walk because this was a journey of crossing bridges and building bridges—a prayer walk around the perimeter of the United States that took place over one of the most critical decades our nation has faced.

In this book, I share with you about physical bridges that made a way for me in the times when my faith was being tested, and spiritual bridges that carried me over troubled waters. I share about times when I found myself in situations with the Red Sea in front of me and the Egyptian army behind me. It was at those times that it took nothing less than *great* faith to part the sea, escape the adversary, and plunge forth on a mission that I tried to avoid for nine years of my life.

This is an "ashes to beauty" story of how God has taken despair, discouragement, and tragedy and worked it all out for good—in faith, encouragement, and triumph.

Until December 31, 2010, there had never been a woman or an amputee to walk the perimeter of the United States. With escorts over the James River Bridge and the York River Bridge, taking part in the Labor Day Bridge Walk over the Mackinac Bridge in Michigan, and being the only pedestrian ever to have had an escort over the Huey P. Long Bridge on Highway 190 East in Baton Rouge, Louisiana, I—a full-figured middle-aged woman, a right-leg amputee—may possibly be the only person to have ever connected every step around this nation.

I believe the only reason this mission was possible is because God ordained this walk and God carried me every step of the way.

Many names and a few towns have been changed in this book, for various reasons. But for the most part the stories are told to depict detail and accuracy of how it really was on this nine-year mission.

Now I invite you to travel with me through the pages of this book as I share my experience, hope, and strength throughout this pilgrimage; as I tell who I was, where I came from, what happened, how it affected myself and others, and where this journey has brought me.

"Testing faith produces endurance" (James 1:3 NASB).

THE JAMES RIVER BRIDGE

I T WAS ALREADY 89 DEGREES on a sultry August morning. The last thing I wanted to do was to ask six police officers to sit in their squad cars and watch me hobble across a five-mile bridge. But it was too late; the asking had been done and the request had been granted. A procession awaited my arrival at the south end of the James River Bridge, a procession that included two state police cars, two sheriff cars, two local police cars, and a vehicle provided by the Virginia Department of Transportation (VDOT).

All I could think about as I approached the bridge was the excruciating pain that I was feeling in my right knee and upper leg. I had worn my prosthetic leg to the place of no return. The foot was broken and secured to the rest of the leg with duct tape. The socket was cracked—also wrapped in duct tape. Each time I lifted the prosthesis, to take the next step, my foot would wrench as it pounded back on the road. My knee would torque in one direction as the upper leg cranked the opposite way.

I could see Deb, my advance person, waiting for me to make my way from a gas station. She had dropped me off there, at the exact place where I had ended the walk the day before. I was about one mile south of my awaiting escort.

Deb had been my pilot car driver since the beginning of the walk. When Deb was only nine years old her mother passed away. She was tossed from one family member to another. She had spent most of her life on the streets and knew how to survive out there.

For the past seven months, Deb had parked herself on the side of the road I was destined to walk. She spent long grueling days in a faded blue 1990 Geo Prism, no more than half a mile ahead of me or half a mile behind me along many abandoned roads. We meandered together up the east coast of Florida and through the lonely, rural backwoods roads of Georgia, South Carolina, North Carolina, and the southern coast of Virginia.

Deb, in poor health and in need of a total knee replacement, slowly and painfully began to limp toward me, making her way along the west side of Highway 17. I could tell by the way she was picking up her pace that she was anxious for me to cross the five-mile bridge. When I caught up with Deb, I was in tears from the intensity of the pain.

"I don't think I can do this, Deb!" I said.

"You can, Carol—you have to! You can't back down now!"

"The pain!" I sobbed.

"You can do this, Carol!" she asserted. "God will carry you!"

As I wiped the tears from my cheeks, a young woman with her little girl approached me. She asked if I would allow her to take a picture of me with her daughter. She explained to me that they

2

had been inspired by an article about my walk in their local newspaper. She had hoped she would be able to meet up with me before I crossed the bridge. I forgot about the pain for a few moments as I embraced the little girl and posed for a picture with them.

I pulled Deb aside to revoice my concern about the amount of pain that I was experiencing.

"I can't do the bridge walk," I said.

"You need to draw strength from your faith," she reminded me. "God will carry you across that bridge."

"Are you ready to proceed?" a VDOT representative asked me. Reluctantly, I nodded.

Deb pointed to an officer and I followed him to my place in the formation. I had three squad cars ahead of me and three cars behind me. The VDOT truck was bringing up the rear with a large yellow arrow directing all of the northbound traffic to the inside lane for the duration of the escort. The outside lane had been completely closed off to traffic for my crossing.

I approached the police car and handed a bottle of cold water to the officer who was driving. I told him that I would have to stop about every mile to dry my leg and sip some water. He nodded and we began to cross.

MILE 1

I couldn't see the other side of the bridge as I set forth from the south end. My head was filled with memories of the preceding months. I thought back to the day I stood before about 200 of my peers and announced that I was taking this walk. Most of them thought I was crazy and asked me to reconsider. I told them to take it up with God because I knew without a shadow of a doubt that I was called to this pilgrimage.

3

It all started when I lost my leg as a result of an injury in an unnecessary surgery. My surgeon attempted to insert a tibial rod in what he diagnosed as a nonunion. The surgeon didn't irrigate properly during the reaming process, which resulted in a burn from inside the bone to the flesh that was being tightly held by his gloved hand.

I underwent 13 additional surgeries that included: debriding (a cutting away of dead tissue) of the wound, a muscle flap from the back of the leg to the front, skin grafts, bone grafts, installation of a halo type fixator (an apparatus that is placed on the outside of the leg with pins through the ankle and the knee to stabilize the bone, and looks like an erector set), removal of the rod, removal of the fixator, and more debriding. I fought a three-year battle, which included over 300 days of hospitalization. I had contracted about every type of infection one could get from a hospital environment. Finally, the infection had spread to the point where I had to make a decision to choose my leg or my life.

By then, my right leg was a mangled mess and was three inches shorter than my left leg. I reviewed the strategies of the past three years in the battle to save my limb. Determined to win this war, I chose my life. An artificial limb would certainly be an improvement over the botched mess I had fought so hard to save. It was definitely time for a different course of action.

The surgeon wanted to remove the leg above the knee because there were only about two inches below the knee that was not damaged. I was informed, if I chose to keep that short stump, I would have to use crutches, a walker, or a wheelchair, for the rest of my life, because the stump would be too short to maneuver a prosthetic leg. I chose to keep the short little stump.

The date was set, December 9, 1992. I arrived at the Cleveland Clinic at 6:00 a.m. to be prepped for the scheduled 8:00 a.m. surgery.

The night before my leg was amputated, I spent some time alone. I rubbed my right foot and gave it a pedicure. I thanked God for the 38 years I was blessed to have my limb, and I asked God to use me as an amputee in ways He could not use me with two legs.

Just weeks after the amputation, I began to speak in schools to sixth and eighth graders about differently-abled people, in hopes of changing some of the prejudices people have toward so-called handicapped people. If my presentations could prevent just one person from being subjected to abuse, it would give some purpose to having lost my leg.

I was walking, but not very well. Definitely not well enough to walk around the country. In fact, I could barely walk the length of a mall. Often times, I would have to have someone get a wheelchair for me so I could get from one end of the store to the other.

In July of 1993 I met an amputee named Jimmy who was planning to walk across the country in hopes of drawing awareness to American veterans with disabilities. He needed a pilot car driver. I was available and agreed to travel to California with him in an effort to support his trek across our country from San Diego to Washington D.C. where he would lobby for better benefits for veterans.

We traveled to San Diego, but Jimmy did not get the sponsorship he wanted so he chose to abort his mission. I tried to encourage him to walk by faith. After all, we sold T-shirts to fund our way from Akron, Ohio, to San Diego, California. Even though we sold enough shirts to meet the needs of each day,

I couldn't convince him to walk by faith, so we traveled back to Ohio.

After I returned home, several people told me that Jimmy was never meant to do the walk, but they believed God wanted me to do a faith walk. I didn't give much thought to what was said since I still wasn't walking very well.

A few weeks later I woke up in the wee hours of the morning with a call on my heart, a strong compelling to do a prayer walk for God. I shook it off and thought that this compelling had happened simply because a few people had suggested the idea to me, which had planted a seed in my brain and my thoughts were working overtime. A few months later the same thing happened. After a year or two, it began happening a couple times a month. This went on for years. It was beginning to happen every week—some time between 3:00 and 4:00 a.m., I would abruptly wake up with this sense that God was calling me to walk the nation and claim it back for Him and His ways.

By the end of 2000, it was clear to me that I was being called to a twofold ministry. God was asking me to do a prayer walk around our nation, to claim this nation back for Him, and to encourage differently-abled people to look at their God-given abilities.

I figured if I was going to have any peace, and if I was going to get any rest, I had better start walking.

"If that is you, God, and you want me to do this walk, you are going to have to carry me because I do not walk very well!" I prayed. "But yes, God, send me; I will walk!"

My walking had improved somewhat. I had a significant limp, a very short gait, and an extremely slow stride, but hey, I was walking!

I spent 14 months preparing for this journey. I downsized from a large home to a smaller home, to a park model camper. I sold things, gave things away, and downsized again into a 31-foot motor home. I walked up and down hills at the campground where I was staying. I started out walking one mile a day, then two miles, then three miles a day. Finally, I was walking three miles three times a day. My goal was to be able to walk 50 miles a week. I would try to get 10 miles a day in, Monday through Friday, and use Saturday for a catch-up day to make up for the times I would fall short of my 10-mile goal.

In October of 2001, I saw my doctor for a routine physical exam. I was referred to a gynecologist because I was experiencing abnormal menstrual cycles with excessive bleeding. After a visit to the specialist and a series of lab work, it was determined that I had very extensive endometriosis and I should undergo a radical hysterectomy as soon as possible. October 16th was the earliest I could schedule the surgery. I was committed to starting the walk on January 1st, 2002, barely 10 weeks after the operation. My faith was being tested, but I was determined to pass the test.

My parents had scheduled to take me on an 11-day cruise, to embark on December 3rd. I asked my doctor to okay the trip. The surgeon agreed only if I followed all of his post-op instructions. I was determined, so I followed his advice. I was not permitted to walk any farther than to the mailbox and back for at least six weeks after my surgery. It seemed like all the training I had done was in vain. I would be in no shape to walk 50 miles a week.

We set sail on the *Celebrity Summit* from Fort Lauderdale at 3:00 in the afternoon and visited eight different ports of call throughout the Caribbean Islands, the Mexican Islands, and Central and South America. I walked about half a mile each day; that was all I was up to doing. I avoided all of the excursions that required the slightest amount of exertion. I spent most of the days soaking in the sun pool-side, and peering from the ship to see all that I could.

Debarkation was only 17 days from when I was to begin to walk the perimeter of our country. The task at hand was more than I could fathom.

The intensity of the heat broke my reverie and brought me back to the walk. I had walked about a mile and I needed to sit down to dry my leg and drink some water. I glanced around and noticed the officers were suffering in the heat as well. Creeping at less than two miles per hour, they had turned their air conditioners off to save their engines. I watched as they wiped perspiration from their brows and necks. I was in agony and so were they. With the intense sun reflecting off the concrete and the water surrounding us, it felt at least100 degrees on the bridge.

I sat down on the side of the road, took off my prosthetic leg, and wiped the perspiration off my stump. It was drenched; I actually poured sweat from the liner. I got up, placed a cross on the side of the bridge, and reached into the squad car for my water bottle.

I felt so much compassion for the officers. I could only imagine what they were going through and what their thoughts might be. We were only one-fifth of the way across the bridge. I wasted no time in getting back to the walk.

MILE 2

My gait was short and my stride was slow. I was doing the best I could, and as my little cousin, Lucy, once said, "I'm going just as fastest as I can!" It was not fast enough for me, and it was not fast enough for them, but it was all I could do.

I had to keep my thoughts off of the walk. I thought about my parents taking me on the cruise. It was great to have their support. Earlier in my life, my family had not been very close. I grew up in the midst of a lot of chaos, conflict, and division.

I am the oldest of six siblings. My parents were teens in love, when I was conceived. It was referred to, back then, as "getting in trouble." My father was a tall handsome football player with auburn hair. He got his height from his mother and he was stocky like his father. He dropped out of high school when he was a senior to marry my mother, just six months before I was born.

Mom was a petite woman of 5'2" and most of her life, until her forties, she had a hard time reaching 100 pounds. She was brought up in a blue-collar neighborhood with hard working parents and four siblings. She finished her education at the end of ninth grade.

I was brought up in an atmosphere of total mayhem. My parents were much too young to be raising six kids. They were barely 27 by the time their youngest child was born, and were not much more than kids themselves. They had very little support from their parents and the responsibilities overwhelmed them. My folks were constantly quarrelling while all six kids were competing for their love and attention.

Often, in the heat of their discussions, my parents would refer to me as a *mistake.* "If it weren't for *that kid*, I would not have married you!" "If we had not gotten into *trouble,* this marriage would have never happened!"—were phrases I often heard. Needless to say, I developed poor self-esteem; after all, I was *that kid, trouble*, and *the mistake* to whom they were referring. I grew up believing I was never wanted and I was the reason for all of the unhappiness in our home.

9

I was not quite a year old when my mother gave birth to my brother, Ken. He was born with cerebral palsy and developed asthma as an infant. He had pneumonia six times before he was a year old. When she went into labor with him, I was literally dropped off at a doorstep at my great aunt and uncle's home. I screamed when Dad tried to hand me over to the strangers, so in desperation, he sat me down on their front stoop and drove off to the hospital barely in time for mom to deliver.

Mama Jo and Daddy Jack, the names I would later give this great aunt and uncle, recalled that they stood and watched me as I sat on the stoop that day. They said I fed crackers to their German shepherd and seemed to be babbling to an invisible friend. I believe this was probably my first communication with God.

I am not sure where I ever heard about God, because it sure wasn't in my home. My Dad didn't seem to believe in God, and my Mom said she believed she *got saved* as a child, but the only time she mentioned Him was in a fit of anger. We sometimes went to church on Easter Sunday and for weddings and funerals, but for the most part, my parents were unchurched. The only time I heard about God or Jesus in our home was when His name was being used in vain.

From the time I was very young I was fascinated with church and I always knew it was a house of God. I would go to church with anyone who would take me. When I was eight years old, I rode a bus to a local assembly on Sundays. That spring, the pastor promised to give a Bible to the person who brought the most guests to the Easter service. I invited everybody I saw. I even knocked on doors in our neighborhood and invited strangers. Sure enough, I won my first Bible. Its cover was burgundy-colored and I will never forget the smell of the fresh printed pages of this cherished prize.

My brother Ken's pediatrician was concerned for Ken's health and recommended that we move to a milder climate. So my parents, just teenagers, packed up everything we had and moved to California with two children under the age of two.

Ken's health improved, but my parents missed their families and became homesick. After a year in California, we moved back to Ravenna, Ohio, and my Dad secured employment as a construction worker. Ken needed annual surgeries to stretch the ligaments in his left leg, and he still had asthma severe enough to need frequent hospital stays. We would catch a bus to the Rainbow Children's Hospital in Cleveland, Ohio, on a regular basis.

My parents didn't have health insurance and the medical bills were overwhelming. Not being able to afford to purchase a house, my parents rented. It seemed like we were constantly moving from one rental to another and we were moved from one school district to another. When I was in second grade, we relocated three times and I attended three different schools.

A lot was required of me as the eldest child. By the time I was six, I had three siblings, five-year-old Ken, one-year-old Helen, and a baby brother named Andy. I had become a little housewife. I mopped and waxed floors, scrubbed toilets, cooked meals, and diapered and fed babies.

In 1962, when I was eight, my mom brought home baby number five, a little boy named Danny. She handed him to me and said that he was my baby. While my friends were playing with dolls, I was raising a son. A year and a half later, Margie was born.

We lived in Kent, Ohio, for two years, my fourth and fifth years of school. I had paper routes to help with the family's expenses—after all, I had a little boy to raise. I had about 70 customers for weekday delivery and almost 200 on my Sunday route. Each day I would walk by Kent State University to deliver the *Record Courier* to local residents and businesses. I remember gazing at the university and hoping to attend there someday. I knew it was a place of higher learning and I wanted to learn about what makes little girls hurt so much.

By the time my parents finally purchased a house, I was 11 years old, had moved 10 times, and would be attending my sixth school. I spent a lot of time staying with different relatives. Mama Jo and Daddy Jack were like second parents to me and my dad's parents' farm was my second home.

My paternal grandmother had become my primary source of stability. She had reared two sons but had always wanted a daughter. Even though she was extremely bothered by my father's teen marriage to my expecting mother, she was delighted when I was born a girl.

At age 38, she did not want to be called "Grandma," so she coached me into calling her Sharlie. Her name was Charlotte. But we spelled Sharlie with an *S* so it wouldn't be mistaken for Charlie. I became the daughter my grandma never had.

Sharlie, a classy woman, was 5'10" with perfect posture. She had beautiful red hair which reminded me of Lucille Ball. Lightly perfumed with a creamy complexion, she always looked like she just stepped out of a salon. Whenever I was with her, she dressed me up in the finest children's apparel and insisted this wardrobe be kept at her house.

Sharlie was well-educated and she and her family had been historically involved at Kent State University. Her father helped build the institution and is the person responsible for placing the big rock out in front of the campus, which is known for the graffiti painted by KSU students, since the beginning of the establishment.

Her grandfather was a construction worker who assisted on laying the cornerstone in the foundation of Merrill Hall. A campus legend and an institution in his own right, he was one of the original nonteaching staff and eventually became the first baseball, basketball, and football coach.

Education was important to Sharlie. When my father dropped out of school to marry my mother, it became a source of contention between her and my parents that would remain throughout their lives.

Sharlie was the secretary at the attorney general's office in Ravenna, Ohio, the county seat of Portage County. She worked in a spacious office and always drove a newer model sports car. Her wardrobe included only name-brand clothing from the finest dress shops.

I spent as much time with my grandmother as my parents would allow. I was served fancy meals and I had steak any time I wanted. Sharlie exposed me to the finer things in life: art, theater, poetry, and classical music. She golfed; I caddied. She bowled; I watched. She played an organ and a violin. I developed a love for music. She taught me to knit. And, she took me to the Lutheran church where she belonged, which was where I began to learn more about God.

I was her princess. We went on shopping trips, visited spas, and I even traveled with her. We stayed in fine hotels and ate in some of the best restaurants. My grandmother taught me etiquette, including how to properly use silverware and how to tip servers and housekeeping.

My grandfather, Papa, was a cattle farmer and owned a sand and gravel business. He was one of 13 children. He was raised by two very humble and modest parents. I think he may have completed eighth grade. At a young age, he purchased 165 acres from

Sharlie's parents and began farming cattle in the front half of his farm, with pastures and hay fields, and ran the sand and gravel plant on the back 40.

Papa was a hardworking man who exhibited no class whatsoever. He was a self-made millionaire by the time he passed away, but I have no memory of him ever enjoying his wealth, at least not sober. He was built like a rock, a stocky man with a red complexion and he began balding in his early thirties. Papa had a severe drinking problem and he could be quite abusive when drunk.

I had a love-hate relationship with Papa. I loved him when he was sober. He would tell jokes and was a fun-loving grandpa. I hated him when he was drunk because he would emotionally and physically abuse my grandmother. I would sometimes be the victim of his drunken indiscretions, when boundaries became blurred with what was appropriate and what was inappropriate.

Though they resided in the same house, my grandparents had separate bedrooms. Sharlie lived her life, and Papa lived his.

Life with my parents was like living on a whole different planet from the fantasy world I lived out with Sharlie. We lived on a three-acre minifarm on Limeridge Road in Freedom, Township, Ohio. It was surrounded by sweet corn and potato farms, with a labor camp right next door that housed seasonal Mexican migrant workers.

My siblings and I made friends with the migrant workers' children and the other poor kids in the area. Our clothes were purchased at department stores and we wore them until they were at least two sizes too small, tattered and torn, weathered and worn. I had the responsibilities of a 30-year-old house wife with household chores and taking care of my younger siblings.

14

Even though Dad made a pretty fair wage as a crane operator for a large construction firm, it was not enough to support a family of eight. With Ken's need for surgeries every couple of years, three kids with asthma, broken bones, childhood illnesses, and hospital expenses for eight births (two stillborn), hospital and doctor bills were bigger than the house mortgage. My parents barely made it from paycheck to paycheck. Things were tough.

My dad would leave for work at 6:00 a.m. and not get home until after 6:00 p.m. He came home tired and hungry and was greeted by my mother who was overwhelmed and ready to share the problems of the day. Dad, tired after a long 12-hour day, wanted to keep my mom happy, so he took off his belt and took care of business. His irritations were taken out on the hides of his kids.

My mother was lonely and had made me her confidant from the time I was about nine years old. She would share the details of the family struggles: marital, financial, and social. I would stay up late at night to keep her company and console her, the best I could.

With the demands my mom put on me and the anger my dad took out on me, I couldn't take it anymore. When I was 11 years old I decided to leave home. I shared this with Ken who was fed up with our home life as well, so he agreed to join me.

Late one night after everyone went to sleep, Ken and I wrote a note to our parents letting them know just what we thought of our home life. Then we ran down Limeridge Road. We threw ourselves in ditches every time a car would pass, to keep from being seen. We made it about a mile from home and hid out in an old barn behind a farm house that was being used for a labor camp by one of the local potato farmers.

Soon after we thought we were safely tucked away in the hay loft, two teen-aged migrant workers climbed the ladder and asked us what we were up to. We told them that we ran away from home. The younger of the two, about 14 years old, asked Ken if he wanted to go out in the night and explore. Ken left with the boy and I was left alone with a much older young man, who was probably 18 or 19 years old. He threw me down and asked me if I was a virgin, a naive farm girl, I wasn't even sure what that meant. "Yes!" I replied, hoping it was the right answer. He told me he was a virgin killer, tore my clothes off of me, and raped me.

By the time Ken returned, the rapist had left the scene. I held my torn shirt around me and wept silently. Apparently Ken thought I was sleeping and settled not far from me and went to sleep. I stayed awake all night and prayed. I felt dirty and violated and I was afraid and ashamed. I prayed that no one would ever know what happened. Even though the man tore my clothes off, forced himself on me, and left me half naked and bleeding, somehow I felt like it was my fault.

Early the next morning the father of the two boys climbed the ladder and told us that if we did not go home he would call our parents. Scared by the threat, we ran all the way home hoping we would get to the note before our parents read it. We didn't make it. My mother was furious and screamed for our father to beat the living tar out of us. After we were whipped with a belt, we were told we were not allowed to get any sleep that day because we had no business staying up all night.

I hid behind an old oak tree where I sobbed until I dozed off to sleep. I was abruptly awakened by my father spraying me with water from the garden hose. I was forced to stay awake all day. I wanted to disappear or, better yet, die!

I didn't tell anyone what happened to me. I was afraid if my parents found out they would beat the life out of me and send me off to some girls' school. I prayed for months that I would not get pregnant.

◊ ◊ ◊

My sisters and brothers were my life. So I stayed focused on trying to help parent them. I worried about their welfare and what should happen to them if my parents were not able to survive their marriage. I washed and ironed clothes, cleaned house, gave the four youngest their baths every night. I cooked most of the meals and packed lunches.

The summer I turned 12, I got a job on the farm that surrounded our home. I felt so grown up! I was making minimum wage, paying social security and government taxes. Even though I had paper routes from age nine, which I considered kid's work, I felt like I was finally gainfully employed.

I divided my pay in envelopes and stored them in a little tin box. I had an envelope for short-term savings, for needs I might have in the winter months, when my only income would be fifty cents an hour from babysitting jobs. Another envelope contained my long-term savings, to hopefully one day fund an education at Kent State University. I had bill money, gift money, and tithe money.

School was difficult, especially in what was then called "junior high." With the stress and worries of my home life, I had trouble concentrating in school and with the responsibilities I had at home, I was not able to complete my homework or study for tests. My grades were a reflection of my home life—poor.

17

Letters were sent home to my parents from grammar school through high school about how my absentee record was affecting my grades. School counselors requested appointments with my mother to discuss the struggles I was having with school because of the number of days I had missed. Mom refused to talk with teachers, principals, or guidance counselors. As far as she was concerned, she was a good mother—her kids were the problem. It seemed like she sent us off to school for no other reason than to be free from the responsibility for eight hours a day.

I was able to maintain grades just slightly below average through middle school. I struggled my freshman year and by the time I was a sophomore, the principal suggested I be placed in a class for students with learning disabilities. I struggled with words all through school and I knew my brain did not work the same as other people's, and I had come to the conclusion that I was just plain stupid, a failure, someone who would never amount to a hill of beans. I began to see myself as the labels I had been given by others.

I was embarrassed to think of being placed in the classroom with the dummies and losers, unfortunately that is the stigma attached to such placement. I was afraid my dad would beat me if I was placed in that class and I believed it would give both of my parents more reason not to love me.

I pleaded with the guidance counselor to allow me to continue with standard courses. After giving me an IQ test which showed that I was of average intelligence, he assured me that I could do well in school if I applied myself and agreed to keep me in mainstream educational classes. He also told me I could go to college if I put mind to it—a seed was planted!

I began staying up late at night reading and studying. I read the Bible and memorized Scripture, thinking God would honor that. I prayed to Him for help with my school work and help with

18

the struggle I had with words and speech. I pleaded with Him to make me a smarter person.

My prayers were answered—my grades improved. I was blessed to have teachers who cared and encouraged me in my school work with positive feedback every time I turned in average or above-average work. The positive feedback was all I needed to believe I could make it through school. I took college prep classes my junior and senior years and made honor roll every grading period. It is amazing how our lives can change if we are able to reprogram our thinking from negative to positive.

At this time, I attended an evangelical church with some neighbors. It was the time with the youth group, and my faith, that kept me from dropping out of school my sophomore year. I survived my childhood on my innate moral standards and through my relationship with God.

MILE 3

I dropped cross #2, as I sat down on the road to dry my stump. I had developed some hot spots and I was concerned that I would get blisters. Knowing how exhausted they must be, I could not bear to look in the eyes of my escorts. I walked over to the car, and reached in for the water bottle, swallowed down some water, tossed the bottle back on the seat, and took off walking, once again, "as fastest as I can!"

My thoughts drifted back to the spiritual struggles I had, as I was getting ready to step forth in this call on my life. Someone asked if I was feeling excited. I didn't feel the excitement one would expect to feel at the commencement of such a feat. I was anxious to see what God was going to do, as I ventured forth in faith, and I was excited to see how He would provide.

It took my faith and all of the courage I could muster to move forth in this journey. Months back, while I was walking the roads of the campground, my pilot car driver, Deb, began to question my sanity and test my faith.

"You have gotten rid of everything, Carol—how do you expect to live out there?" she asked.

"I don't know!" I exclaimed.

I walked and prayed, "God, how will I make it out there?"

After some time with God, and pondering His Word, I came back to report, "Glory money. I will live on glory money!"

"And what is glory money?" she asked.

"My God will provide all of my needs according to His riches in Glory!" I quoted Philippians 3:19.

"Okay then, are you going to eat this glory money?" she asked.

"I don't know! Let me ask God?"

Once again, I walked, prayed, and listened.

"I am going to eat steak!"

"What?"

"Steak, Psalm 50:10 says, 'God owns the cattle on a thousand hills!' I'm working for Him, He is my provider, so I am going to eat steak!"

"All right then, what about Nubby?" Deb blurted. Nubby is the nickname that had been given to my residual limb. Deb was concerned for me, because I had been hospitalized on several occasions, with a reoccurring staph infection on my stump. The infection was supposedly caused from *overdoing it,* in mediocre tasks like walking the stretch of a mall, doing lawn work, helping a friend move, or even doing nothing but a few household chores. The infections were severe enough to have me declared permanently and totally disabled.

Deb had seemingly valid concerns, but I was called to walk in great faith, which could not waiver because of her fears.

"My stump is fine when I walk for God!" I explained. Then I took my prosthesis off, after walking three miles, and exhibited the healthy, pink stump.

"I can do all things through Christ who strengthens me."
Philippians 4:13 NKJV

Besides being burdened with Deb's fears, I had my own apprehensions. I had to get my affairs in order and address some issues.

I was prideful. I never really thought I could trust or depend on anyone for financial security. So I prided myself in being as independent and self-sufficient as possible. It was difficult for me to think of relying on others for anything, and I knew God was going to use others to provide everything for me on this walk. I had to swallow my pride and cast my cares on God, Who cares for me. Besides that, "God opposes arrogant people, but he is kind to humble people" (James 4:6 GW).

I was also concerned about my witness. I was called to walk the nation and pray for unity, yet there was so much division and hostility in my own family.

◊ ◊ ◊

On July 9th, 2001, I attended Papa's funeral. My dad's eyes were swollen from crying as he gazed down at a stranger. He had been estranged from his parents for over 20 years and didn't even know the man in the casket. There had been two occasions in my life

21

when I had been away from my family for 10 years at a time, and my daughter and I were straying apart.

I had learned about generational curses in Bible school and I was convinced we had a few curses to contend with in our family. I said a prayer and walked over to my dad.

"I am not going to view the body of a stranger called Dad or have you look at a stranger known as your daughter someday, after one of us passes on. I would like to make peace and put this curse to an end!" I pleaded.

I gave my dad a hug.

"I love you," I said. "Forgive me for the times I wasn't there. From now on, I'm going to be the best daughter I can. And, I will do everything in my power to maintain a relationship with you."

My dad reached down and hugged me.

"I love you, Carol."

I smiled at him, wiped the tears from his cheeks, and walked away to find my daughter; she needed a hug too.

It was my forty-sixth birthday. After gathering with the family at Sharlie's house, I went to play miniature golf with my daughter and son-in-law. I was on my way to building better relationships with my family.

My daughter, Laurie, who had been subjected to abuse by her father and had abandonment issues from my absence, was suffering through her own issues. I did not want to be away from her while she worked through the horror and neglect of her own childhood. The thought of leaving her to pursue this faith walk was eating me up.

I stood before a pastor friend, after a church service, where she had preached, in Louisville, Kentucky, and told her that I would like for her to join me in prayer for Laurie.

"And, how many times are you going to take this concern before God?" she asked.

"As many times as it takes!" I replied.

"You have to walk in that faith of yours, Carol! You have to walk as though your daughter will be okay."

I knew I had to do this walk and I had to put my daughter's healing in God's hands.

◊ ◊ ◊

Another of my biggest concerns was snakes. I was terrified of snakes. My brothers used to throw them on me when we were kids and I developed a crippling fear of them. I would not go anywhere where I thought I might see one of these reptiles. I was so afraid of snakes that if someone told me they had seen one at their house 10 years before, I would vow never to visit them, ever! I was sure I would see thousands of snakes on the perimeter of the United States, especially near the water and certainly in the South.

I prayed for God to give me victory over this fear. One day in October, a few months before the walk began; I was traveling home from a speaking engagement in Allentown, Pennsylvania, when I stopped at a park to take a walk. About 100 feet into my stroll, I thought I saw a shiny black stick lying on the ground just a few feet to the right of me.

I looked over and saw the stick looking back at me. It was a four-foot-long black snake. My first impulse was to scream and run the other way, but I felt a tremendous peace instead. I watched that snake slowly slither away and I continued on the hike. That was a miracle! The second miracle is that I came back down that same trail! God had given me victory over this fear. I was ready for my assignment.

23

On January 1st, 2002, at 3:00 p.m., 30 of my friends and family members gathered with me on the most southern point of South Beach, Miami, Florida. We stood in a circle and prayed for our country and for this mission. A minister friend, Deanna, sang a song, *Walk by Faith, Not by Sight*. I planted a four-foot cross and headed north with both of my parents and about five friends at my side. I did not notice it but others did—a sky writer wrote "God is Great" right over where I was walking.

Later, Deb told me she was praying that I would not look over my left shoulder, when I was walking along a hedge of bushes, as I headed toward my designated starting point; because there was a very long snake slithering on the bushes right beside me, at shoulder's height; the reptile seemed to be purposefully positioned. Was it there to tease, to taunt, or perhaps to torture? Woman and reptile, shoulder to shoulder—Deb said this sent shivers down her spine.

"It was like seeing the age-old war between darkness and light!" she commented. "And it was taking place right before my eyes!"

She did not want me to notice; she knew I hated snakes and she was concerned that I would abandon my mission if I had noticed the serpent. At that point in my faith walk, she may have been right on! As I look back, I am so glad that I kept my eye on the goal that day.

I thought about the day ahead as I labored through the deep sand along the shore. Concerned about scar tissue that could form if I would try to do too much, too soon, after my hysterectomy, I took heed to what my doctor warned about, trying to walk 10 miles the first day. I decided to go for six.

By the time I had walked three or four miles, my friend, Jerry was the only one left walking with me. As we completed the sixth mile, we turned to get in the pilot vehicle and I noticed the car parked beside us had JESUS LOVES YOU written in big letters across the back window. It was refreshing to know I was on the right track.

The days were long, back in the beginning of this journey. It took me 12 to 14 hours to trudge through the 6 to 10 miles a day. As I walked, I left a cross each mile with a tag which read:

If you find this cross in your hands please *don't throw it away! Please pass it on to someone to the west of you [this was to be changed to the south, when we walked across the north, to the east when we walked the west coast, and to the north when we walked the south. I did it like this so the crosses would be passed throughout the United States], and tell that person that "God loves you!" Ask that person to pass the cross on and keep it going. These crosses are placed in the ground as, I, a right-leg amputee, walk around the perimeter of the United States and pray for our country. As I walk, I encourage differently-abled people to focus on their God-given abilities, not their disabilities. I would appreciate hearing from you if you have passed the cross and the Word of God's Love.*

All of my contact information was printed on the backside of the tags.

The crosses were being used to stake out this country for God, as I walked and prayed for our nation and for the church at large.

There were three prayers that I prayed often, and I walked in faith that God would hear these prayers, and have mercy on this country, which was founded on His principles.

25

I prayed that we would get beyond the idea that the church is a building. According to the Bible, the church is the people! I prayed that the people would be the church to the nation, by revealing the fruit of God's Spirit, and the love of God, by living lives full of, "love, joy, peace, patience, kindness, goodness, faithfulness, gentleness, and self-control" (Galatians 5:22 NLT).

I prayed from 2 Chronicles 7:14 that God's people would humble themselves and pray and seek His face and turn from their wicked ways, so He would hear from heaven and forgive our sins and heal our land.

I prayed that we could be a part of answering Jesus' prayer, as recorded in John 17:20. Jesus prayed to God, that we would be one with each other, as He and God are one. Jesus' plea to God was for unity among the believers.

There is so much division in our homes, our families, our communities, our counties, our states, and our country. Because He gave us a free will, God cannot answer His Son's prayer without the cooperation of His children, you and I. "So then, let us aim for harmony in the church and try to build each other up" (Romans 14:10 NLT).

Remember, united we stand, divided we fall! I pray that the unity among His people begins in our homes, our congregations, our work places, and our communities. I pray that Jesus' prayer to God is answered by His people living and loving together.

MILE 4

I was over halfway across the bridge, where I could see the other side. There was light at the end of the tunnel. Blisters had formed on my stump, I could feel my face baking from the sun's rays. The temperature had risen to the high nineties, with high humidity.

I am sure the heat index was well over 120 degrees. I could not go forth in my own power, so I relied on Christ, who gives me strength (Philippians 4:13).

I slipped to the ground as I was dropping the third cross. As I dried my stump, I could see the officer was holding the water bottle out the window. I quickly grabbed the bottle and took a swig of the very warm water. I was feeling extremely dehydrated. I was praying that the six officers and the person driving the VDOT truck had enough liquid to sustain them, for at least another hour.

As I pushed forward, I could hardly believe this was really happening. It was just a week before when I had visited the district office of the Virginia Department of Transportation, in Elizabeth City.

After I had studied the maps, I realized I would not be able to continue north along the coast. Toll Road 13 extends an excess of 20 miles over and under the Chesapeake Bay, and there is no way a pedestrian could survive the tunnels with the carbon monoxide. I had to find another way to cross the waterway.

I discovered three places to cross the water, two major routes, Interstate 64 or 564, which both have tunnels, and Highway 17 which crosses the James River, probably the best bet. I had no idea that the bridge spanned five miles and had no shoulder, with traffic traveling in excess of 55 miles per hour. I only knew that if I was not able to cross that bridge, I would have to walk eastward to Hopewell, just outside of Richmond, which would add about 100 miles to the trip.

I walked into the VDOT office and asked to speak with whoever might have the decision-making authority, over the jurisdiction of the James River Bridge. I was referred to William A. Key, who assured me that someone would be there to drive me over the bridge. I told him, "That is not an option! This is a prayer walk

27

and it is important to me and I believe it is important to God, that every step is connected."

He said that if I got the police department from Newport News, north of the bridge and the sheriff's department from Currituck County, south of the bridge, and the Virginia State Police, to coordinate an escort across the bridge, in alignment with the local department of transportation, and submitted my request to the Commonwealth of Virginia Department of Transportation that, maybe, something could be worked out.

I walked out of there thinking I was just told "No." I looked up and said, "God, I know you are in the business of opening doors—if this is the way you want me to go, you are going to have to open the bridge!" That was July 26th. I submitted my request that very day, and began making phone calls to the law enforcement offices. By July 30th, I was granted written permission to cross the bridge, on August 1st, as long as I was willing to follow the "Special Provisions" as outlined in the letter of approval.

Special Provisions

1. Marked police vehicle escorts with blue flashing lights will be required for this crossing, providing traffic control. A minimum of two police vehicles will trail the walker and the pilot vehicle in front of the walker. However, it is highly recommended that the third escort vehicle in front of the walker be a marked police vehicle. I have attached excerpts from our *Work Area Protection Manual* of a mobile operation on a four-lane roadway, which outlines the spacing of the vehicles. This support should be solicited from isle of Wight County, City of Newport News, and/or Virginia State Police.

2. Crossing time will be restricted to Thursday, August 1, 2002, 9:00 a.m. to 3:00 p.m.

28

3. The walker is required to wear a reflective safety vest and stay to the right side of the roadway while crossing.

4. Notify the office of Mr. Mike Dangerfield, facility manager, one hour prior to crossing and once clear of the bridge.

Well, the answer was not "No!", and apparently this is the way God intended this walk to go! The walk started promptly at 11:00 that morning with the blessings of Mr. Dangerfield. There were three cars, meeting the minimum of two, behind me, with three police cars, instead of one pilot car, leading the procession. All of that and the safety vehicle of the Virginia Department of Transportation following with the big arrow pointing traffic to the left.

Yes, this was all happening and I was shaking my head in wonderment!

I was about halfway through the fourth mile and I felt the blisters breaking inside my liner. By now I knew that my nose and ears were sunburned. The heat was almost intolerable, and I was feeling extremely dehydrated. I wasn't sure I would make it to the other side without having a heat stroke. I needed purpose in the walk. I thought of meaningful moments along the journey.

The Pink Ribbon

My mind drifted back to January 3rd, which was the third day of this walk around the perimeter of the US. I was walking with Deb and our friend Jerry. We were just a few miles into the day's walk. Jerry, a thin, fair man in his forties, who had been a runner for years, was walking at a much faster pace than I was able to hobble. I followed about 100 feet behind Jerry with Deb, 20 feet or so behind me.

We were walking on a very narrow sidewalk near the beach, in Broward County, three miles north of the Dade County line.

I looked down and saw a pink strap on the sidewalk. It appeared as though it had fallen off of a dress or something, perhaps from New Year's Eve. It had landed in the shape of a breast cancer awareness ribbon. I looked up and Deb was standing on my left side staring down at the ribbon. Jerry had turned around and joined us. He was also staring at the ribbon. We all three began to pray for all the people with breast cancer and for God to work in a mighty way with miraculous healings.

A few weekends later, Deb and I went to see some friends who had promised to be at South Beach, Miami, Florida, on January 1st but didn't show up. They wintered on the west coast of Florida, so we had to travel across the state to visit them.

Our friends, Pat and Rita, took us out to lunch and we shared with them some of the things we had experienced the first few weeks of the walk. When we told the story of the pink ribbon, the couple began to sob. Rita explained to us that the reason they were not there when we started the walk was because, a few days before that date, she had found a large lump in her breast. They were so upset that they completely forgot about the kickoff for the walk.

January 2nd, Rita made an appointment to see an oncologist and a few days later, she found that the mass had completely disappeared. Rita and Pat were so touched by our testimony of prayer, they began to thank God and give Him the credit for Rita's miraculous healing. The couple encouraged me to keep walking and to keep praying!

Port Everglades

Just days later, Jerry and I were walking in Fort Lauderdale. As we approached a causeway that over looked Port Everglades, Deb joined us in the walk. All three of us felt a need to stop and spend extra time on a bridge and pray over the port. That made sense to us because a lot of evil leaves and enters our country at our ports. We prayed against any drug trafficking that might be taking place in the waters, and we prayed against other violence that often takes place at sea.

Not long after that, we were having dinner with some friends. In a discussion about the walk, I told about different places where we felt that we needed to pray harder. When I mentioned the port, we were informed that the biggest drug bust in the history of Fort Lauderdale, took place right after we passed through the city.

It was encouraging to think our prayers were making a difference.

Mile 5

It had to be at least 2:00 p.m., which is probably the hottest time of the day in Virginia, that time of year. By now, I had moved from tearing up, now and then, to a steady salty, flow that stung my face as it streamed over my sunburnt cheeks. I glanced at the officer in front of me who was also wiping tears from his cheek, as was the patrolman who was the driver, just to my rear.

Exhausted, I fell to the ground dropping cross #4 on the bridge. My prosthetic leg slipped off from perspiration. I must have poured an eighth of a cup of sweat out of my well-worn liner. I dried Nubby. After struggling for a few minutes, I was able to reattach my prosthesis and lift myself up.

I stumbled to the car for a sip of water. The officer, with tears welling up in his eyes said, "One more mile, sweetheart, one more mile."

I was so touched by his compassion, I was able to muster a smile.

As I painfully hobbled toward the goal, I thought of more inspiring situations—memories began to flow…

Lemonade Stand

Routinely, Monday through Saturday, Deb would take me back to the place I had left off walking the day before. She would then drive beside me or park the car and wait for me to pass her and get about a half of a mile ahead. Then she would pull up to see if I needed to take a break or use the restroom. If I needed a restroom break, she would take me somewhere to use the facilities and bring me back to that exact spot.

At the end of the day, we would note precise landmarks so I would be able to return to the same spot the next day. Deb would drive me to the 31-foot RV, which we were using for our home base. It was usually parked at a Walmart or a truck stop. Every weekend, we would move our home 50 miles farther down the road.

Sometimes, one or more people would join us on the walk. On these occasions, we would often park a vehicle ahead of us, and Deb would then drive that person to my location, so they could walk with me toward their car. Other times, we would just all walk together, away from the other walkers' vehicles. When the day was completed, Deb would give the walkers a ride back to their cars.

One day while walking near Daytona Beach, a woman, Renee, from one of the local churches, joined me on the walk. On that particular day, we proceeded away from Renee's car, heading north on A1A.

After we had ventured five miles, we decided to take a lunch break. There was a lemonade stand/deli kind of place, right across the street. I went inside and waited for Deb to take Renee back to get her car.

I was pretty thirsty, so I decided to get some lemonade to sip on, while I waited for the other two to join me. When I went up to purchase my beverage, there was a jock type, college-aged man in front of me. He fumbled through some coupons despite the fact that he did not appear to be hurting financially. I believed the clothing and shoes, which he was wearing that day, probably cost over $500.

I felt God prompting me to buy lunch for this young man. This didn't make sense to me as I stood there in my second-hand clothes and my half-worn walking shoes. But the prompting was strong so I stepped forth in faith. I was shaking and feeling uneasy, but I told the cashier, "I would like a small lemonade, and I would also like to purchase lunch for this young man!"

Both individuals looked shocked, so I exclaimed, "I am a minister and sometimes ministers do this type of thing!"

The young man threw me a dirty look, the cashier seemed a little confused, and I was a whole lot embarrassed. I reached in my pocket and pulled out a wadded ten-dollar bill and paid the woman, then went over to sit, and sip on the ice-cold beverage. The apparently ungrateful young man gave me another dirty look shaking his head as if to say, "How dare you?" He grabbed his carry-out bag and headed for the door.

When Deb and Renee returned, we got in line to purchase lunch. Renee ordered first—then she offered to pay for Deb and me.

The cashier jumped back, and exclaimed with delight, "So that is how God works, she bought lunch for a young man and you come in and buy lunch for the two of them!"

It was not about the young man at all—at least, I don't think so. God wanted to make Himself real to this young cashier, and I am grateful for being obedient that day, even though it was way out of my comfort zone.

The Donut Shop

I was finishing my walk one evening near Daytona Beach, when a stranger handed me $5 and told me to get some coffee. The next day, I told Deb to drop me off where I had finished walking the day before and meet me at the donut shop, which would be about eight-tenths into my first mile.

When I arrived at the donut shop, Deb and I went inside. The first thing I noticed was the Christian music. I asked the man behind the counter if he was a Christian. When he replied yes, I told him that I was doing a faith walk around our country and I was praying for unity in the hearts of the believers.

He was so touched by the walk that he would not accept my $5 for the coffee. He wanted it to be on him. While Deb and I were enjoying our morning beverage, the man approached us with a handful of Christian literature and asked if I could pass it on.

I left the donut shop, with literature in hand, not knowing exactly how I would distribute it. I tucked some tracts in some bus stop booths along the way, and handed some of them to people I passed on the sidewalks. In my eighth mile, I saw a sign that read BOOKS FOR PRISONERS. I went inside and asked if they would accept Christian literature. The woman was glad to pass the donation on to the prisoners.

I continued walking another two miles and stopped for the day. Deb and I took a drive to see what the path was like ahead. As we headed back to our RV for the night, we decided to stop at a Waffle House for dinner. As we were waiting to be served, we noticed someone, who could have been homeless, walk into the ladies room. About 10 minutes later, while we were actually ordering our food, the woman came out of the restroom. It appeared as though she had bathed while in there.

As the woman walked by to be seated behind us, she was counting some change from a small purse. Deb and I looked at each other, and I remembered the $5 that the man at the donut shop refused to be paid. I told the waitress to give the woman whatever she wanted and we would pay for it. She ordered a sandwich and a cup of coffee. Her order came to just under $5.

As I left the Waffle House that night, I was in awe of how far the $5 had gone. I marveled at the fact that when the man at the donut shop refused to be paid for our coffee, he had no idea how by the end of the day; he treated two missionaries, ministered to prisoners, and fed a homeless person. Who knows how far this one random act of kindness spread once the prisoners read the Christian literature and all was said and done!

Sky Writer

There was a day early in the journey, when I woke up a little off balance. As we began to walk, I put my head down to pray. I was feeling tired, sore, and a bit discouraged. Deb and Jerry were walking with me and they simultaneously chimed, "Carol, look up!"

"I know—I am trying to be more cheerful!"

"No, look up! Look up in the sky!"

I looked up to see GOD BLESS USA written in big puffy clouds of smoke, left behind by a small airplane. My heart smiled as I watched the words slowly fade and blend into the heavens.

For the next few weeks, over 200 miles of the walk, we saw messages of God's love painted across the sky. I never met the sky writer, but was informed that we were both interviewed by the same TV news reporter, and apparently, he began to leave his trails of hope across the firmament on January 1, 2002—the exact day

I began to leave a trail of crosses across the earth. I do not believe in coincidences, but I do believe in *God* incidences!

Brian and Jason

One day, earlier that summer, Jerry and I were walking near Myrtle Beach. Jerry is a good friend of mine; he was a contract nurse at the time, and would walk with me whenever he was able to get away from work. Being an intercessor, he felt right at home on a prayer walk, and I enjoyed his company.

Jerry, as usual, was walking at a much faster pace, and was quite a distance ahead of me. I noticed he had passed a young man who seemed to be struggling. By the time I got to this young man, he had fallen to the ground and was hugging his duffle bag. Jerry had turned around and headed back to us.

I introduced myself to this weary traveler, and asked if there was anything I could do to help him. The young man, in his mid-twenties, told me his name was Brian and he worked the night shift. He said he arrived home from work early the previous morning and found his wife in bed with another man.

In his devastation, he took off walking toward his home town, Raleigh, North Carolina. He had been walking all day the day before, through the night, and thought, by then, he had traveled over 30 miles toward his destination. He walked away from his home, his wife, and two little girls—aged seven and two.

Brian had not been wearing a shirt and his back was blistered with second-degree burns. He was exhausted and dehydrated. We were in front of a small independent hamburger place so I got Brian some water and Jerry carried his duffle bag as we looked for shade. I escorted Brian to a picnic table. I contacted Deb by cell phone and asked her to meet us there.

By the time Deb got to us, Brian was not quite as dehydrated and I was sharing with him about the prayer walk. Deb got some aloe lotion from the car and Jerry nursed Brian's sunburns. Brian asked if he could use my phone to call his mother to let her know that he was okay and on his way to Raleigh.

After making the call, Brian asked about the cross I had in my hand. I told him that I planted one every mile. Jerry and I talked to him about our faith and he asked if we would pray for him. After praying for Brian to have a safe trip and for God to carry him through this difficult time, he thanked us and informed us that he did not own a Bible. I asked if he wanted one. He said he did, so I went to the pilot car to try to find an extra Bible to give him. I searched for several minutes before realizing I had given all of our extra Bibles away.

I felt God urging me to give *my* Bible to Brian. Yes, *my* Bible… the one that had been given to me as a special gift at my ordination. *My* Bible…the one that I had used when preaching sermons over the past several years! *My* Bible…the one that I read, the one I studied from, the one I highlighted. God wanted me to give *my* Bible away. Imagine that! After a long sigh, I reached in the back seat of the car and grabbed *my* Bible. I walked over to Brian and handed him *my* Bible along with one of my business cards.

He tucked the business card in *his* Bible and asked if he could have one of the crosses. I told him that he could walk with me to where I had planted the last cross, and that he could pick that one up, and take it with him.

I asked Deb if she would drive Brian farther north so he could try to get a ride with a truck driver to Raleigh. I told her that Jerry and I would be fine. We were walking through a residential area with plenty of places to get out of the sun and numerous public restrooms en route.

37

Deb agreed to transport Brian, so he placed *his* Bible and the cross in his duffle bag and got in the front passenger's seat. Deb drove him to Fayetteville, bought him some lunch and gave him a little cash. After heading back toward the walk, Deb called Brian's mother to let her know we did all we could to help him get home.

Later that evening, I called Brian's mother. Brian had made it home, but he was not there, at the time, so I was not able to converse with him. She told me he had explained to her about meeting us and how we were able to help him. Brian told her that he was not able to get a ride at the truck stop, and had walked several more miles before someone gave him a lift.

He was okay but his duffle bag had been stolen. He had stashed the bag in a ditch, while he ran to a truck stop to use a restroom. When he came back the bag was gone. She said he was mostly bothered by losing the cross he had picked up and the Bible I had given him.

Weeks later I received a phone call from another young man.

"Reverend Carol Cruise?"

"Yes!"

"My name is Jason. I found a duffle bag in a ditch near a truck stop north of Fayetteville. It has a Bible, a business card, and a cross with your name on it. Do you know who the bag might belong to?"

I told Jason the story about Brian and that I had his mother's phone number. Jason said he would like to get the bag to Brian. I told him I would call Brian's mother and see what we could do about returning the bag.

Jason went on to say that he had been getting in trouble time and time again and wanted to live a better life. When he found the bag, it inspired him to take his Bible out of his closet and to get right with God. He said that he had not been in church for years, but he would be there the next Sunday.

I called Brian's mother and she gave me the go-ahead to pass her number on to Jason so he could make arrangements to return Brian's belongings. She thanked me for our help and concern.

I called Jason with Brian's mother's phone number. A few days later, Jason called me back and said he had talked to Brian and had made arrangements to take the duffle bag to him. We had no idea that when we ministered to Brian, we would ultimately be ministering to Jason as well!

1,000 miles

A week or so later, in Ahoskie, North Carolina, I hit 1,000 miles on the walk. Arrangements had been made with the local news to meet me at Higher Ground Church at 3:00 on Saturday, June 29th, where I would plant my one-thousandth cross.

Until this point, that was the most difficult day of the journey. I had a speaking engagement in Winston-Salem on Sunday evening, June 23rd, which was not unusual. I did not walk on Sundays, so on Saturdays, after I finished walking, I would often travel up to 10 or 12 hours to where I would be speaking on the following day.

This particular week, we had a 250-mile trek on Monday, and had stopped at a produce stand en route. While checking out the fruit, the business owner told us that he had noticed the magnet on the side of our car and he asked about the ministry.

After hearing about the walk, he told us that his family was going through some tough times with a daughter who had gotten pregnant out of wedlock, and a son who was using street drugs. We ministered to the family and prayed with them, and did not make it back to the walk until about 6:30 Monday evening.

I believe this was a blessing in disguise, because as soon as I began to walk, I came upon a roadblock of logs, right on the path where I was walking. I got goosebumps as I realized I had been spared from being on that path at the exact time tons of logs avalanched off a flatbed semi.

Thank you, God, for giving us the assignment at the produce stand!

I got about five miles in before dark and had 56 miles to make it to the Higher Ground Church in Ahoskie. I walked 10 miles on Tuesday, 10 miles on Wednesday, 10 miles on Thursday, and 16 miles on Friday. Saturday morning, I was only 10 miles from my goal, but had walked 46 miles in the previous four days and that was much more than I was used to walking in the summer heat. My average was less than 50 miles in six days.

I started the day off physically exhausted. Jerry had come up to join us for this milestone in the walk. At 2:30, I had completed nine miles but did not have enough energy to go on. I sat down at the pilot car and made a cross to mark the thousandth mile. I cried out to Deb and Jerry that I was not sure I could make it as I plodded away from the car and slowly headed north on Highway 17.

About halfway through the mile, my knees began to buckle. Jerry carried the cross for me and Deb stepped in behind me and began singing praise songs. I joined in with the singing and, miraculously, felt God carrying me.

By the time we were within one-tenth of a mile from the church, I could see the news cameras and people waving crosses they had found along the way. I felt supernatural strength as I took the cross back from Jerry and held it high above my head. We marched victoriously onto the church property.

As I approached the north end of the bridge, only humor could keep me going. I know God has a sense of humor—after all He called *me* to do this walk!

I was parched. I had finished my last sip of water about a mile back. My mouth was dry and tasted salty. I remembered back a week or so when entering Virginia on Highway 17. I was walking on a blacktopped road through the Great Dismal Swamp. It was extremely humid that day. I am sure the temperature had climbed to over 100 degrees. I was in about my eighth mile. Deb was parked ahead of me. When I approached the car, I asked her for some water.

"You drank all of the water!" she cried.

"How about some Gatorade?" I asked.

"No, all out of Gatorade!"

"Do we have any soda?"

"No, you drank all of the soda too!"

As I walked away from the car, I heard what sounded like a metal can rolling toward me. Looking down I saw a Diet Cherry Pepsi next to my foot!

Deb told me later that what happened next would have made a good Pepsi commercial. I reached down and picked up the soda, then held it to my cheek. It was ice cold! I scanned the area, and could see no logical place from where this Pepsi could have rolled. Then I looked up to the sky and said, "God?"

"Even God has a choice in sodas!" I chuckled.

As I walked off the James River Bridge that sultry August day in 2002, I knew, without a doubt, that God had carried me that first thousand miles, and that He would most definitely carry me the entire 10,000-plus miles it would take to make it all the way around the country!

I planted the fifth cross at the north end of the James River Bridge, and the seven men who escorted that walk, formed a line with me while pictures were taken. There was not a dry eye in those photos. I glanced back to where I had planted the cross, it was gone. I smiled, thinking one of the men who had accompanied me that day, had picked up the cross.

Who would have ever thought that God would call *that kid, trouble, a mistake*, to such a journey as this? He can use what one might consider useless to do mighty works! God is in the business of turning ashes into beauty! We just have to be willing ashes!

Who would have thought that God would call a middle-aged, overweight, female amputee who could barely walk to the mailbox, to walk 10,467 miles around our nation? I certainly was not qualified for this mission. God is in the business of calling the unqualified and qualifying the called! Moses, David, Paul, Peter, Carol, you!

We need to quit saying, "I can't" to the Author of our call, the One who wants to show you He can! Let go and let God!

February 13, 2002

Hello,

My name is Adam and I spent last night in the clink at Sharps waiting for the remarkably slow process of being ticketed and released. Seeing as how my van was in Titusville and I was south of Port Saint John, I decided to walk back to Titusville and give sticking my thumb out a whirl. It didn't work very well, and I wound up walking the whole way. On my way, I found a wooden cross lying in the grass as the sun was trying to sneak past the cloudy horizon. It was yours. I think it had a 239 or 231 for a number on it. I found it on the northbound side of US-1 just north of 405. Not being one to normally in-volve myself in such things, I felt like it was some kind of sign to keep walking and decided to take the cross along with me. Well, I made it to US 50 and walked across the street (walk-ing west) to the Walgreen's on the corner there to try and make a call and I stuck the cross nicely in the landscaping next to the telephone and made a wish for someone to carry the cross further.

I'm sorry I didn't do more. I was very tired and I had originally intended to bring it further west and give it to a person, but I had been up for some 24 hours already and had just walked 10 miles or more. The pay-phone didn't work for me and I left in frustration absentmindedly forgetting the cross I had placed so nicely in front of the shrubbery.

I would like to think at least I saved the cross from obscu-rity on the side of the road and being run over by mowers.

Good luck, dear ladies and to the right-leg amputee, I wish to thank you for brightening up my day in more ways than you know.

Adam

43

BRIDGES

CROSSING OUR NATION'S CAPITAL

Soon after crossing the James River, I was given police escort over the Coleman Bridge, which crosses the York River. I was greeted on the north side by a crowd of VDOT workers who cheered me on and supplied me with a bottle of cold water and a safety vest.

By early September I had made it to Fredericksburg, Virginia, picked up US 1, and headed north to our nation's capital.

I was beginning to have some struggles with Deb, who was very fearful of the road ahead. She was worried about the route I was taking and our safety through the cities.

I had a new prosthetic leg made back in April and it was not fitting well. I had switched back to the duct-taped leg shortly after being fitted for the new one. The duct- taped leg was worn beyond repair. Somehow, I had to make the new leg work. The wear and tear of the day was about all I could handle.

I told Deb I was having trouble dealing with her fears. I went on to remind her that God would take care of us and we needed to proceed in faith. "For God has not given us the spirit of fear, but of power and of love and of a sound mind" (2 Timothy 1:7 NKJV).

We spent a lot of time arguing. One evening, after the day's walk while sitting in the RV, in a parking lot in Alexandria, Virginia, we had a heated discussion during which we said some unloving things to each other. Deb left the camper and went to a bus station to purchase a one-way ticket back to Ohio. In retrospect, I believe we were both stressed out from having spent so much time together over the past several months.

That night, I hardly slept. I felt great remorse for my part in the quarreling, and very badly about some of the things I had said to Deb. I prayed and asked God to forgive me for my unkind and unloving behavior.

Deb called me the next morning to let me know she had made it safely to Ohio. We apologized to each other and agreed that we needed a break.

Jerry traveled up from Florida to assist me on the walk. We walked three miles that evening.

The next day, we walked 12 miles, which took us into Washington D.C. The following day, on September 19th, we reached the White House. Being just one year after 9/11, the grounds were crawling with security personnel. I wasn't sure I would get away with it, but I successfully planted cross #1,250 at mile "0" right in front of the White House. Every guard must have blinked at the same time while I planted that cross!

I will never forget the walk through the city. I could feel a spiritual battle going on within me all day. I felt tempted to do things I would usually never think of doing. I actually thought I was losing my mind. Keeping my eyes focused on the next step, I concentrated on praying for the city and our government leaders.

My stump was bleeding from breakdown of the flesh. Jerry, a nurse, explained that he would normally tell someone to clean the wounds, leave them exposed, and elevate the limb but he, too, sensed we were experiencing spiritual warfare and suggested I push onward. By the time we got through the city, my stump was miraculously healed.

I was glad Deb was not with us that day. She would have been overly concerned about the condition of my stump and would have tried to discourage us from traveling through the inner city.

That weekend I drove back to Canton, Ohio, to take some things to Deb and to preach at New Hope, the church I attended when I began this journey.

I met with Deb and we decided that she would finish the year with me. She would then move to Florida to stay with some friends and seek medical attention for her ailments. She would be assisting with the street ministry at a small church in Fort Lauderdale.

I felt good about these decisions. Deb had been suffering for years with health problems. I was glad to know she would be getting much needed medical attention, and would be pursuing her own call to ministry.

ASHES TO BEAUTY

After spending time with Deb in Akron, I drove to Kent to visit my daughter, Laurie. At the time, she was a graduate student at Kent State University, working on a masters degree in education.

She had been haunted with memories from her past as she worked her way through undergrad school with a bachelor of arts degree in psychology. She had blocked many of her childhood memories, which her psyche kept tightly stored, while she was too young to deal with such violations.

Laurie worked her way through college, burdened with having to be ready to take the stand at a court hearing that was rescheduled time and time again while the case against my surgeon was tied up in litigation. It seemed like there was a hearing date set for every exam week. Finally, halfway through her junior year, I settled out of court and was able to help pay for her education, buy her a better car, and take her on a nice vacation. However, because of my medical bills and the cost of prosthetic legs, the money, from the much-too-lean settlement, was gone within a few years.

As we visited, we had a real breakthrough. Laurie had been angry with God since being abused by her father when she was a child. She had come to believe that God did not love her and she did not deserve to be blessed.

She remembered how when she was a child, I taught her to pray the "Now I lay me down to sleep…" prayer and, at the end, she would say "God bless…" and list everyone in our home. She would say, "God bless Mommy, God bless Daddy, and God bless Susie" (Susie was her little beagle). Because she was the one saying the prayer, what she did not say was, "God bless Laurie!"

After Laurie would settle in bed, her God-blessed mommy would leave to work third shift at a factory, and her God-blessed Daddy would hurt her in ways little girls should never be hurt. Understandably, this left her feeling that God did not love her, nor did he want to bless her.

This went on for quite a while before I became aware of it. I had been badly beaten, raped, spit on, and emotionally abused by Dale, her father and my husband, for almost 10 years. I was not aware that he had been inappropriate with my daughter, until one evening, while I was fixing dinner; he insisted she watch him take a shower. She was eight years old.

I love my daughter so much and I would do anything to take her pain away. I held her in my arms and I told her that

48

she had done nothing wrong. She deserved to have parents who loved and protected her. It was not her fault that bad things happened to her. I told her that God did not cause her to be abused. Man did. Her earthly father did. I asked Laurie to forgive me for not being there for her.

I told my daughter that I believed God loves her and wants to take all of the bad and use it for good. I said that her heavenly Father wants to bless her and He wants to turn her ashes into beauty. I explained how she could be used to counsel other women who have been subjected to abuse and neglect.

Laurie had a hard time receiving this word, but she did admit that she had seen how I have become a stronger person for everything I have been through. I held her real close to me and asked her to try to let God work in her life. I told Laurie that I believed God could heal her from her injuries and He can use one's past to make a better future.

Laurie walked me out to my car. She said she had a lot to think about. As we said good-bye, I asked her to please take care of herself.

My daughter, Laurie, wrote this poem for me while I was struggling to save my leg.

MARCH

A step on a crack, and everything changed.
A soldier of swift feet could not march anymore.

We used to promenade, ballet steps in the sand.
Until one sorrowful day, when four prints became three.

She carried a torch all the years of her life.
Encountered fierce battles, she never lost a fight.

Brave little soldier, march in your mind.
Your feet will carry your body one day.

The 1990 ignoble war shed mawkish blood.
Her battery fought strong armed with heavy artillery.

But the united strength just wasn't enough.
The Soldier left paralyzed, while the enemy fled, AWOL.

Every morn the baron flies slower and weaker.
I pray he never lies faint at her door.

Brave little soldier, march in your mind.
Your feet will carry your body one day.

Keep close the medallion of the loving Madonna.
She will work the miracles and Father's hands may heal.

The apocalypse shall come, victory songs will be sung.
The dove may fly gaily as she parades through life again.

Finally the closure came, as the white flags arose.
The enemy was defeated but an infinite battle endures.

Brave little soldier, march in your mind.
Your foot now carries your body away.

Laurie

OVER A DECADE OF TRAGEDIES

Harmed at Home

As I drove back to Akron, I reflected over a decade of trials and burdens. Having such poor self-esteem, it was not surprising that I ended up with an abusive person. Dale had threatened to kill me if I ever tried to leave. After a couple years of marriage, he began threatening my life if I had anything to do with my family. Later I found out that he had been sleeping with my sister, who was only 15 years old at the time. He didn't want me to find out about this so he bullied me into staying estranged from my family. I was not permitted to leave the premises, except for work and specific times that he approved, which were for grocery shopping or taking Laurie to dance and piano lessons.

Surprisingly, he allowed me to take Laurie to church on Sundays. I discovered later, this was the time he pursued my sister, my cousin, and his boss's daughter, to name a few—all teenagers. What self-esteem I had left dwindled down to nothing. I was living my life in total fear.

The day after the shower situation, while Dale was at work, I mustered enough courage to call for help. I asked a friend to pick us up at the end of the road because Dale had locked a chain across the end of our long winding driveway. There were trees all through the yard, so it was not possible for anyone to drive in or out without him first unlocking the chain.

A friend from church met us at the road and drove us to a battered women's shelter, where Laurie and I spent the next several weeks hiding from Dale. I made the mistake of letting Dale's parents know where I had taken Laurie. My mother-in-law gave Dale the number and he called the shelter and threatened to kill me. The house mother was concerned about the threat and thought it might put other residents at risk, so we were asked to leave.

We were moved to another shelter that was not kept clean. Laurie had a dust allergy and became ill with asthma. Out of desperation, Laurie and I stayed with families of people I worked with. Since I was the only woman in my department, we ended up staying with two different Christian co-workers and their families. Both of these men had witnessed the wrath of Dale when he showed up at my work place one night in a fit of anger. Both had expressed their concerns to me about bruises on my face and arms and they were concerned about the safety of both me and my daughter if we continued to stay with Dale.

Uncomfortable with sleeping in the same house with a male co-worker during the day while his wife was at work, I chose to sleep in my car in a parking lot. I would leave work at 6:00 a.m. and drive to the place we were staying, get Laurie ready and drop her off at the local elementary school. While she was at school, I parked in a church parking lot and slept until 2:30, when I would pick Laurie up from school and drive to our temporary home. Once there, I assisted Laurie with homework, helped with dinner, then spent some quality time with my daughter until 8:30. This was the time Laurie would get tucked in for the night and I would then get ready for work to be there by 9:45.

Concerned Dale would show up at work or find out where I was staying, I consulted an attorney and requested a restraining order. I was told that nothing could be done unless he actually broke into my place of residence and tried to harm me. This was in the early 1980s when there was very little protection for battered women. I asked the attorney if he had any suggestions. He said I should get as far away from the man as possible. I had a friend in Texas, so I got a leave of absence from work and headed for Texas. We stayed there a few weeks, until Dale calmed down a bit, then I drove back to pursue a divorce.

Laurie and I bounced around from one home to another until I was able to buy a small trailer and make a little home for us. I leased a room to a friend who agreed to be there at nights with Laurie while I worked at the factory.

Harmed in the Work Place

Several months after the divorce, I met Chuck. He was a much older man who was going to take care of us. This sounded good; almost too good to be true. I could not remember a time when I ever felt "taken care of," because I was always taking care of others. We got married not even a year after my divorce from Dale was final.

Chuck taught school and had the summers off. I was laid off from my factory job in early summer. We spent most of the summer of 1982 on Chuck's houseboat on Lake Cumberland in Kentucky. We had a great time. It seemed like one big vacation.

Late summer, I was called back to work and assigned to a machine that I was not trained to operate. This machine pulled plastic tubing through the center of a circle of spools of synthetic yarn that spun around the tube, to reinforce it. Then the tubing would be sent through an extrusion line. The end result was hydraulic hose that is used on semi tractors and other heavy equipment. After the tubing was reinforced, it would feed onto a reel. When the reel was full, the operator would cut the tubing and set up a new reel. Unlike the reinforcing machines I usually ran, this particular tubing was inflated with high-pressure air then fed through a solvent bath.

The first time I attempted to change the reel, I cut the tubing, and one end fell into the solvent. The stream of high-pressure air caused the solvent to spray, drenching me with the adhesive.

I asked to go home and shower, but was told I could wash off in the ladies room and get back to work. I was back to the machines within 10 minutes.

Within a few weeks I had a urinary infection that I was not able to fight off, even after two rounds of antibiotics. I was hospitalized with intravenous antibiotic therapy before I was able to fight the infection.

The next month, I was hospitalized with pneumonia again and it took intravenous antibiotics to battle the infection. Soon I began to have some severe allergy symptoms. I was diagnosed with an immune deficiency that probably resulted from my body being exposed to the chemicals in the solvent.

I was hospitalized for seven weeks in Chicago, Illinois, for tests. This was the closest place to home, where this type of immune deficiency was being treated. It was about the time the AIDS virus was being detected on the west coast. I was frightened but had no history of intravenous drug use or promiscuity, so I was highly unlikely to have AIDS.

As my immune system began shutting down, my body was not tolerating the clothes I was wearing, the food I was eating, or the air I was breathing. I was placed in a very sterile environment and told that I may have to spend the rest of my life in a bubble. This was not acceptable to me. I took the matter to prayer and began to meditate on being healthy and strong. Within a few months, I had a miraculous healing, and was back in the world again.

I quit my job at the factory and began taking college classes at Kent State University as a psychology major. I was determined to find out where all of my inner pain was coming from. I also helped manage Chuck's student rentals; I obtained a real estate license, and began selling real estate to pay for my education and to help with the bills.

The Loss of a Son

Toward the end of 1982, with Dale no longer in my life, I reconnected with my family and made a decision to get each member a special gift for their birthdays in 1983. I chose to give them each a Bible with their name engraved on the front cover. Danny's birthday was the first in the year, June 8th, Helen's birthday on June 26th, and Ken's on July 2nd. I went to a Bible Book Store and picked out three Bibles, a black one for Ken, a white one for Helen, and a burgundy Bible for Danny. I left them at the store so they could be engraved with their names.

A week later, I got a call that the Bibles were ready and I could come and get them anytime. I had a lot going on, so I decided to pick them up the following week. But on Friday, as I was running some errands before meeting Chuck and a group to go on a Christian retreat for the weekend, God spoke to me: "Pick the Bibles up now!"

I shook it off because I had people waiting for me. So I kept driving and once again I heard from God. "Pick the Bibles up now!"

I shook my head and kept driving. I knew Danny's birthday was the next day, but I hadn't given him a birthday gift for 10 years and it wasn't going to hurt to wait until Sunday evening when I got back from the retreat, I reasoned.

"Go pick the Bibles up!" I couldn't stop the message.

God kept saying, "Go get the Bibles now!"

I turned the car around and headed for the Bible Book Store. I ran inside grabbed a few book markers; one had the *Footprint in the Sand* poem on it and the other had *Daniel* on it but I did not stop to read them. I grabbed a birthday card, paid for the merchandise and the Bibles, and ran to the car.

Once more, I was high-tailing it home because I had people waiting for me.

"Take the Bible to Danny now!" God's voice whispered.

"I don't have time!" I argued.

"Now! Take the Bible to Danny now!" God insisted.

"Please, God, I have people waiting!"

"Now!" I heard again.

I turned the car around and headed to the sand and gravel plant behind the Cruise farmhouse, where Danny worked with Papa, our dad, and my uncle. As I drove into the plant, I noticed Danny standing under a hopper with his hands pulling a lever, as gravel dropped into the bed of a dump truck. As I got closer, I noticed Danny was staring off in space like he was connecting with someone or something in another world.

I parked the car and signed Danny's card, *I love you, Carol.* I had never signed a card like that before. I had always signed cards simply, *Love, Carol.* I ran up to Danny. My presence brought him back to the moment. I handed him the Bible and card wrapped in a bag with floral print from the bookstore. I was in a hurry, so I kissed him on the cheek and scurried off to the car so I could head home to join the group for the weekend retreat.

I don't remember anything about the get-away. I don't even remember who we went with. What I remember from that weekend was a phone call I received from my dad on Sunday afternoon after we had returned home.

"Carol, this is Dad. You have to come to the hospital! Danny has been badly shocked!"

I thought he said, "Shot!"

I dropped the phone and screamed for Chuck to drive me to the hospital. It was about a 30 minute drive but it seemed like hours before we pulled into the hospital parking lot.

When I walked in the big glass sliding doors of the emergency room at Robinson Memorial Hospital in Ravenna, Ohio, on June 9th, 1983, one day after Danny's twenty-third birthday, I saw my family members standing in the dreaded room.

The room where families are escorted to be told they had lost a loved one.

My mother was sobbing in Andy's arms. My brother-in-law was holding Margie while she sobbed on his chest. Helen sat on a chair with her face buried in her hands. Ken stood speechless with tears running down his cheek. Nobody had to tell me! I ran to my dad, threw my arms around him, pounded on his back and screamed, "Who did it? Who shot Danny?"

"No, Carol, not shot! Danny was badly shocked! He was electrocuted!"

Danny had been helping a friend erect a CB antenna when electricity arced from a high-power line and struck the pole that Danny was holding with both hands. The current entered his hands and was not able to escape his feet. Instead, it blew his tennis shoes apart and he died suddenly as every organ in his body exploded from the current. A spokesman from the electric company told us that it was a freak accident and probably wouldn't happen again in a thousand years. It had to do with the humidity, the temperature, and other specific conditions. Apparently, it was Danny's time to go to heaven!

I helped my parents pick out a casket and make funeral arrangements for their youngest son. My mother picked out cards with the *Footprints in the Sand* poem to be used as the memorial cards with his personal information, the little cards that are placed beside the guestbook for people to stuff in their Bibles or store away in a drawer, I guess to remind them they had attended the funeral.

Danny was buried a few days later. His wife placed the Bible in the casket with his body. I picked it up and the two book markers fell out, the one with the *Footprints in the Sand* poem and the other one which read, *I call you Daniel to walk with me in all eternity*. I felt chills run down my spine as I placed the Bible back in the casket. God let me know he had called Danny to be with Him!

That was one of the most difficult days of my life. I did not only lose a brother but I lost the little boy that was handed to me when I was eight years old, a little boy I tried so hard to take care of and provide for when I was merely a child myself. In a way I had lost a son!

A Broken Leg

As I was healing from my traumatic childhood, the abuse of my first marriage, and the loss of a brother who had been like a son, I began, for the first time in my life, to be my own person. I lived a life with many hats: Daddy's little girl, Sharlie's princess, Mom's confidant, the big sister, Danny's mother, Dale's victim, Laurie's mommy, Chuck's project; but never Carol, whoever that was!

Soon it was evident that Chuck did not appreciate the growth. He would much rather be taking care of someone. It became apparent that Chuck had some real control and anger issues. As I became more independent, he became more angry and controlling.

Laurie was beginning to show symptoms of depression and other problems. I am sure she felt a total loss of control with what she had been subjected to by her father, and now with Chuck's control issues. She was desperate to have some control in her own life and her living situation. Not only that, I was in such desperate search of my own identity that I neglected to be there for the struggles my daughter was experiencing.

Chuck had two children, a son, Ben, a year older than Laurie and a daughter, Christine, a year older than Ben. His kids lived with their mother in Perry, Ohio, about two hours away from where we were living in Rootstown, Ohio. We would meet his ex, half-way between Perry and Rootstown, about twice a month to get his kids for the weekend.

In the summer of 1988, we decided to build a house in Mantua, which was about an hour closer to Perry. Christine, who had been attending a Catholic school, was ready to start high school and really wanted to go to a public school. Because her mother was totally against this decision, Christine had to choose to live with her father to be able to make that choice. So she came to live in our new house and attend school with my daughter.

By fall, our house was almost completely constructed and we had moved into our new home. The girls were enrolled in the Crestwood School District. By the time the snow was flying we had the exterior completed except for some siding on the inside of our front porch.

We had very mild weather during the last week of December. A few days after Christmas, Chuck and I went outside to hang the last bit of siding around the door on our front porch. In an attempt to hang the piece right over the door, and not realizing what time it was, I propped the ladder on the door. I climbed up and carefully placed the last piece of siding. As I began to climb down the ladder, Laurie opened the door from the inside. She was taking our dog, Fuzzy, for a 3:00 walk, which was her responsibility each day.

In a split second, I envisioned the ladder, with all of my weight, falling into my 15-year-old daughter and causing her serious injury. I jumped back and fell. As I landed, my foot slid on a handsaw, and I was on the porch rolling and screaming in pain.

I cried out to Chuck that I had broken my leg and he rushed me off to a 24-hour urgent care unit. It turned out that the leg was broken in two places. I was put in a full leg cast and scheduled to see an orthopedic surgeon on Tuesday, December 31st.

Alone with Reality

I was housebound for the next several months, with a lot of time to think about things. I constantly read self-help books and came to the conclusion that I was drinking too much and was an adult child of alcoholics.

Even though my parents were not alcoholics, they were both raised by fathers who were, and had many of the abusive characteristics, typical of people raised by alcoholics. This explained the neediness and immaturity of my mother, and the anger issues with my father. Mom didn't get the nurturing she needed and deserved from her parents. Dad was the brunt of his alcoholic father's anger and neglected by his mother who was busy escaping from her abusive husband.

I became aware of unhealthy patterns in my own life. I did not like being with men. I was more attracted to women who seemed to be much more sensitive and nurturing. I disassociated during sex with both of my husbands. I married my first husband to escape a very unhappy home. I married my second husband out of desperation to have someone to help take care of and protect my daughter and me.

Here I was feeling, once again, trapped in a very unhealthy environment. I was on a lot of pain medication and began to drink daily. I was going crazy and feeling desperate.

I ended up spending time in the stress management facility at Akron General Hospital. While I was there, I made some decisions. I needed to get out of that second marriage. I needed to attend some recovery meetings, and I needed to heal from psychological abuse and get on with my life. And, I was determined, not to be a victim of another man…ever!

I began attending Adult Children of Alcoholic meetings and realized I was possibly developing a drinking problem, so I also attended some AA meetings.

Leaving a Second Husband

I told Chuck that I was not happy in the marriage and I wanted out. He agreed we needed to separate and shared that he was aware that I did not enjoy being with him and that I disassociated during times of intimacy.

I rented a room from my dear friend, Rachel, an elderly widow who lived alone and was looking for a housemate. She had two bedrooms on the second floor of her home that I was able to rent for Laurie and myself.

Even though Laurie was not happy with Chuck, she begged me to let her stay in Mantua where she had several friends she was very close to. She wanted to stay and graduate from Crestwood High School. I reluctantly agreed.

Chuck and I discussed the situation and we agreed I could come back to the house on the weekends to be with Laurie. So on either Thursday or Friday, I would travel back to Mantua with a car full of groceries and stock the refrigerator for the girls, cook some home-cooked meals, and spend some time with my daughter. I would leave on Sunday evenings to go back to Cuyahoga Falls to live with Rachel.

Rachel had two sons about my age. She was like a second mother. Since she did not have a daughter, she enjoyed taking me out to eat and to go shopping with her. We enjoyed each other's company.

My leg was still in a cast when I moved in with Rachel, so I was not able to return to work in real estate. I continued with school and secured a part-time position on a suicide hot line. I was living on credit cards and student loan money.

A Severed Finger

One day, in late October of 1989, I was using a knife to attempt to loosen an aluminum cap on a Pepsi bottle. I was gripping the bottle tightly with my left hand. The knife slipped and severed my left index finger. It was hanging by the skin.

I grabbed a towel, wrapped my hand, and ran to Rachel. I told her that I cut my finger off. In disbelief, she asked me to show her. Both of us in shock, she took me to the emergency room.

I underwent a five-hour surgery in an attempt to reattach the finger. I woke up after surgery to find my left hand in a cast with the fingers exposed from my knuckles. The finger had been reattached and a hole had been drilled in my finger nail. My hand was in a fist position. There was a rubber band stretched from the nail to a little hook midway up the cast.

Later the surgeon explained to me that it was a miracle he was able to reattach the finger. He had to make an incision from the outside corner of the base of my finger downward across my hand at an angle, to reattach the tendons. Each day, I was to stretch the rubber band with my finger to exercise and strengthen the reattached tendons. I would need months of physical therapy to restore full use of the hand and finger.

I trembled at the thought of possibly losing my appendage. I thought I would have gone through the rest of my life looking like a four-fingered freak. I graciously thanked the doctor for saving my finger.

After a few days, I was discharged from the hospital with instructions to schedule therapy two times a week and to see the surgeon every other week.

It cost me a leg to save a finger.

In late November, I was attending a twelve-step meeting one evening, when the weather became very treacherous. As I was walking from the meeting place to my car, I began to slip on ice and I twisted my right leg.

A few days later, I limped into my surgeon's office for one of my post-op checkups. He examined the finger and said it looked great. He asked me why I was limping. I explained to him how I had broken my leg eleven months prior, and how I had twisted it the night before walking across an icy parking lot.

He asked if he could x-ray the leg and I agreed. After he examined the x-rays, he told me the leg was still broken and I should have a tibial rod inserted. He said he could schedule the surgery in two weeks. This doctor was my hero. He saved my finger. I did not question his opinion, so we scheduled the surgery for December 29th.

I was awake for the surgery. The pain medication and Valium kept me from caring a whole lot about what was happening to my leg. I recall hearing heavy-metal music, a drilling sound, and the hammering of the rod being inserted.

The following morning, an intern who had attended the surgery, came to visit me in my hospital room. He told me that I was the most stoic person he had ever met and that mine was the most barbaric surgery he had ever attended.

Later that morning, Dr. Mentry, the man who operated on my leg, the man who saved my finger, my hero, came to see me. He pulled the sheet away to examine the incision. I looked down and saw two bandages; one over my knee where the rod had been inserted, and the other, halfway down the front of my shin bone.

I asked the doctor about the second bandage. He told me that I had somehow gotten burned in surgery. He explained to me that he had a tight grip on my right leg throughout the procedure. He believed that the intensity from the heat caused by friction from his glove during the reaming process caused the burn.

As he pulled the bandage away, I could see the tibia was exposed. Dr. Mentry assured me the injury would be fine. I would have to clean it daily, by applying wet sterile gauze and tapping it dry with sterile gauze. Being on a morphine pump I didn't think much more about the situation.

Over the next couple days I became aware that my roommate was being treated for a dripping staph infection on her left arm. The nurses would change her bandages then come over and attend to my dressing without washing their hands.

On January 3rd, I was discharged from the hospital with a prescription of antibiotics to prevent infection. I was scheduled for a follow-up exam in two weeks.

Two weeks later, when I showed up for the post-op visit, I was experiencing substantial swelling, redness, and pain at the site of my *friction* injury. I expressed some concerns with Dr. Mentry. He became irritated with me and said I was being overly concerned and should continue cleansing the wound with wet and dry gauze.

A few days later, I was working on the crisis line. During my break, while I was cleansing my wound, my supervisor walked in. She took one look at the site and insisted I head straight to the burn center at Akron Children's Hospital, for a second opinion.

I left the crisis center and headed for the hospital. Once the leg was examined by several burn specialists, I was informed that

I had a very serious infection that could cause me to lose my leg. I was told that the bone should have never been left exposed, and I should see a plastic surgeon immediately.

I was given a referral to the infectious disease center at Akron City Hospital. I was at the center within a couple of days and hospitalized with three different types of intravenous antibiotics.

The same day I was admitted, Dr. Ewsami, a plastic surgeon scheduled me for a surgery which would involve debriding the wound, a muscle flap from the back of my leg, and a skin graft from my thigh.

This was the beginning of a three-year battle, of 15 surgeries, in attempts to save my leg.

Would You Know an Angel if You Smelled One?

I had been asked to speak at a convention in Phoenix, Arizona, in October 2002. Deb and I headed south on 77 to 65, then we headed west along Interstate 40. We drove about 400 miles the first day, and pulled into a Flying J for the evening. As we were exiting the freeway, we saw an older gentleman who was walking toward the truck stop.

"Oh, look at grandpa!" Deb chuckled.

The following morning, the man was hitchhiking on the entrance ramp.

"Do you want to give grandpa a ride?" Deb asked.

Both Deb and I felt compelled to give this old guy a ride. We stopped the vehicle and invited the man into the camper. He introduced himself as Art, and thanked us for the lift.

Deb was driving— I was sitting behind the driver's seat on a bench at one end of a fold-down table. I was sewing a banner. Art

65

sat across from me on a sofa. He stared at me a few minutes and asked, "Are you two ladies traveling alone?"

I said, "Yes, God takes care of us!" I shook my needle at him and continued, "And He takes care of anyone who messes with us!"

I shared with Art that I was preparing to speak at a Christian conference in Phoenix. He said he was traveling to Vegas.

He was interested in the fact that we were Christians and I was going to be preaching in a few days. He told us that he sold Bibles door to door for many years. He was very knowledgeable about the Scriptures and helped me prepare for the sermon.

I shared with him about some of the spiritual struggles we had along the way. He said he encountered the devil once.

"I told him to get lost, you have no business in my life, and that was the end of that!" he exclaimed.

What a novel idea! I thought."

After another 400 miles, we pulled off at another Flying J parking lot for the night. Art headed for the building. I prepared dinner and took a plate of food into the truck stop in hopes of finding Art and offering him something to eat.

Art was nowhere to be found, so I went back to the RV to call it a night. The next morning, we found Art on the entrance ramp and invited him to continue west with us. This time, he sat up front with Deb. We had a wonderful talk about God and His ways. Art had such deep insights about spiritual things, especially the Kingdom of God.

We agreed to take him with us until we got to the place where we would turn and head south on 17 toward Phoenix. Art would then try to get a ride from there to Vegas.

After we parted ways, I told Deb, "I enjoyed listening to Art. I think he may be an angel."

She said, "No, I don't think angels smell like that!"

I told her that I would hate to get to heaven and God would say, "You wouldn't know an angel if you smelled one!"

BACK FOR THE FUTURE

After a three-day convention in Phoenix, Deb and I made a quick three-day journey to Maryland to continue in the walk.

Deb was more anxious than usual. While we were in Phoenix we had been informed that there had been a sniper, who was randomly shooting people all around the D.C. area. In fact, a person had been shot and killed at a gas station in Fredericksburg, where I had planted one of the crosses. Apparently, the shootings had taken place on the same path where I had been walking and during the same time period. I was so glad we did not know this at the time. It would have been too much for Deb to handle!

We got back to where Jerry and I had left off, right outside of Washington D.C. I could not get permission to cross the Chesapeake Bay, in Maryland, so I walked into Baltimore on US 1 and journeyed northeastward toward the Susquehanna River, in hopes of being able to cross the river in Dublin. I was denied permission to cross on US 1, so I headed north on 136 to Pennsylvania.

I remember thinking, *What kind of perimeter walk is this? I am not even on the coast!* I couldn't understand why God would not make a way for me to cross the river in Maryland and why I had to take a *detour* into Pennsylvania.

Once I crossed the state line, I headed north on Highway 74. I turned east on 372, where I was finally able to cross the Susquehanna River over a tall bridge with steep grades on both sides. As I walked off the bridge, I planted a cross near a telephone pole.

It was good to be making my way back out to the coast, after all, this was a *perimeter walk.* I picked up Highway 202 somewhere near Downingtown and followed it into New Hope where I crossed into New Jersey.

By the time I made it to New Jersey, it was almost Thanksgiving and winter was raising its head with cold, wet, freezing weather. I remember the last day I walked in 2002. I was filled with emotion. I had spent hour after hour, day after day, walking the east coast and planting cross after cross to mark the miles I had walked. My hands were cold. I clenched cross #1,451, in my right hand, as I treaded forward in a downpour of freezing rain.

As I thought of breaking for the winter months, I began to grieve. I fondly remembered a day in mid-March, when I was walking just north of Kingston, Georgia. I was singing *Amazing Grace* and kind of swaying and dancing as I made my way along the lonely country road. A still small voice spoke, "Look up!" I gazed up at the trees to see that they were, ever so gently, swaying to my song. I was dancing with God!

For the past 11 months; I had walked with Him, I had talked with Him, and I had cried out to Him, I had breathed Him, smelled Him, and even tasted Him in the air. With tears in my eyes, I planted cross #1,451, at a small church, on Highway 518, in Hopewell, New Jersey. I was going to miss Him!

IN MY ELEMENT

I had trouble walking on ice and snow with the prosthesis. Because of the harsh winters in the northern part of our country, I took the winter off.

I drove the motor home to Virginia to store it for the season. When I was not traveling throughout the southern states of our country, to various churches where I had scheduled speaking engagements, I worked for my friend Jen who has a landscaping business in Williamsburg.

I worked eight to twelve hour days raking, mowing, shoveling, planting, and hauling away leaves and other debris. I was in my element. I really enjoy the outdoors and hard physical labor. I always did!

When I was a child, even though my Dad had a bad temper, I was a real Daddy's girl. He would sometimes allow me to join him on fishing and hunting trips. And a time or two he let me mow the grass and help with yard work but I would usually see a snake and abandon the chore.

When I stayed on the farm with Sharlie and Papa, I enjoyed going to the barn when Papa would do his chores. I liked to watch him feed and milk the cows and sometimes he would let me help. In the summers he would let me ride the tractors with him while he plowed and tilled the fields.

My mom called me a *tomboy*, and insisted I do household chores and act more *ladylike*. I never felt very *ladylike*.

When I was in my early thirties, my second husband and I bought an aquatic weed harvester. I spent the summers cutting weeds at Portage Lakes and other bodies of water throughout northeastern Ohio.

I've always been happiest when I was working outdoors, so spending the winter working in Virginia with the landscaping job was right up my alley.

NOT SO HOPEFUL IN HOPEWELL, NEW JERSEY

I returned back to that small church in Hopewell, on April 8th. Because Deb was no longer my pilot car driver, I had several people sign up for a day here or a few days there, to help out with the walk. A couple different people committed to come out to spot me for a week or two.

A lot of time was spent traveling to and fro to pick up pilot car drivers. I was either traveling long distances to get someone or waiting for days for a driver to arrive at my location from several states away. Needless to say—2003 got off to a very slow start.

I had arranged for the Guardian Angels to escort me through New York City. They were scheduled to meet me on the east side of the George Washington Bridge on the Tuesday following Memorial Day. The bridge was about 70 miles from Hopewell so I had to press forward to meet that deadline.

My sister Helen traveled to New Jersey to be the first of several pilot car drivers for the year. She was committed to help me for about a week before she would have to return to her home in Washington, Georgia.

When we got to Hopewell there was still five inches of snow on the ground from winter. The cross I had planted five months earlier was not in the flower bed where I had left it. Somebody had moved it to a different bed. I picked up the little cross and attached a note to it with information about my return to the walk after a winter break.

I was able to cover 30 miles while Helen was spotting me. I continued on 518 which eventually became Highway 27. I walked Highway 27 up to a few miles south of Newark before Helen headed back to Georgia and I returned to Virginia.

I had about 40 miles to walk to get to the George Washington Bridge. I worked for Jen for several weeks then she was able to take off work to spot me. Toward the end of May, Jen and my friend Gwyn, also from Virginia, traveled with me back to New Jersey.

As I was walking toward Newark on US 1, I strolled by a television cameraman. I stopped to chat with the gentleman but he didn't seem to speak English. I didn't think too much of it.

The next day as I was traveling through the city, I had a *God* sense that I was to turn left, walk one block, turn right, walk another block and turn left back to Highway 1. I told Jen and Gwyn my plan, and Jen pointed out that I was going out of my way. She asked if I was sure I wanted to add the two extra blocks to my walk.

"No, not really, but I really believe God wants me to do this!" I responded.

"Okay, whatever!" she muttered.

So I turned to take the detour. I was about halfway into the turn when people began to come out of their homes and applaud me as I passed through their neighborhood. I was in a Hispanic section of the city and I couldn't understand what was being said to me as the folks cheered me on. Some of them pointed toward the sky as they applauded. As I waved and smiled, it soon dawned on me, that these folks knew what I was doing and they were excited to be a part of this journey. Apparently, without my knowledge the Hispanic cameraman covered this walk.

I was about 15 miles from the bridge before Jen and Gwyn had to return home. Up to this point I had not taken the RV out to the walk. It was still parked near Jen's house. I traveled to Virginia with my friends and drove the motor home north to Allentown, Pennsylvania, so it would be stored closer to where I was walking.

Jerry had traveled to Ohio with his grandmother for a conference over Mother's Day weekend. He dropped his grandmother off with some relatives in Pennsylvania then he joined me as I walked the George Washington Bridge on Thursday, May 15th.

GUARDIAN ANGELS

Some local members of the Guardian Angels greeted us in New York City to escort us through upper Manhattan and the Bronx. They were young men in their early to mid-twenties-well built, they stood tall appearing confident. They were adorned in uniforms which consisted of black pants tucked in black combat boots; a white t-shirt with *Guardian Angels* on the front, and a burgundy beret tilted slightly on their heads.

After introductions, it was determined three of the angels would be escorting us the first day in the city. Two walked with us while the other drove a silver van with *Guardian Angels Escorting Service* written on the sides of the vehicle. I walked and chatted with each young man throughout the day. Both of them had a very sad story to tell me about their own lives and by the end of the day, I had spent hours ministering to each of them.

We covered 10 miles and the angels took us back where Jerry had left his pickup truck. Jerry and I went downtown where Jerry's friend Bradley hosted us in his New York loft apartment, only a few blocks from Times Square and a short distance from Ground Zero.

The next day the angels picked us up and drove us to the place we had left off the day before. This time, two of the angels from the previous day and a third guard whom we were just meeting, would accompany us. I walked with the new guy and he too seemed to be very troubled. I shared my faith with him, hoping to encourage him in his struggles.

That day, each of the three angels picked up a cross which I had planted. Two of them wanted to have a cross to remind them to keep their faith. The other guard asked if he could replant his cross at a place where an eight-year-old girl had been killed. The youngster was being carried by her mother as the two were headed

72

to a church service, when mother and child got caught up in a gang-related cross fire. The bullet lodged in the little girl's chest and killed her.

At the end of the walking day one of the guards drove the van back toward New York City and took a detour to the place where the child was killed. He stopped the van and the angels got out of the vehicle. They walked to a spot on the sidewalk where the men stopped and bowed their heads. Jerry and I sat quietly in the van as we peered through the windows to see all three angels take off their berets and weep as the guard placed the small cross in the ground. There was dead silence in the van as we were escorted back to the loft apartment. This was the last day we spent with the New York City chapter of the Guardian Angels.

We were getting closer to Connecticut and farther away from the high-crime area. Jerry spotted me as I walked up to a McDonald's restaurant within six miles of the Connecticut state line. He drove me to Allentown then left to get his grandmother in Ohio before heading back to his home in Florida.

AN EMMAUS ROAD TO DAMASCUS

I found myself getting more and more discouraged as I had difficulty getting someone to come out to spot me on a regular basis. A day here and a day there was all I had. It seemed like I was spending more time driving than walking. I thought about giving up.

On May 20, I decided it was time to take the RV out to the walk with me, in great faith that I would be able to stay out there and not have to travel so much to get helpers. I left from Allentown with Gina, who agreed to spot me for a few days.

73

After we returned to New York, Gina informed me that she did not have a driver's license. I recalled that there was a bus route along US 1 where I was walking. I drove the RV to the McDonalds where I had quit walking the week before. Gina and I took off, in hopes of finding a bus stop 8 to 10 miles ahead. Sure enough, there was a bus stop near the end of our tenth mile but we had to change buses three times to get back to the motor home.

The next day we did the same thing, we drove the motor home to the place we left off the day before and headed north on foot. This time, we had to walk four miles out of our way before we found a bus stop. We walked a 14-mile day to cover only 10 miles.

The following day was one of the rainiest days I had walked thus far. I drove the RV to the exact place where we had ended the day before. I put on a rain poncho and kept my cell phone tucked tight up under the plastic shield.

As we began walking, I had to lean forward to press through the wind and rain. I began to grumble to God—just loud enough for *me* and *God* to hear what was coming out of my mouth.

"God, I am not sure I am still on the right path. Please show me if you want me to keep going! You carried me 1,451 miles last year. I don't even have 100 miles in this year, and it is almost June!" I grumbled.

Knowing that by the end of November, I would have to break for winter, and the way winters are in the north, it would be May before I would be able to walk again. I thought about how this would be the case all the way across the north and I did the math.

"God, if I continue at this pace, I am going to be an old lady by the time I finish this walk!" I protested.

"What kind of a path am I on anyway?" I whined.

74

"This is not a perimeter walk! Look at the detours! Last year I had a full-time pilot car driver; this year I spend all of my time waiting! Couldn't you have used me better when I had two legs, God? God, if you want me to finish this walk, you had better hit me over the head with a two-by-four, because I am ready to quit and go home!" I mumbled.

Big mistake! Not a good idea to ask God for a two-by-four! God has God-sized two-by-fours. No sooner had this come out of my mouth when I heard my phone ringing. I very carefully pulled the phone out from under my poncho and held it under my hood.

"Hello!" I grunted.

"Hi, are you Carol Cruise?" the caller questioned.

"Yes, I am!" I answered.

"I am a police officer and I live in Baltimore, Maryland. Last night, well sometime in the wee hours of the morning, I was in a near accident as I was crossing a bridge in Pennsylvania. As I was descending off the east side of the bridge, I was traveling at an excess of 70 miles per hour, and a car pulled in front of me!" the woman reported.

I listened intently as she continued.

"I slammed on the brakes and my SUV was airborne. My life flashed before me while I soared through the air! I landed within a few inches of a telephone pole on one side and a steel pole on the other…I know I could have been killed if I had hit either pole!" she continued.

She paused for a moment.

"I was really shook up, got out of the vehicle, and found the young man who had pulled in front of me, standing next to me. He asked me if I was okay. I told him I was all right and the boy left. I wondered if the SUV was okay, so I got back in the vehicle and backed up! I do not know how I saw it, because it was pitch-black outside, but there was a little cross pushed two-thirds of the way in the ground!"

After another moment of silence, she continued.

"You're the only person I have shared this with. My life will never be the same! I know it was divine intervention that I am still alive! Thank you for walking this walk! God bless you!"

I began to ask this person some questions, but I had either lost her call or she chose to hang up. Her call showed up as a private number so I was not able to get back to her.

Yes, I was hit by a God-sized two-by-four! God loves that police woman so much, he carried a one-legged, middle-aged, overweight, woman on a course to plant a cross right where He knew she would land, on that particular morning.

God said to me, "Whose walk is this anyway? Is it your path, Carol, or is it My path? Are you giving Me a few years of your life, or are you giving Me your life? Is it My timing, Carol, or is it your timing? Who was it who woke you up in the middle of the night, Carol? Was it Me, or was it you? If you had done this walk when you had two legs, it would have been incredible, but doing it on one leg is miraculous, I get the glory!" God scolded.

While on my Emmaus journey, pondering how God had abandoned me, He was with me the whole time, right beside me directing my path and paving the road. Like the Apostle Paul on his journey to Damascus, I got hit over the head with a God-sized two-by-four.

I looked up and raised my hands to the sky and in all my humility, I said, "I am so sorry, God! This is Your walk, it is Your path, and it is Your timing. I don't care how long it takes, I give You my life! And, yes God, You get the Glory!"

That was the first day of the rest of my life! From that day forward, I have been determined to live my life for God, on His path, in His time, His way!

I will never forget that bridge on Route 327, in Sunnyburn, Pennsylvania. I will never forget how God opened bridges and closed bridges to get me there. No, I will never forget planting that particular cross on the east end of that particular bridge...the bridge crossing that changed my life forever, and the bridge crossing that changed the life of a complete stranger!

December 4, 2002

I recently found a cross in my front yard, with the note of intent. The note says mile #1,354.

My children (twins, five) state the cross had been there several days BEFORE I saw it, so I do not know when it was actually placed, but sometime in the last week is my guess.

I cannot imagine the walker placing it in my somewhat remote, uphill, off-the-main-road yard. I am guessing someone I know has passed it on to the west, and we will also do so, probably to an unsuspecting person, and will let them wonder if "the walker," sorry cannot make out actual name: Reverend Carl Cruise? Has left it for them.

I would appreciate more info on this mission, and where mile #1,354 originated. I would like to see if there is a tracking system for the crosses to see how far, and where they end up. God's touch is all encompassing, and it would be wonderful to see the movement of His love!

We looked in disbelief at the cross in our yard (my first thought was that someone's beloved pet had died in our yard and they had left a memorial cross). Read the note, said a prayer, and chuckled. It was a delightful little surprise. Thank You, and Praise be to God.

Note: I have answered each and every email, letter, and phone call!

"God, Please Send Me a Partner"—2003

Three Crosses on the Side of the Road

The winter months were full of travel and speaking engagements. Since I didn't have a car, I spent many hours on buses traveling from state to state from north to south and east to west. I would often think of the roads traveled on foot and how God carried me every step of the journey and how he protected me even in the winter months when I was not on the walk.

One time I was traveling from Canton, Ohio, to Richmond, Virginia. I had to change buses in Washington D.C. The bus station was crowded with weary travelers. There was an hour wait before my connecting bus was announced.

I put my bags at my feet and looked around the terminal. I spotted a very hefty African American man across the room. I really couldn't help but spot him; he had a glow about him that caused him to stand out in the crowd. He began to sing gospel music. I became mesmerized by his singing and lost touch with my surroundings. I was brought back to reality by a young man singing in my ear. He was reciting a song about *three crosses on the side of the road*—actually the only words I caught from the song.

The young man was only about six inches from me and singing right into my ear. Quite surprised, I turned and stared at him for a few minutes. He told me his name was Stephen and he was a Christian. He said he thought maybe I was too, because I seemed to be enjoying the gospel singing across the way.

About that time, an announcement was made that our bus had arrived and we were directed to the proper gate. I got in line behind the gospel singer—Stephen followed. Passengers were counted as we went through the gate and the count stopped with me. I was the last person to be given a seat on that particular bus headed to Richmond.

As I was climbing into the bus, I looked back and saw Stephen standing in front of a long line of people waiting for the next bus to leave for Richmond.

I usually sit in the handicapped seating behind the driver so I have more leg room to extend my prosthesis, but I noticed the bus driver had put his personal belongings there. Instead of asking permission to move his things, I took the first available seat which was in the back of the bus.

The bus driver stood up and turned to look back through the bus and a few minutes later, he moved his things from the handicapped seat, got off the bus and returned with Stephen—*just* Stephen! The driver pointed to the seat and told the boy to sit down.

As we began our six-hour bus trip, the gospel singer, who was sitting right in front of me, began to sing. Soon several people in the back of the bus began to sing with him and I joined in. After a couple of songs, a man began to share his testimony. We sang a few more songs and people from the front of the bus began to turn and stare at us. Some gave us dirty looks. Stephen looked back and smiled. I waved. Another person shared a testimony. We sang another song. I shared my testimony. We sang more songs.

Several hours into our trip we were still singing and praising God, when the bus began to swerve from side to side. At one point it seemed like the driver had lost control. He had both hands clenched on the steering wheel and seemed to be hyperfocused on the road. As the bus swerved some more we, the folks in the back of the bus, began to pray for our safety. It was a rough ride for the rest of the way to Richmond.

When we pulled into the bus station, people began to stand. The bus driver parked the bus, stood up, and ordered everyone to sit down.

"The brakes are going out on the bus. We almost collided with a semi-truck back there. I believe if it were not for the passengers in the back of this bus, we would have all been killed. God showed favor on us because of their faith!" the driver announced.

I got off the bus and looked for Stephen. He was nowhere to be seen. It was months later before I heard the words to the song about three crosses on the side of the road. I believe the song was about a bus colliding with a semi-truck.

Even when we seem to be traveling alone—we are not alone! God is always with us!

JUST BE KOZ

I began to walk in a new light. Even though I was aware that God was always by my side, I began to pray for God to send me a partner who would share the vision and be equally dedicated to the ministry. God is the author of companionship! After all, God gave Aaron to Moses, Noah had his whole family, Abraham took

Lot, David had Jonathan, Ruth stayed with Naomi, and Jesus sent the disciples two-by-two. Certainly, God had a companion for me.

Meanwhile, I continued to go down through my list of people who signed up for a time. My friend Koz was next in line. I went to Canton, Ohio, to pick her up for her adventuresome mission experience. She was packed for the trip and ready to go!

We headed toward Connecticut, to where Gina and I had left off by planting cross #1,546 a few miles north of the state line.

Not far into our trip, while traveling on Interstate 80 in Pennsylvania, I turned abruptly and unintentionally onto an exit ramp. Just as I began exiting off the ramp, Koz and I witnessed an accident. A semi-truck sideswiped a car then proceeded to hit and flip another vehicle. If this mysterious exiting had not taken place, we probably would have been in the middle of very serious accident. It was like an angel had grabbed the steering wheel and headed us off the road, so our lives would be spared.

About 100 miles before reaching Connecticut, we had a blowout in our right rear tire. I pulled the car off the very next exit ramp where we found a garage. It did not take long for the repair and we were on the road again.

Just after getting back on the highway, I hit a yellow barrel in a construction zone, with the awning support posts on the passenger's side of the motor home. The column was torn loose and the awning encasement hung down the side of the RV. I pulled off onto the emergency lane, and Koz, who is afraid of heights, climbed up the ladder mounted on the back of the camper and disconnected what was left of the awning.

It certainly seemed like there was a force that was trying to prevent this walk from taking place. We very cautiously pressed on in our mission.

After finally reaching our destination, Koz and I began making our way through Connecticut on US 1. New England has a very good transit system, so we decided Koz would join me on the walk and we would use public transportation to return to our home base each evening, which happened to be the parking lot of a supermarket.

Koz was at a turning point in her life. She had just ended a very dysfunctional relationship and was desperately looking for a new flame. She seemed to be relationship dependent. I encouraged her to *just be Koz*, and simply seek a relationship with God because He would meet the desires of her heart.

We struggled through the next several days. We were walking up and down hills in the heat of the summer. My prosthesis is held on by a liner that adheres to my skin. When I perspire the liner gets too wet and slips off. It was extremely hot and humid so I had to stop about 8 to 10 times each mile to dry the sweat from my stump.

Koz was with me for a week. With the intense heat and the poor-fitting prosthesis, we were only able to cover 35 miles. But as we witnessed God's hand in our protection and provision—our spiritual relationship with each other—grew by leaps and bounds. I believe by facing her fears, exerting herself to the max, and in spending time in God's presence, Koz's relationship addiction became more of a *God dependence*. She is in fulfilling relationships today with God first, herself in God second, and spouse third.

COULD I HAVE SEEN THE DEVIL?

My closest friend, Wendi, was next to join me on the walk. She signed up for a two-week stretch while on her summer break from working in a school system as a special education specialist.

Wendi wanted to walk with me instead of spotting me with a car. She is a powerful intercessor and I was delighted to have her by my side.

I appreciated Wendi's willingness to take part of her summer for this mission and I wanted to really cover some miles while she was with me. I remember walking the best I could, but with the summer heat I was only able to cover seven or eight miles a day.

Each day we would leave a vehicle ahead of us and use public transportation to get back to our starting place. Sometimes our days were exceptionally long. On one occasion we spent all day trying to figure out how we could position a car at the end of a bridge in New Haven, so we could walk to the car at the end of the day's trek. By the time we mapped out our route, planted the pilot car, and drove the RV back to the day's starting point, it was late afternoon.

We walked into New Haven in a downpour about 10:00 that evening. I heard preaching and walked toward the source and noticed we were standing in front of a large church building. I ran up the steps and went inside. Soaking wet and wearing shorts and a tank top, I did not go into the sanctuary. Instead, I sat out in the foyer and listened to the preaching. Then I remembered I had left Wendi in the rain so I opened the church door and motioned for her to join me. She sat beside me for a while then someone came out and invited us to join the service. It was an inner city youth revival and we felt blessed to be there.

It was after 11:00 before the service was over. Wendi and I made our way back to the street and across the bridge. At the north side of the bridge, there was a dark path that led down to where we had parked the van. When I began to enter the path, I sensed an eerie presence. As I walked deeper into the darkness, I saw the most awful looking creature I had ever encountered. I gasped and jumped back.

Wendi sensed the presence but claimed she did not actually see it. I began to run back toward the lights on the bridge.

Wendi said, "No, Carol, we have to go toward the car!"

She grabbed my left hand and raised it up. She sang praise songs as she dragged me down the hill.

It had been prophesied about a year earlier that I would encounter the devil on this walk. I actually thought the minister, who spoke this prophecy, had lost his mind.

"The devil is not omnipresent, like God is, and can only be in one place at a time. Why would he bother himself with me?" I chimed.

"Because you are walking one of the most powerful nations on earth for God, and he certainly doesn't want that to happen!" exclaimed the minister.

Well, let me tell you, if that wasn't the devil, I hope I never have to encounter him. It was a creepy creature that appeared to be neither male nor female. It was dressed in a brown cape and lurked in the darkness. Its presence was disturbing. Maybe the prophet was right. Maybe the devil came out to see what we were up to. Thank God, he has no dominion over us. I remembered Art's words. "Get lost—you have no business in my life!" I informed Satan.

Wendi and I made it to the car and were safe and sound in the RV by midnight.

COULD I HAVE SEEN GOD?

As we continued up the coast of Connecticut, Wendi and I enjoyed each other's company. Wendi told me that she had just interviewed for a position at work that she had been waiting for, for over three years.

A few days later, while walking, Wendi received the news of her promotion. She was delighted. It was around my birthday so we decided to go out for dinner that weekend and celebrate my birthday and her new position. Saturday after walking eight miles, we got cleaned up and went out to a fine seafood restaurant on the Atlantic Ocean.

The next day Wendi followed me in her van as I moved the RV ahead to Westerly, Rhode Island, which would be our next home base. We talked to each other on walkie-talkies as we traveled up the road. At about 10:00 a.m., Wendi reminded me that her home church was about to begin their worship service and asked me if I would pray. After closing the prayer, Wendi informed me that she was going to continue praying, so I laid the walkie-talkie in the passenger seat and enjoyed some quiet time as I drove.

After about 15 minutes, Wendi called out to me on the walkie-talkie. She asked me if I would find a place to pull over. As I drove north on Interstate 95, I scanned signs at each exit for a truck stop. Wendi called again—this time, there was urgency in her voice.

"Will you please find a place to pull over?" she pleaded.

Wendi followed me off the very next exit ramp and into the parking lot of a warehouse. Wendi got out of the vehicle and headed toward the camper, I could see tears streaming down her cheeks. My heart began to race as I opened the side door of the RV.

When Wendi stepped into the camper, I noticed a bright glow around her. I backed up. I didn't know what else to do, so I dropped to my knees. Wendi knelt down, leaned over me, and began to pray. I felt her tears dripping on my neck and back. It seemed like eternity before I could move.

Wendi stood up and I followed. As I turned to face her, she appeared taller and was still surrounded by a bright light. I had never experienced anything like this. I was unable to speak and seemed to be paralyzed. I believe I was seeing the same kind of glow Moses exhibited when he came down off Mount Sinai.

Wendi knelt down and began digging for something under the fold-down table that was between two bench seats. I found this to be odd because I had items stored under there, but not anything she would know about or be interested in. She stretched and reached to the back corner of my stash and pulled out a small board. Then she reached back and got a second board, then a third, and the fourth. These were small, rough cut one-by-twos, all cut to about 10 inches long. I kept them tucked away and would pull them out to use for extra support under the table or bed when extra heavy people came out to stay in the camper.

I watched curiously as Wendi positioned the boards in the form of a two-by-four. She stood up and gently clobbered me over the head.

"I got your two-by-four, Carol!" she sobbed.

I had told Wendi that God would have to hit me over the head with a two-by-four, if He wanted me to have a full-time partner on the walk—I did not want to mistakenly join up with the wrong person.

Even though I had prayed for a companion, I had never considered Wendi. She had two young daughters who needed her at home. I was puzzled. She began to tell me that while she was praying in her van, God revealed to her that she was to be out there with me full-time on this walk. She shared with me that God promised her that He would take care of her girls, Courtney, 15, and

Molly, 11. She went on to say that God let her know this ministry was going to be blessed abundantly and He would supply all of her needs.

She began to sob even more. "I am grieving everything God is asking me to sacrifice; my home, my girls, my family, my job… the job I prayed for, for three years! God is asking me to give all this up for Him."

Again, I was speechless. I held her in my arms as she sobbed.

I couldn't move and could not believe what I was hearing or seeing. There was such an anointing on Wendi, I knew that God was speaking through her!

Quite some time passed before I was able to utter, "Wendi, you are my best friend and I love you too much to ask you to leave your daughters, to join me out here. God loves you more than I do. Surely we must not be hearing His voice correctly!"

I looked into her eyes. Even though I was having a hard time believing, I knew. Yet still operating in denial, I babbled, "Maybe He is just calling you for the summer and spring breaks!"

She shook her head. She knew, and deep down, I knew too.

Wendi was not able to begin full-time right away. There were a few things she had to take care of first. The next week we crossed into Rhode Island and made it through Westerly before Wendi returned to Ohio.

MAXINE

I had to drive to Scottsboro, Alabama, to fetch Maxine, my next pilot car driver. She was an unemployed truck driver who was willing to come out to spot me with the motor home, for as long as I needed her.

Once we returned to Rhode Island, I instructed Maxine to move the RV ahead of me a little at a time and I would call her on the walkie-talkie if I needed her—at the times I would need a restroom, drink of water, or to take a short break; otherwise, she was to stay put until I caught up with her.

I asked her to please stay on the right side of the road to prevent situations where she would have to back up, because I wanted her to avoid possible liabilities that might be caused from something being in her blind spot, when backing up and making turns.

Maxine, having been through truck driving school, was somewhat insulted by my being overly cautious. I think there may have been some passive aggressive issues, because many times when she pulled forward, she either backed up or crossed the road. In fact, a few times, I looked ahead and saw her backing across the road.

I asked her over and over again to please stay on the right-hand side of the road and to avoid backing up. She seemed frustrated with me for repeating myself, but she still insisted on doing it her way. Both strong-willed individuals, it became obvious we were having a power struggle. Finally, Maxine and I came to an agreement on how she should move ahead and things were going better.

I talked with Wendi just about every day. She was a constant source of encouragement. One time, while Wendi and I were conversing, I mentioned that Maxine was actually keeping the RV on the right side of the road as I had asked her. Wendi encouraged me to give her positive feedback. So when I got to the motor home, I thanked Maxine for doing such a great job. We exchanged smiles—after all I love Maxine, she is a friend, and I wanted things to work out.

Maxine, a talented song writer and musician, has a beautiful voice. After I finished walking each day, she would play her guitar and sing. Sometimes I would sing along. She was one of several musicians who donated songs for two CDs that were recorded and presented to me for fund raising.

I was constantly getting phone calls from well-meaning friends asking what state I was in. When I was walking Florida, the calls were kind of annoying and discouraging. People would say things like "Are you still in Florida?" "I can't believe you are still in Florida!" "When are you going to be through Florida?" I was walking as fast as I could and the calls actually got on my nerves. Well, I shared this with a friend in Virginia. She told me to tell people that I "was in the state of grace!" I told this story to Maxine and she wrote a beautiful song about being in the *State of Grace*.

One day Maxine pulled ahead of me to a Y in the road and veered to the right. By the time I got to the Y, she was nowhere to be seen. Not knowing which way she went, I went to the left. Hours passed and I had no idea where Maxine was with the motor home. I tried to call her but the battery was dead in her cell phone.

I decided to call Wendi. She quickly answered the phone and told me she was on her way to Wednesday night prayer meeting. I asked if she would request prayer for me because I had no idea where I was, I didn't know where Maxine had gone with the RV, my phone battery was almost dead, I had no money in my pocket, and it was getting dark. She said she would ask the group to pray for me and we ended the conversation.

I planted a cross and dropped down on a stoop in front of a restaurant. I put my face in my hands and began to pray. After a few minutes I looked up and rubbed my eyes. It was getting dark and I wasn't sure if I was seeing what I thought I was seeing, but there appeared to be 100 or more crosses, right across the street from where I planted cross #1,700. I walked across the street, and sure enough, there were rows and rows of crosses made out of debris from what was left of a nightclub that had burned to the ground. 100 people had vanished in the flames of that fire. I was in Warwick, Rhode Island.

I walked back across the street to the restaurant and noticed a police officer was pulling in. By then it was dark. I walked to the squad car and explained my situation to the officer. I asked him if there had been any accidents reported involving a Fourwinds motor home. He told me that there had not been any automobile accidents reported that evening, but he would keep an eye out for my R.V.

Minutes after he had pulled out of the parking lot, Maxine pulled in. She had no explanation other than she just got lost!

I took the driver's seat of the motor home and we headed to Ohio to get Wendi, who had planned to be on the walk for another week before school started.

◊ ◊ ◊

When we arrived back in Warwick, Rhode Island, it was nightfall. There was a memorial ceremony taking place at the ruins, where there had once been a nightclub. It was the six-month anniversary of the tragic fire.

Each of the 100 crosses had been made into a shrine, as the victim's family members and friends stood around holding lit candles. The three of us stood there and respectfully observed as poems were read and songs sung.

As the mourners began to quietly leave the site, Wendi and I walked together while Maxine drove ahead.

It was great to have Wendi's company. As we walked together, we talked about the possibilities of her being out there on all of her school breaks. Before we knew it, the week was over and she had to return back to Canton to start the school year.

A few days after Wendi left, I was on the phone with her when I noticed Maxine was about to run into an awning over the entrance of a very elite restaurant.

"I've got to get off the phone! Maxine is about to take off an awning of a restaurant!" I screeched as I abruptly ended the call.

I screamed for Maxine to stop. Apparently she did not hear me, and she drove the RV through the carport which was at least six inches lower than the top of the camper. Within seconds the awning was torn away from the carport and the air conditioner was ripped off the motor home.

The irate owner approached me from the front of the vehicle as I came walking up from behind. Maxine sat in the driver's seat with a blank look on her face. I knew she felt terrible. I asked her to stay seated while I discussed the situation with the owner.

I apologized to the disgruntled businessman and explained to him that even though Maxine was driving, I am the responsible owner of the vehicle. He calmed down a little bit after I handed him my insurance information and told him I would be releasing Maxine from her position.

My insurance agent informed me that over $20,000 of defacing was done to the restaurant. I got estimates for the repairs needed for the motor home. It would cost over $1,200 to have a new air conditioner installed and the damage repaired. I was responsible for a $500 deductible. It could have been a lot worse, but this was still a lot of money for a small shoebox ministry.

I took the driver's seat and began heading to Allentown, Pennsylvania, to stay with my friends Bobby and Colleen, while the air conditioner was being replaced on the camper. After the repair work, as we headed back toward Rhode Island, we stopped at an A&W Root Beer stand to have lunch. I realized we were sitting at a fork in the road. I could go one way and head back to the walk, or I could go the other way and head home to Ohio.

I gave Maxine a ten-dollar bill and asked her to get us some burgers, fries, and a couple of root beers. Meanwhile, I called Wendi and asked her to pray about our situation.

After eating our lunch, I looked over at Maxine and explained that I was no longer comfortable using the motor home as a pilot vehicle. I handed her a piece of paper and told her to pray and write what she thought God would have us do at this point. I told her that I would do the same.

I prayed for a few minutes then I wrote on a piece of paper. I peeked over at Maxine as she handed me her slip which read, *Go get Wendi and send me home.* I showed her what I had scribbled, *Go to Ohio and get Wendi and help you get back to Alabama!*

As I was pulling out of the parking lot, I gave Wendi a call. She asked me to come and get her.

"Everything has gone wrong since I have come back from the walk; I don't feel like I *fit* here anymore! I am supposed to be out there with you!" she informed me.

"I am on my way!" I replied.

GOD'S PERFECT TIMING

I drove back to Canton, Ohio, and purchased a bus ticket to Scottsboro, Alabama. I gave Maxine a hug, thanked her for helping out, told her I loved her, and sent her on her way.

93

Things were going better than expected for Wendi. She had a talk with her ex-husband, Terry, and her two girls. All three seemed to miraculously accept the call on Wendi's life.

"We can't argue with God!" exclaimed Terry.

"No, can't argue with God!" mimicked Molly."

Courtney was very quiet but seemed to be okay.

Wendi had called me, over a year ago, and asked what I thought about her having Terry as a housemate. I asked if she thought there was a chance she and Terry might get back together. She said she didn't know. She went on to tell me that she was struggling financially and Terry was renting elsewhere, so it seemed practical for them to share the expenses of one place.

I cautioned Wendi about how this looked to the outside world, and told her I was not sure it was the best decision. What did I know? Our ways are not God's ways—He knew what He was doing. He was lining up things for such a time as this. Courtney and Molly did not have to be uprooted and change school systems. What a blessing!

Wendi submitted a letter of resignation and a two-week notice. Her supervisor wanted to discuss the situation and called her in to talk. She dangled the contract in front of Wendi like a carrot and offered to tear up the letter and hold her job for a period of six months, just in case things did not work out on the walk.

Wendi hesitated for a brief second and said, "This is a faith walk, and it would not take much faith if I had this job to fall back on. My answer is no!"

So the position Wendi had wanted so badly, the job she had prayed into existence, was gone. Her supervisor gave her the next two weeks off with pay and suggested she take care of any health needs before her insurance coverage ended. Wendi spent the next several days scheduling appointments, packing, and preparing for a very long journey.

There was something I needed to attend to, before I could go back to the walk. The prosthesis that Cleveland Clinic had provided for me the year before was not working out. I desperately needed another leg. So I went to Cleveland Clinic Orthotic and Prosthetic Center to see about having a new prosthetic leg made.

As I walked into the clinic, the staff people began to call out to me by name, "Hi Carolyn!" "How's it going, Carolyn!" "Good to see you, Carolyn!" One salutation after another—this seemed odd!

Gee, they are getting friendly here! I thought. *I wonder how all of these people know my name?*

John Redding, my prosthetist, was wearing a big smile, as he came out to meet me in the waiting room. Again, this seemed odd. John was usually very somber. As I accompanied him to the fitting area, John informed me that I had been featured in the July/August issue of *inMOTION* Magazine. This is a national medical magazine that goes out to prosthetic places all over the country.

I had been interviewed for the magazine by Brandie Erisman, in February of 2002. Brandie told me the story would appear in the July issue. The story was not featured at all that year, so I figured it had been rejected.

Here we were a year later and the article finally came out. I was handed a copy of the magazine and I could see that Brandie had updated the material by visiting my website.

John examined my stump and shook his head.

"There is really no way I can fit you with a prosthetic that will be more comfortable than this, unless I make a brace that fits around the top of your thigh and perhaps your waist. You wore your stump out!" he exclaimed.

I said "Praise God! He carried me so far on a cosmetic prosthesis which was never intended for this type of wear and tear, so He will certainly carry me in this uncomfortable walking leg."

I chose not to have the alterations, and limped out of the building.

As I was crossing the parking lot, I got a phone call from Jimmy, at Myrtle Beach Brace and Limb in South Carolina. He had seen the article in *inMOTION* and asked if he could make a leg for me. I explained to him what I had just been told at Cleveland Clinic. He said he was a Christian and believed in miracles, and was certain he could make a prosthetic leg for me.

Wendi and I headed down to Myrtle Beach to meet Jimmy and to see about a new leg. Jimmy, a delightful man, ran a one-man prosthetic and orthotic business, which his father had started many years earlier. He greeted us with love and got right to work.

His techniques did not seem as modern as I was accustomed to. He made a mold of my stump and grabbed parts and pieces from here and there, then sent me off with a test socket to try for a few days.

Wendi and I traveled to Virginia Beach for a speaking engagement. The service was at 9:00 a.m. Afterward, we drove to Williamsburg, Virginia, for an 11:30 a.m. service at a church where a friend of mine ministered.

At the later service, my test socket cracked when I knelt down to pray. Other than the crack, the leg seemed to work just fine. We returned to Myrtle Beach for a final fitting. Jimmy sent me off with some new liners and a leg that seemed to be working out for me. He had added some inflatable cushions for a more comfortable fit.

It was amazing how God worked this out! I believe the article was not published in the summer of 2002 because there was divine timing and purpose for the article to be published one year later.

Four Squares in Massachusetts

Since I had driven the RV home to get Wendi, we had two vehicles to get back out to the east coast. I drove the motor home and Wendi followed me in her van.

One day we walked away from the van, hoping we could catch a bus back at the end of the day, but after walking 11 or 12 miles we still had not seen a bus stop. We were in the small town of New Bedford, Massachusetts.

As we walked up to a Methodist church, I said, "It is Wednesday evening. I am sure there will be some midweek meetings at some of the local churches."

We stood in front of the church for a few minutes. There were some cars in the drive but neither of us felt led to go into the building and ask for help.

Instead, we continued walking another few blocks. I noticed an A-frame sign on the sidewalk which read ALL ARE WELCOME. We stopped at the little store front and noted that it was a Four Square Church. I pulled at the door. It came open so we went inside.

We were welcomed by an outgoing young man who seemed excited to greet us. He said he had been at the park watching his nephew play basketball and realized he had to head over to the church to unlock the doors. He told us this was a responsibility he had taken on, but had not always been so diligent about being there by 6:00 p.m. We shared our story and thanked him for being there on time.

After a few minutes people began to gather for an evening service. The pastors, a husband and wife team, prayed over us and took up a collection to help us on our journey. They said they saw a real anointing on us and this ministry. It was prophesied that we were leaving a path of fire behind us with each step that we take for the Lord—a revival fire.

One of the women offered to drive us back to the van and spot us the next day. We were told that there were two more Four Square Churches right on our path and that there were sure to be folks from those congregations who would be willing to help us.

Sure enough, a few days later, we walked right up to the Onset Beach Four Square Church. There were people at the building who invited us to help in a soup kitchen on Saturday and I was asked to share at the Sunday service. We were cordially invited to park our motor home in the drive for the weekend.

By midweek, we found ourselves at the Plymouth Four Square Church. And it was the folks at this church who helped us move forward.

As we continued to head north on 1A through Marshfield, we noticed another Four Square Church. We saw that there was someone in the building so we went in to say hello and to share our mission. We met a charming middle-aged woman, Lindsey. She was one of the intercessors of the congregation and was there for a Tuesday morning prayer meeting.

She told us that she was the one who "cleaned house" in the church. This means she was blessed with the gift of discernment and was very sensitive to evil and wrongdoers. She would pray for protection and she would alert the leadership of the church to anyone who was there to cause division or harm, or anyone who was not walking in the Spirit of God. She discerned an anointing on us and the ministry (familiar words).

Lindsey took a liking to us and invited us to join her at her home for a swim and lunch. Later that week, she invited us back for dinner.

The pastors, a husband and wife team, asked us to share our testimony at the church and again a love offering was collected and support was given. After the service we visited with some of the folks. There were some concerns about our walking and especially walking through Boston. "People just don't walk around here!" "It is not safe to be out there!" "There is someone attacking women at the shopping centers!" "It just is not safe!" were a few of the remarks.

We were told about the Big Dig and how the city was torn apart for that massive underground transportation project. One person told us that her husband had ventured that way a few months back, "but for the most part, people just avoid Boston!"

"Great!" We were headed right for Boston and, *for the most part, people just avoid that city!*

We moved the RV from one shopping center to the next as we got closer and closer to Boston. We noticed there were no other pedestrians out, except for a few people on bicycles or walking (because they had lost their licenses due to drunk driving), we were the only pedestrians.

Several police officers stopped to ask us "Where you headed?" and "Are you all set?" A few people stopped and asked if we were hunting vampires. One person even asked if were after *the* vampire—I guess they noticed we were carrying wooden crosses. But, for the most part, people kept to themselves.

When we did have an opportunity to talk with someone about what we were doing, we were warned about the crime, and about the hazards of the Big Dig.

As we walked into Boston, we saw earth movers, cranes, bull-dozers, dump trucks, and other heavy equipment parked along the city streets. There were also several mounds of dirt piled throughout. Even though there was no actual work taking place, there was evidence of new construction and the road signs were confusing.

We had some difficulty maneuvering through this wide-spread construction site so we stopped at the police station to ask for directions. The police officers rolled their eyes at us in disbelief that we were doing this walk. We were given maps and sent on our way.

We needed to find Atlantic Avenue, but we couldn't. So we stopped to ask a newspaper vendor how to get there. He told us he didn't know where Atlantic Avenue was, so we continued on.

I needed a restroom. I stopped in several places of business and asked if I could use the facilities, just to be informed there were no public restrooms. I went into a Subway and was told there was a restroom next door. Went next door to be told the key was in the business down the street…ventured down the street to be redirected back to the Subway. Not getting anywhere with my pursuit of a restroom, I meandered back to find Wendi approaching a pedestrian.

I caught up with Wendi just in time to hear her ask the woman if she knew where Atlantic Avenue was. She leaned forward and whispered to Wendi, "I can show you, but you know this city just isn't the same any more, since…"

"I know, I know!" Wendi replied. "The Big Dig!"

I cracked up laughing and began dancing! I needed a restroom! And it was almost to the point of emergency!

The woman led us back to where the newspaper vendor was and exclaimed, "This is Atlantic Avenue!"

There it was—Atlantic Avenue, right by his newspaper stand! We turned the corner to see construction in action and some Port-o-Johns set up for the workers. I shouted, "Thank God for the Big Dig!" as I ran toward the portable restrooms.

We followed the path which was laid out for us by the Boston police and made our way to Chelsea where we connected with 1A.

SALEM ON HALLOWEEN NIGHT

We walked into Salem, Massachusetts, on Halloween night. As we walked through one of the suburbs, we noticed most everyone was dressed in costume. We strolled by a small boutique, where the business owner asked us if we were dressed as crusaders. We were both wearing shorts and white tee shirts that read *Walk by Faith*. We were also carrying wooden crosses.

I looked at the woman and said, "No, we are going as a right-leg amputee and her pilot car driver, who are on a prayer walk around the perimeter of the United States!"

The seemingly confused woman said, "Ohhhh!"

A gentleman who had overheard the conversation said, "God bless you!"

A few blocks down the road, I heard a voice call out from behind us. I backed up and saw a man crunched down in a dark alcove, "Are you headed to Salem?" he asked.

"Yes, we are!" I replied.

"They're expecting you!" he whispered.

This sent chills down our spines! Who was expecting us? And why?

Somehow we missed a turn and got off track. We asked for directions and were told we would have to take back roads to get to US 1. Late and getting darker by the minute, it was scary. There were no lights or sidewalks and we didn't have flash lights. We found ourselves walking beside a chainlink fence. There were things tied to the fence that shook and rattled as the evening wind howled. We were probably only on this road for twenty to thirty minutes, but it seemed like forever before we saw Salem's street lights.

As we approached the town, we could see hoards of witches and people dressed in about every costume imaginable. It's estimated that over 60,000 people travel into Salem every Halloween to celebrate the annual Witch Festival. This year was no exception. There were invitations for spell castings and palm readings announced every 20 minutes.

"There are still two spots open for the 11:00 spell casting!"

"The 11:00 palm reading is full, sign up for the next palm reading at 11:20!"

Unbeknownst to us, due to heavy traffic, the bus route had been changed for the duration of the festival. While waiting at the bus stop, we witnessed some domestic violence in the street in front of us and for the first time that day, there was not a squad car to be seen. It was an eerie place to wait for a ride and it was over an hour before we were able to catch a bus back to our vehicle.

It was probably midnight before we made it back to the van, to find that Wendi had locked her keys in the vehicle. We waited in the dark for AAA to come to the rescue.

We drove back to the RV and began to move it forward to find ourselves right smack in the middle of town in bumper-to-bumper traffic. I was in the lead with the motor home and Wendi was tucked in behind me with the van. The traffic was progressing less than a half a mile per hour.

We discussed the situation over the walkie-talkies. Both of us exhausted, we concluded, out of desperation, we should pull down a side street and find a place to park...any place! We turned right at the first street we came to. Shortly after the turn I pulled to the back of a hospital parking lot. Wendi followed. This became our home base for the rest of the weekend.

The next day, Sunday November 2nd, was Wendi's birthday. We visited the Four Square Church in Salem which met at a coffee house. An informal setting, nobody seemed to notice when we walked in a little late.

The pastor sat on a stool and played his guitar as he led the praise music. After a few songs, he paused, and someone came forward with some artwork and a poem.

Then the pastor shared some announcements. We learned that he and his family, and a few others, had moved out there from California, to do mission work and plant a church in Salem. It was intriguing to hear how this small congregation of about 30 people had been so active in the community. During the Witch Fest, they had served 6,000 cups of hot cocoa, maintained a stage with ongoing Christian music, and had a tent set up for Psalm readings.

After the service, we spent some time socializing and told about the walk. Since it was already November, and winter weather was right around the corner, we did not commit to speaking at the church at that time; but we were asked to come back and speak after our winter break.

Meanwhile, we needed a place to park our motor home for the next week or so before we headed back to Ohio. A young couple, Pete and Nancy, offered to let us park the RV at a mansion on the ocean. The owners were out of the country for an extended period of time and Pete was the one who took care of the property. He and his wife actually had living quarters in the house, and there was a guest suite available.

We didn't need to stay in the mansion because we had the motor home, but we did need a place to park and plug in. Pete gave us directions and we met him at the mansion where he directed me onto a very large patio in front of the home, a spot that was large enough to park 20 buses.

We spent the night there. The next day it was raining and both Wendi and I were feeling sick. Wendi seemed to be coming down with pink eye and I was battling a bad cold.

By the end of the day, we were walking in freezing rain and snow was on the way. After planting cross #1,863 at a T-Rail Station in Hamilton, Massachusetts, we made a decision to use that as our starting point when we returned in the spring of 2004.

JUST ASK!

We headed back to Ohio for the holidays. On the way home, a friend, RJ, called me and said he was buying a new car and he really believed God wanted him to give us his Cavalier. He had actually contacted me several months earlier and asked me if I wanted to purchase the car for a small amount, only about half of the Blue Book price, and he said he would accept small monthly payments.

At that time, I could not buy the car because I did not have a steady income. We lived on random donations we received and free will offerings that were sometimes presented after speaking engagements, nothing consistent enough to warrant a car payment.

Now he wanted to give us the car and I could not see how I could even afford to receive it as a gift. I didn't have the money for the license plates, registration, or insurance. Besides, we had Wendi's van and we were already trusting to be able to afford all of those expenses, so we could keep her van as the pilot car.

By the time we reached Canton, Ohio, we began to have multiple mechanical problems with the van. As we were driving into town, I received another phone call from RJ. This time he was practically begging me to take the car. He told me that he got an exceptional deal on his new car and he believed God was blessing him financially because he was willing to give the Cavalier to us.

Well, the van was falling apart and we did need a reliable pilot vehicle, so I decided to accept the car, and thanked RJ for his generous gift!

We made arrangements to get rid of the van and meet RJ in Streetsboro, Ohio, to pick up the new pilot car.

We drove the motor home to where Terry and the girls were living, and parked it in the parking lot of a business behind the house. This is where we stayed for the rest of the year, so Wendi could be near the girls.

After the first of the year in 2004, we moved the motor home to a friend's house for the rest of the winter. I had scheduled speaking engagements across the southern states from Kentucky to Florida to California for late winter and early spring. Wendi traveled with me for the winter and we made it back to the walk in late April.

We drove the Cavalier back to Hamilton, Massachusetts, to the T-Rail Station and I took off walking. After 10 miles, we got in the car and drove around aimlessly trying to figure out where we would stay for the night. We had left the RV back home because we were planning to return to Ohio to attend a conference in May.

We headed north on Interstate 90 and found a rest area. We moved everything from the trunk to the front seat of the car. We then put the back seat down to make a platform that extended into the trunk. We positioned a roll-away bed mattress there and put two sleeping bags side by side.

After dark we each took a side and tried to get some rest so we could walk again the next day. After only an hour of the cramped sleeping quarters Wendi began suffering from severe claustrophobia. She got out and walked around. She would try to get some rest, then walk some more. Neither one of us got much sleep that night.

Our sleeping conditions were horrible and our food supply was scarce.

The next day, after we walked, we sat in the car pondering our situation. Then I decided to call the pastor of the Four Square Church in Salem, Massachusetts. I had a speaking engagement scheduled there for Sunday, and I hoped he would be able to help us with lodging. "Ask, and it will be given to you..." (Matthew 7:7 NASB).

The pastor and his family were pleased to have us come and stay with them for the week. We were given rooms in the upstairs of their home and they offered us breakfasts, gave us food to pack lunches, and treated us to dinner every night. We soon realized *we had not because we asked not*, as recorded in James 4:2.

By the end of the week, we had made our way along the coast-line of New Hampshire and across the state line into Maine.

◊ ◊ ◊

In May, we drove to Dayton, Ohio, to attend a conference over Mother's Day weekend. We had stopped in Canton to pick up Molly, so she could spend the weekend with her mother. After the conference, we took Molly back to Canton and picked up the motor home at our friend's house.

Because we were moving away from the cities and into a more rural area along the coast of Maine, Wendi thought it would be good to have a bicycle with us. We could walk away from the car each day and Wendi could push the bike as we walked, then ride back to where we left the car, load the bike on the back and come up the road to where I was walking. Having a plan, we loaded a bike in the motor home and we caravanned back to Maine.

We parked the RV and the car at the place where I had left off before the conference and took off walking. After about eight miles, Wendi headed back toward the car on the bike. Shortly into her trek, she realized the brakes were not working well and the bike was not mechanically sound. So she got off the bike and pushed it toward the car.

A woman saw Wendi pushing the bike and stopped to ask if she could help. After giving Wendi a ride to the car, she handed her a piece of paper with the name of a Christian social worker, Marge. The kind stranger suggested we pay Marge a visit and told Wendi how to get to her office.

"She will be excited to hear about your walk and will want to help!" she added.

Wendi shared the information with me and we made a decision to take a break halfway through the next day and pay Marge a visit.

Now it was time to find lodging. We knew we had to ask if we were going to receive. Wendi followed me in the car as I drove the RV up the coast into York, Maine. I pulled into the parking lot of the first RV park we came to and went inside to ask if we could park the motor home there for a few days while we walked through the area.

I approached the owner of the park and explained what we were doing. I told him that we do not even need one of their rental sites.

"Could we please park the motor home on a patch of grass for a few days, while we walk through this area?" I asked.

"We are self-contained!" I added.

He folded his arms in front of his chest, shook his head, and said, "No, I don't think so!"

I walked out of the office, shook the dust off of my feet, and motioned for Wendi to follow me. We pulled out of the parking lot and across the street to another park. I went inside and approached the owner. No sooner had the words left my lips, when he said, "Yes, I would be happy to help you!"

As we followed him he announced, "Welcome to God's most beautiful sanctuary!"

He took us to a site with full hook-ups, overlooking the ocean, and told us we could stay as long as we liked and thanked us for asking him.

The next morning, we worked on the bike brakes a little and decided to take a different approach. Wendi dropped me off to walk and drove the car a few miles ahead, parked the car, and rode the bike back toward me.

Once she reached me, I had walked about a half a mile. She joined me on the walk, and pushed the bike as we headed toward the car.

We did this one more time which put us at about five miles for the day. We took a lunch break and set out to find Marge.

Marge's office was located behind a thrift store. She was overjoyed to meet us and wanted to do everything she could to help. She got on the phone to a local bike shop. The owner was willing to give us a $400 bike for half price. Marge donated the $200, and the bike was purchased. She also provided us with four new tires for our pilot car, paid our cell phone bill, and gave us food and other supplies for the road.

We developed a friendship with Marge. She invited us home to meet her husband Rob and her daughter Kelly. On June 18th, Marge came out to stay with us at a campground in Wiscasset, Maine, when we planted cross #2,000 at a teen dance club. The three of us went out to eat to celebrate this milestone.

December 30, 2003

Dear Reverend Cruise,

On Sunday the 23rd of November, which would have been my father's ninety-third birthday, had he lived that long (he was a Methodist minister), my husband and I took a ride through the countryside west of Gloucester, Massachusetts, where we were spending the fall on a sabbatical. In the grass by the side of the parking lot where we left our car, near a candy shop in Wenham, Massachusetts, I found one of your crosses. It had been raining and the card was wet, but readable because of the plastic. When it was getting time to leave Gloucester (where I had had an intention of spending the fall to do inner work and daily meditation, and where we had had a truly wonderful reconnection to church in a little Episcopal church there named St. John's), I gave your cross to a dear friend in Reading, Massachusetts, who is a spiritual director and a lay Franciscan. She also has trouble walking due to some medical problems. I was very moved by your message and your effort, and send prayers with you in your journey.

Thank you for your service.

Mary

CHRISTIAN TOURETTE SYNDROME—2004

BLESSED BY THE BAPTISTS

One Sunday morning, while camping at a state park just north of Camden, Maine, Wendi and I found ourselves driving around looking for a church to attend. We noticed a Methodist church, a Catholic church, a Presbyterian church, and a few other places of worship.

All of a sudden, "We are going to a Baptist church!" came rolling off my lips.

Wendi often diagnosed me with having Christian Tourette syndrome—I open my mouth, something comes flying out, and I sit there looking shocked, like, where did that come from? Well, that is exactly what happened. The minute I spoke the words, my mouth flew open, my breathing increased, and I almost hyperventilated.

I could not believe that I was actually suggesting that we go to a Baptist church. I had avoided Baptist churches for years, especially since the start of the walk.

When I was a child, I would sometimes visit a Baptist church with my aunt and cousins. According to that particular pastor, it was an abomination for women to wear slacks, or for people to dance, be in the same swimming pool with the opposite sex, and to do pretty much anything that was fun. Also, it was not acceptable for a woman to preach, or teach for that matter, if there were men attending the session. There was so much condemnation spoken from that pulpit, I thought for sure there was no way I could ever go to heaven.

When I was about 12 years old, I attended a Christian and Missionary Alliance Church camp for a week. That weekend I made a decision to turn my life over to God and to live for Him. Some people call that "getting saved" or "getting born again." I see it as a decision to accept Jesus Christ as my Lord and Savior.

At the time that I was making that choice, a voice deep within told me that I would be speaking all over the world about this decision. I remember feeling horrified because, just as I was taught at that Baptist church that I attended as a child, my pastor at the Christian and Missionary Alliance (CMA) church also spoke against women preaching. So I chose to keep this revelation a secret for years.

Later in life, after marrying my second husband, we decided to attend our local Baptist church, and again I experienced a whole lot of condemnation, enough to assure me that I was not heaven bound. We really were not living much of a Christian life, especially according to the teachings of that church, so we did not attend the church much longer than a few months.

But even when my relationship with God grew and I became more spiritual in my walk, and my life resembled more of what one would think a Christian life would look like, I still had a bitter taste in my mouth about both the CMA churches and the Baptist churches. I chose to attend assemblies where I learned about the love of God. After all, "there is no condemnation, for those who belong to Christ Jesus" (Romans 8:1 NLT). Certainly as a Christian, I do belong to Christ Jesus! By then I was certain, "God did not send His Son into the world to condemn it, but to save it" (John 3:17).

I am sure I was not the author of the suggestion to go to the Baptist church—it came straight from God Almighty! Wendi and I noticed that the Baptist church van had pulled in front of us and we began to follow it. It made several stops to pick up congregants and we kind of felt like we were stalking the church van. Before anyone came to the same conclusion, we took note of the church address and headed for the building.

Once inside, we sat in the back of the sanctuary. The pastor preached a whole lot of condemnation and I once again, had that "not worthy" feeling that I felt as a child. I looked up and secretly asked, "God, why do you have me at this Baptist church?"

When the service was over, we quickly headed for the back door. We were stopped by a friendly older gentleman, John. He asked if we would join the congregation in the basement for some food and fellowship. I looked around, and I saw the pastor leaving the building and heading for the parking lot. We graciously received the invite and headed downstairs.

We were greeted by several wonderful people. After sharing our story with John, he asked if I would share my testimony with the folks. Afterward, a free-will offering was collected to help us on our mission. John happened to own a restaurant in town, and asked us to stop by in the morning for a blueberry pancake breakfast. Who could turn down blueberry pancakes in Maine? We were on! As we were pulling out of the drive, I thought of the social time, the offering, and the invitation. We were very blessed by the Baptist folks and I thought to myself, *So maybe this is why God wanted us to visit the Baptist church!*

The following morning, while we were immensely enjoying our blueberry pancakes, John stopped by our table with a young woman who had asked him to introduce us to her. He referred to her as an angel, so we will call her Angel, because she most certainly lives up to the name.

Angel asked if there was any way she could help us. Wendi told her how each day she dropped me off at the same spot and how she used her bike on the road. She went on to explain that we were headed for an area with curves and steep hills where it was not safe to ride a bike. I asked Angel if she would be willing to drop us off in the morning and pick us up when we finished walking. She said she would be happy to do that for us.

The next morning, Angel was there bright and early to take us out to walk for the day. She asked if we had dirty laundry that she could wash for us. Yes, we had dirty laundry, but we were reluctant to let anyone wash our clothes because they get really smelly from our perspiration. She insisted and so we humbly consented.

After a 10-mile hike, up and down the hills, and around the curves, we called Angel and gave her our location. She was there within minutes and we shared the events of the day with her as she took us back to our RV. We opened the camper door and found our clothes freshly laundered and stacked neatly on our beds. Yes, Angel is an angel indeed! Could God have led us to the Baptist church so we could be blessed by an Angel?

One day a few weeks later, as we were making our way up US 1, we saw a couple walking toward us. They began calling out our names.

"Hey, Carol!"

"Hey, Wendi!"

"Wendi and Carol!"

I asked Wendi if she had called the newspaper. She said she had not. We were really puzzled by running into two strangers who knew us by name. As we got closer, they introduced themselves as DeAnne and Gary. They told us that they attended the Baptist church in Camden and were really touched by our testimony. Gary said they really wanted to talk to us after the social time, but were not able to because we were surrounded by so many people.

We chatted with them for a while and they asked if we needed anything. I usually couldn't think of a need in the world while I was walking, so I immediately said, "No, we are all set!"

Wendi reminded me that the RV was parked at a construction site and we needed a more secure place to park.

"Oh, yeah!" I said, "We do need a place to park our motor home."

They cordially offered space to park in front of their house and invited us to stay in their home. We were each given a room with an ocean view on the second floor. There was a room between our bedrooms that had a balcony that overlooked the ocean. Both rooms had a private access to this oasis and we each had a private bath. It was like living at a beach resort for a week.

Every morning, DeAnne and Gary would fix us a nutritious breakfast and send us off with a packed lunch. We returned in the evening to a home-cooked meal. Maybe this was why God sent us to the Baptist church!

We were invited back to DeAnne and Gary's home to attend a small group meeting on the 4th of July. We were excited to return to the home of our new friends and equally excited to get more acquainted with some of the people from the Camden Baptist Church.

There was a couple there who were celebrating their fiftieth wedding anniversary. They gave us contact information for a pastor friend of theirs who was an interim pastor of three different churches in the Calais, Maine, area, and they were sure this friend and his wife would be so blessed to help us when we got there. Cailais was over 200 miles ahead of us. This very well may be the reason God had us visit the Camden Baptist Church!

DownEast Christian Church

A few weeks later, while journeying north on Highway 1, once again we found ourselves looking for a place to worship on Sunday. Because we had missed a turn to a particular campground, we pulled into a Methodist church parking lot to turn around.

I blurted, "I don't want to go there!"

Where did that come from? Once again, Christian Tourette syndrome! This time, I was more blown away, because I really *did* want to attend the service there on Sunday.

We sat in the parking lot for a few minutes, puzzled by my spastic blaring, but because it was not yet Sunday, we did not concern ourselves about my spontaneous outburst! We continued our search for the campground.

After several wrong turns, we felt like we were on a wild goose chase. We could not find the campground. We followed the signs and asked for directions and we still couldn't find it. On our last pass around we noticed a sign for a different campground, so we decided to try to find that one instead.

On our way to the new campground, we approached a cute little full-Gospel church. When we saw it, we knew that we had been divinely diverted to this place.

When we finally reached the camp, the owner donated a site for the next few nights.

Sunday morning came and I was dressed up in slacks and a nice blouse, but in my recollection, women who attended full-Gospel churches wore dresses and they had long hair. I asked Wendi to peek inside to see if my clothes and hairstyle would be acceptable. She peeked and nodded yes.

Once inside, we noticed two empty seats near the aisle in the center of the sanctuary. We hurried to the seats because the praise and worship was about to begin. We joined the singing then enjoyed the sermon. The pastor, Pastor Clive, was an elderly man with a very kind face and he had a precious way of delivering his message. He had greeted us during the service and asked what brought us to their fellowship. We shared our story and he asked if he and his wife, Anna, could take us to breakfast the next morning.

We enjoyed a wonderful breakfast with the pastor and his wife. Clive asked a lot of questions. After giving more detail about our journey and sharing some of our personal lives with him, he asked me to preach at his church and offered the church parking lot as a place to park our motor home for the next week. We accepted the invitation. We were delighted to have a home base for a week and I agreed to speak the following Sunday evening.

We attended the Tuesday night prayer meeting. Pastor Clive carried a huge burden for his county and the amount of sin that was taking place, including a lot of incest, domestic violence, and drug and alcohol addictions. He lay prostrate with his face buried in his hands, as he wept and prayed for the people in Washington County. We cried and prayed with him.

The next Sunday, after a few praise songs and a brief Bible lesson, Pastor Clive pulled out our grocery list, which he had asked for earlier in the week. He read the list to the congregation and insisted every item be given to us. He said, since cereal was on the list, and we did not specify what kind, he would give us Cheerios because that was his favorite. As each item was mentioned, a hand went up in promise of meeting the need.

Throughout the day, church members showed up at our camper with precious gifts of food. One woman brought fresh eggs, each wrapped separately in paper towels. We received milk and bread, cooking oil, toilet paper, paper towels, and even items that were not on the list. These gifts came from the meek and humble, hardworking citizens, of Harrington, Maine, Washington County.

Thursday morning while I was walking, Wendi backed into a broken culvert pipe when turning the car around. The gas tank was punctured and it was not safe for her to drive the car. Being hundreds of miles from family and friends, we were not sure how to handle this predicament. I called AAA and had our car towed to the nearest town for a repair that we could not afford. We sat and prayed about our situation and felt led to call Pastor Clive. He sent a couple from the church to pick us up. They took us to their house for dinner. The church paid to have our car repaired. Yes, our biological family and longtime friends were hundreds of miles away, but our Christian family was right there when we needed them.

Sunday evening while preaching, I found my eyes drawn to a map of the county, which Pastor Clive had mounted on the side wall. In fact, I was so drawn to the map that I had a difficult time staying focused on the delivery of the message.

After I finished speaking, and before I sat down, I asked Pastor Clive and the congregation to look at the map. I pointed out that, because of the way the county was shaped and the route I would be taking, I would be walking the southern border, then heading up the east coast, before turning westward across the county again.

"If the congregation would coordinate a walk to cover 23 miles and meet us as we head west we could seal off most of the county in a prayer walk," I explained.

Pastor Clive was ecstatic! He jumped up and asked, "Who will make the crosses?" A blind man named Phil raised his hand.

"Who will walk?" Several hands went up!

We had a plan. The folks from Down East Christian Church were going to be a part of the walk, and seal off their county in prayer. Plans were made to meet us the following Saturday, July 31st at 4:00 in the afternoon, at the corner of County Road 193 and Highway 9.

BIG LAKE CAMP MEETING

When we had reached our turning point at the intersection of US 1 and Highway 9 in Calais, Maine, it was an exciting day on the faith walk. The east coast had been walked and prayed for. By now we had heard from hundreds of people who had found the crosses we had planted. We heard how lives had been changed and how the crosses were being passed all over the world. Crosses had traveled from the east coast to the west coast, to over 30 states, several different countries, and three continents. We had been encouraged enough by these cross stories to keep on keepin' on!

Two newspaper reporters greeted us at the turn, and wrote reports from the same interview. After the pivot, we walked a few miles westward, before we began looking for lodging. Wendi pulled out her contact information to find the number for the pastor that was given to her at the 4th of July meeting, at DeAnne and Gary's (the folks from the Baptist church).

After contacting the pastor and his wife, we were invited to park the motor home at their recently built apartments. There was an unoccupied unit that was opened for us to use the kitchen, shower, and laundry facilities.

We were also invited to attend a camp meeting that was taking place all week at Big Lake which was only a few miles from the apartment building. This was exciting for us and as soon as we showered, we headed to the camp. The camp director, Stan, introduced himself and asked us to be their guests at the camp and join them for meals and services.

We had 54 miles to cover the next week, in order to meet the DownEast people at our appointed time on Saturday. Each day was full. We got up about 6:30, headed for the meeting grounds, had breakfast, packed a lunch, and headed out to walk. Monday through Thursday we walked 10 miles each day and we covered eight miles on Friday.

After walking, we headed back to the apartment to shower, then to the camp for dinner, prayer meeting, evening service, and a gathering in the social hall for snacks and fellowship. We usually got back to the RV by 10:30. We were in bed by 11:00, to get some rest so we could do this all over the next day.

The temperature was in the high 90s that week and we were walking on a newly blacktopped highway. The terrain was very hilly. Cars raced by at a very high speed, oftentimes over 90 miles per hour. The stress from the heat, climbing the hills, and the fast traffic, wore on us.

By Saturday we were exhausted. We still had six more miles to walk on the hot asphalt. We calculated our miles and the time we were supposed to meet the DownEast folks and a newspaper reporter. We determined we should start walking about 10:00, walk to within a mile of the intersection of Highway 9 and Route 193, take a long lunch break, go back out about 3:00, and we should be at the intersection at 4:00.

As we got closer and closer to the intersection of Route 193, we became overwhelmed with excitement. Wendi and I began to pick up our pace as we sang songs and rejoiced in the accomplishment of an entire county being walked and prayed for.

When we got within two-tenths of a mile of the intersection, we could see a man and two children from the DownEast Church walking toward us. We noticed cars pulling into a vacant parking lot at the intersection, and our hearts pounded as we raced toward the goal.

We met with the excited congregants of DownEast Christian Church and gathered as we planted a cross to represent 23 miles of their journey and 2,272 miles of our journey. Then we joined hands in a circle in the parking lot to commemorate the cause and accomplishment.

After a time of celebration we went back to Big Lake Camp. We were given the use of a couple of kayaks to enjoy some time on the lake.

Later in the evening while visiting with some of the folks, we spent time with Stan and his wife and family. Stan asked us to stop in to see them when we got near Littleton, New Hampshire. He told us they would like to have us over for dinner. This would be about 180 miles down the road.

We really enjoyed our week at the camp. We attended campfires with the youth and we enjoyed fellowship with the adults. All in all, it was a great camping experience. But, it was time to move on! So, we said our good-byes, hugged necks, and made plans to move on down the road.

THE GIRLS

The next morning we moved the RV to a small campground behind the only convenience store on Highway 9, the Airline, between Calais and Bangor. I don't know why it is called the Airline— maybe because cars and trucks *fly* back and forth on this 90-mile stretch of highway.

By midweek, we walked to Bangor, where we picked up Highway 2 which we were on most of the way across the country, to Seattle, Washington. As we walked through the city, I felt heaviness in my heart for the people in that part of the state. I'm not sure what the heaviness was all about, but I sensed there were a lot of folks who had been hurt by the church and by hypocrisy in the church. I remember walking and praying and crying out to God to heal the hearts of the people and to correct the hearts of the church. Bangor was definitely a difficult city to walk through.

As we made it to the west side of town, we found a home base at a small campground right on US 2. It was a nice park with a pool, clean shower room, and laundry facilities.

We were especially glad to be at a campsite, instead of a parking lot, because we had plans to have Wendi's two daughters with us for a week while they were still on summer break. We were permitted to leave the RV at the site while we traveled to Ohio to pick up the girls.

We had barely enough money in our ministry account to get the girls and bring them out to the mission field. There we were with two girls—Courtney, 16, and Molly, 12. They were going to be with us two weeks. This was their vacation. We had $50 to buy food and gas for two weeks, and to get them back to Ohio.

Some people would consider this irresponsible, but we were living a life of faith. Now our faith would have to cover the girls, too. I was not about to share the financial situation with the girls and have them be concerned about whether or not they were going to be able to eat or get home at the end of their vacation.

Instead, the next morning after we all had some cereal and milk, I asked Wendi to take me out to the walk, to where I had left off before we left to get her daughters. I gave her $10 so she could get burgers for herself and the girls for lunch and take them to see a dollar movie. We had soda in the camper so they would be all set for the day.

Wendi dropped me off to walk, handed me 10 crosses and a couple of bottles of water, and she and her daughters headed off to begin their vacation. I walked and prayed and walked and prayed and walked and prayed. I talked to God about the financial situation and told Him I thought it would be so nice if we had just a little money so the girls could have a good vacation with their mother.

Early in the afternoon, before Wendi and the girls came out to pick me up, I got a phone call from someone who was putting $500 in my personal account. I began to weep for joy.

We had been given the campsite for the week, so the girls had a nice place to hang out, go swimming, or watch a movie on the VCR in the motor home. And now I was able to give Wendi some money so they could venture out a bit.

Friday, after I walked, we traveled down to York, Maine, where we stayed with Marge and her family. Marge is really interested in the fine arts as are Wendi's two girls so it was a nice visit. The next day we drove to a state park and went sightseeing, played miniature golf, and took the girls to have some Maine lobster for dinner. We still had more than $300 left.

The next morning we went to the DownEast Christian Church where I was scheduled to preach. Wendi sang a song and Courtney and Molly sang a duet. After I spoke, Pastor Clive took up a free-will offering. Before he handed the basket to me, he reached in and pulled out some cash for each of the girls. This vacation was getting better by the minute—now the girls had some spending money.

On most mornings, the girls slept in until after Wendi dropped me off to walk, but one morning they got up early and joined me. We had always referred to our placement on the walk as being in the *field* (meaning the mission field). I think it was a good experience for them to see what their mother's life looked like in the field. The girls were real troopers. They walked three or four miles with me and they each planted a cross.

Molly had made some crosses for us at the retreat over Mother's Day weekend. Now she and her sister were able to be a part of planting crosses to mark the miles we had walked.

It was great to have Wendi's girls with us. They were so young and full of life. Molly, a beautiful slender blonde, was gifted in both academics and the arts. I always thought of her as an old soul. Wise beyond her years, she was 12 going on 30.

Courtney, an adorable little brunette with a smile that could brighten a coliseum, was a late bloomer who skipped and bounced through each day with the innocence of her youth. Being an extremely bright individual, learning seemed easy and effortless to Courtney. She was a child prodigy in music who had been singing since she first learned to talk. From the time she was a toddler, she felt right at home on stage and had the charisma to own the platform. Wendi would often comment, "I did not need a babysitter for Courtney when she was little, I needed someone who was willing to be her audience."

With Molly being mature beyond her years, and Courtney holding on to her youth, the girls seemed more like twins than two sisters who were four years apart. I believed there would be a day when Courtney would blossom and not only catch up but probably surpass her peers in maturity and responsibility. And she has!

Before we knew it, it was time to take the girls back to Ohio so they could get ready to start a new school year. We were able to use the money I had been given for preaching to cover travel expenses, so there was money left in my personal account to give to Wendi to help with the girl's school clothes.

After the fact, I felt comfortable sharing with the girls how God had provided for us to have them with us for two weeks—how we had lived on Glory Money!

PEEPING IN NEW HAMPSHIRE

One morning in September as I was walking down a hill on US 2 in Dixfield, Maine, I had just watched a fawn frolic and play in an open field. I was in an extra good mood and had a skip in my step. A car came to a stop and the passenger opened her window and called out to me. She seemed so excited to meet me, and said she and her husband had visited the coast near Calais, Maine, and they found one of the crosses on US 1.

She went on to share that she was having a bad day and asked her husband to take her out for a country drive. They had barely gotten started in their ride when they came upon me skipping down the hill. She noticed the cross in my hand and realized that I was the woman who had planted the cross she had found some 200 miles back. Vivian shared with me that her not-so-good day had gotten much better. She exclaimed that she had been very touched and inspired by the cross she had found and now she was actually meeting the person who planted it!

Vivian introduced me to her husband, Harold. She asked me if I could give her some more information about the walk so she could share it at her church. I told her that my pilot car driver, Wendi, had brochures in her car and that she was sitting in the blue Cavalier at the bottom of the hill.

They said they would stop by the car to get a brochure. By the time they turned around and drove up behind where Wendi was parked, I had made it to the bottom of the hill, had reached a mile post, and was ready to plant a cross.

We chatted with Harold and Vivian for several minutes and they invited us to their house for a meal.

A couple of days later we joined them for supper and they shared with us that they would try to catch up with us down the road. Before we left, they gave us a case of local maple syrup and claimed that Maine maple syrup is the best in the nation. It was fabulous, especially on pancakes made with Maine's famous *wild blueberries.*

This gift was most precious to us because it provided us with gifts to give others. Wendi and I are both gift-givers by nature and because we were living by faith we seldom had means to shop for others.

One day as we were driving up a hill near Warham, New Hampshire, we noticed a man pulling a cart along the road. He was toting a backpack which had a large sign that towered above his head. The sign read LOVE LIFE. He smiled and waved at people driving east and west on US 2. Wondering what he was all about, we waved and smiled back at him.

The next day, while walking in Shelburne Village, New Hampshire, I met up with this gentleman. He told me his name was Steve Fugate and he was doing a perimeter walk around the United States. He had left Florida about the same time I did. He headed east across the Tamiami Trail and up the Gulf Coast. Then he headed across Louisiana, Mississippi, Alabama, and Eastern Texas. He told us that he avoided the desert and headed northwest into northern California. He shared with us that people would tell him, "That is not a perimeter walk!" and he would reply, "This is my perimeter walk. When you do your perimeter walk, you can do it any way you want!"

"This would usually shut people up!" he snickered.

What are the chances two people doing a perimeter walk, each leaving the same point, at about the same time, heading in opposite directions, would meet up with each other? Around a city, maybe, but not around a country! Besides that, very few people have ever walked a perimeter walk. I was in awe! There we were, face to face—east meets west!

Steve was delightful to chat with and seemed to be *loving life*. We shared our story with him and he shared his story with us. He told us that his son had committed suicide. He was in so much pain in his grief that he didn't know what to do with himself, so he just started walking and encouraging people to *love life*, in hopes he could prevent someone else from committing suicide. He would stop and talk to strangers along the way and reach out to people who seemed to be living in desperation.

I prayed that his efforts would prevent others from having to go through the pain of losing someone to suicide. Wendi and I took a liking to Steve.

We told Steve how the church had been very instrumental in our support and supply. He explained to us that he had a very different experience. He told us that he is a *believer*, but did not want to be known as a *Christian*. He said, "Nobody in those buildings ever did anything for me!" He also expressed concerns about hypocrisy in the Christian community.

Even though we had met many wonderful Christians who were living good and Godly lives, we also had some heartbreaking experiences. I will elaborate more on that in future chapters. I felt very sad about Steve's experiences and his deductions about the church.

We told Steve that we camped along the way and that we had our motor home parked about 20 miles behind us. He told us that he usually found a spot off the beaten path and set up a tent; he would sometimes stay in hostels so he could take a hot shower and sleep in a real bed.

We invited him to stay in the camper for the night so he could shower, do his laundry, and enjoy a home-cooked meal. He was delighted. He told us that he had walked into a hostel that morning and, for some reason, just turned around and walked out.

After I had finished 10 miles, we headed toward the campground. We saw Steve pressing forward eastbound on Highway 2. We stopped to check on him and Wendi asked him if he wanted a ride.

"We can bring you back here tomorrow and you won't have to miss a step."

"No, I think I will walk to the campground then I will take off from there tomorrow!" He had six more miles to go, for a total of 22 for the day.

When we got back to our site, I showered and made dinner for the three of us. Wendi showered while I was cooking and she straightened the camper and put bedding on the sofa for Steve.

As it was getting dark, we saw Steve making his way up the long winding drive to the campground on the top of a hill.

We had a delightful dinner at a picnic table and great fellowship on into the night. The next morning after breakfast we exchanged contact information, and sent Steve on his way with a packed lunch and some extra food and water. We tidied things a bit and headed off for a day on the road.

We enjoyed the beauty of New Hampshire as the color of the leaves constantly changed—new every morning. Autumn is a big tourist season in this part of our country. Hotels, motels, inns, and campgrounds, had signs, WELCOME PEEPERS; people venture out hundreds of miles to bask in the beauty of God's handiwork in the changing of the season. The mountains are brilliantly painted in blotches of exuberant yellows, reds, and oranges, with a myriad of softer and more subtle patches of rose, browns, and mauve.

I scaled Mount Washington, probably the highest point I had climbed thus far. Winded from exertion, I was ready to head down the other side, confident that there was no mountain high enough to deter me as long as I drew upon God for my strength!

We made it to the western part of the state, almost to the Vermont state line when Vivian and Harold informed us that they were on their way out to meet us on the walk.

They had driven 80 miles to meet up with us. We were walking near Lancaster. They took us out to eat on Saturday evening. We visited a Community church in Lancaster on Sunday morning.

After church they treated us to lunch at a Chinese restaurant, then we ventured off to explore some covered bridges and an old Catholic cemetery. We had a great time with our friends.

Before Harold and Vivian said their good-byes, they blessed us with tickets to Santa's Village, a local amusement park. What a special treat. We had very little money to spend on ourselves for entertainment, so it was nice be given an opportunity to enjoy a local attraction.

PROMISED PROSTHETICS

The next week, Wendi attempted to call Stan, the camp director from Big Lake Camp Meeting. He was a person we met through a connection we had made in Camden, Maine, because we were obedient and went the Baptist church. She got an answering machine so she left a message.

The next day, Stan's wife, Riley called and invited us to dinner and to park our camper in their driveway for a couple of days. She also invited us to attend their church on Sunday.

In a conversation over a wonderful spaghetti dinner, I asked if Stan knew of a prosthetic place in the area. I explained to him that I had a real problem with my liner. It had worn to the point where, when I stepped up, the prosthesis dropped to the ground before I could step down into it. I shared with him that this was a situation that caused me to slow down tremendously in the walk because of the discomfort.

Stan informed me that he knew of a prosthetist in Littleton, where he worked as a police officer. He went on to say that he believed the man was a Christian and he was sure he would be able to assist me. He looked up the address to Promis Prosthetics and I made an appointment for the next day.

In the morning when Stan packed lunches for his two children, he packed lunches for Wendi and me as well. They were the most precious lunches with sandwiches, lunch cakes, fruit, and chips. Most of all, our lunches were packed with the love of a Christian brother.

We set out for Littleton for the appointment at Promis Prosthetics.

Dick Roy, the CEO, was pleased to meet us. He guided us in the direction of his examining room. I told him about the walk and how many miles we had covered so far.

Bewildered he said, "You are doing what? On *that*?" as he pointed to my prosthetic leg.

I explained to Dick how the leg was a real Godsend. I told him about my trip to Cleveland Clinic, about *inMOTION* Magazine, and how Jimmy had read the article and offered to build the prosthesis.

"How would you like to wear a leg like this?" Dick asked as he tossed me a high-tech, ultralight, prosthetic that weighed less than three pounds.

"I would love to wear a leg like this, but I cannot afford this leg!" I gasped.

"I am going to give you what you need, not what you can afford!" Dick replied. "I would like to fit you with one of these lightweight walking legs and it won't cost you anything!"

Shocked, I answered, "I would be very blessed to have a leg like this!"

Dick got right on it. He made a cast of my stump to fit me with a new prosthetic. I continued on with the uncomfortable liner for a few days then returned to Promis to pick up the test socket, which fit like a glove. Dick asked me to wear the socket for a few hours then return to his office.

I reported back to Dick that I had no problems with the socket so he asked me to return on Friday for a final fitting.

As I was strolling on a country road in Vermont, I noticed a sign to watch for handicapped people. Then I noticed a farmhouse. There was an older woman at the mailbox by the time I got to the house. I asked her about the sign and she told me about her husband, Andy, who had been ill and had to use a walker or wheelchair to get around.

The woman, MaryJo, asked me what I was doing. I told her about the walk and how we stayed in a motor home at night. She was a sweet woman and asked if we would like to park our RV on her farm while we walked the remainder of Vermont. She invited us in for lunch and introduced us to Andy.

We made arrangements to move the motor home to their farm on Monday evening.

On Friday, when we went back to pick up my new leg, I was wearing a red, white, and blue shirt with stars and stripes. Dick looked surprised when he saw me walk in. He told me he liked my shirt then he handed me my new leg. The socket was a colorful red, white, and blue flag motif. We all chuckled about how my shirt matched the new prosthesis. That prosthetic leg carried me over 1,500 miles and was the first of three legs provided by Promis.

I had no idea what God had in store for me when the words came blurting out of my mouth, "We are going to a Baptist church!" I want to summarize just some of the blessings that came from this one act of obedience:

- We were treated to Maine's famous blueberry pancakes.
- We had an Angel wash, dry, and deliver our laundry.
- We made wonderful friends, some of them for life.

- We spent a week in a beautiful home overlooking the Atlantic Ocean.
- We were invited to a 4th of July celebration.
- We were blessed financially.
- We were given a place to park our motor home for a week at a beautiful apartment building with facilities to shower and wash our laundry.
- We were invited to a camp meeting where we enjoyed food, fun, and fellowship for a week.
- We were treated to a spaghetti dinner and had our lunches packed by a police officer.
- I was provided with three walking legs and eight liners.

The moral of this story is that if God asks you to go to a Baptist church, *go to a Baptist church*! For that matter, whatever God asks you to do, do it!

June 30, 2005

Dear Reverend Carol,

I thought that I lost your contact information and just found it. You were walking through Colchester, Vermont, and you stopped to talk with my boyfriend, Gary, who was walking our much loved German shepherd, Rami. It was a few days later when he took a slightly different route and found your cross #2,598. As asked, we handed the cross off to family south of us who happened to be located in Marlboro, NY. My sister-in-law was then going to bring the cross further south to her brother in New Jersey who has been in a wheelchair since an accident

20+ years ago left him a quadriplegic. I do hope they both have had a chance to contact you. Your story and strength is very inspiring. We wish you well as you continue on your journey and will keep up with your progress on your website.

God Bless and God Speed,

Joanni and Gary

Note: As we walked across the northern portion of our country, we requested on the tags that people pass the crosses to the south.

HOME SWEET HOME—2005

LAKE CHAMPLAIN

We went to church with Stan's family and the next day we moved the RV to Andy and MaryJo's farm. By then it was late autumn and winter was right around the corner. Each evening for the next week, we stopped by the farmhouse for a short visit with Andy and MaryJo before we retreated to our home parked in the barnyard across the country road.

Vermont is another beautiful place in the fall. We passed swiftly through the state enjoying the smell of dried leaves and chimney smoke from hickory, maple, and oak burning in the wood burners and fireplaces.

We were in the north heading east, closer and closer to our home state, Ohio. Soon it would be snowing and we would call it a year for the faith walk, and we'd be home to spend the holidays with our families and friends. Each day we walked in great expectation of getting 10 miles in—10 miles closer to home.

While walking along Highway 2 in Vermont just north of Burlington, Wendi noticed trash bags that were strung along our path just off the road in a shallow swampy ditch. The bags were new. They looked like they had somehow been unraveled from the roll. She began to pick them up.

Throughout the afternoon, we kept hearing a sound of movement along the roads edge. At first we thought we were hearing grasshoppers moving through the dead foliage. Then Wendi spotted a snake.

"A snake!" she called out.

Then as we heard the movement again, she cried out, "Another one!"

We heard the sound again and she shouted out, "Another one!"

She began to head into the grass to pick up another bag and I shouted, "Forget the bags, there are snakes everywhere!"

I heard the sound, she shouted, "Snake!"

We began to realize that every time we heard the sound, it was a snake slithering away from the edge of the pavement.

I couldn't even look down. After the seventh time Wendi announced, "Snake," I lifted my hands in the air and cried out, "Jesus, Jesus, Jesus!" He knew I had issues with snakes, so I was expecting Him to do something with this brood of vipers. Or, at least for them to flee at the name of Jesus! It was so unnerving to know there were nests of the reptiles all around us.

No sooner had I called out to Jesus when I saw the biggest snake I had ever seen in my life. It was coiled up about eight feet in front of me. I screamed!

Wendi, coming up behind me, cried out, "I see it too, Carol!"

We both froze for a minute then I ran into the road. Wendi yelled at me to get out of the road and to just move to the other side. I scanned the other side of the road and saw that it was marshy over there too.

I screamed, "They're everywhere!" she grabbed my arm and dragged me to the other side of the road.

I then saw the car ahead of us and headed for the vehicle as fast as I could.

"We are going to walk really early tomorrow, so that maybe we can be done before the sun is warm enough for the snakes to be sunning themselves on the road!" I deduced.

Then I realized we were at a place where I had to decide if I was going to stay on Highway 2 and go straight ahead across a bridge, to the string of islands in Lake Champlain. It kind of reminded me of the Florida Keys, the way the islands were all connected by bridges. The other option was to turn on Highway 7, and head north along the east side of the lake, and cross at the north end of the water near Swanton, Vermont.

Having encountered all of the snakes, my first impulse was to turn and head up Highway 7. I could only imagine hundreds of snakes coming up from the water's edge to the warm pavement of the road. Then I realized the snake, the big one, was so out of character for a snake. I had been screaming and heading toward it for several minutes before I saw it. It is not natural for a snake to stay still while someone is tramping toward it and making a lot of noise in the approach. Everything I had experienced and heard about snakes was quite the contrary. They move away from the vibrations of movement and noise.

Yet, this one was there, staring at us. It was not like the others that looked like very large garter snakes. This one was *ginormous* and the most awful shade of green. It just stared at us. Was it manifested? Was there something or someone who did not want us to go that way? My *gut* said to stay on Highway 2, my *fear* said

137

take Highway 7. I decided to go with my gut because "God has not given us a spirit of fear; but of power, and of love, and of a sound mind!" (2 Timothy 1:7 KJV).

TUESDAY NIGHT BIBLE STUDY

We were faced head-on with blustery winter weather as we traipsed northward over the islands of Lake Champlain. The locals were friendly and hospitable. We always had a place to park and food to eat.

One evening as I was getting in the car after a 10-mile trek, a woman walked over and stuck her head right in the window. She said she had seen an article about the walk and asked if we would attend a harvest dinner hosted by the local AA group. We accepted the invitation and asked for the details.

Saturday evening, while we were lavishing over turkey and dressing—definitely not something we had enjoyed much of over the past few years, the same woman walked up to us and told us there was another dinner open to the community on Sunday afternoon at the Catholic church in Alburgh. We graciously thanked her for the information.

Sunday morning we got up, attended a small church on the islands, and headed north to Alburgh for the harvest dinner. After standing in line for a while, we were informed there was an $11 charge for the meal. Disappointed, we stared at each other for a moment. We rarely spent $11 for *two* meals. I remembered we had a little money stashed in the glove box. Wendi went to the car and came back with enough money for one meal.

Since we had driven over an hour to get there (our motor home was parked at the south end of the islands and Alburgh is at the north end), we decided we would see if we could buy one dinner to share. I explained our situation to the woman collecting the money, and she accepted what we had as full payment for two meals, saying, "We are a church you know!"

We found a seat and began to eat and enjoy fellowship with the locals. Halfway through our meal, a gentleman came to our table and introduced himself. Luke told us that he had seen our story in the local newspaper and had been discussing it with his co-workers the week before. He went on to say that he was a Spirit-filled Christian and would like us to attend a Tuesday night Bible study which he had started there at the Catholic church.

"Would you share your testimony?" he interjected.

We were delighted to accept his invitation to the Bible study and I agreed to speak.

By Tuesday, we had actually walked past the church. So we cleaned up at a rest area and were at the church by 6:00. Luke met us in the parking lot and told us, to his surprise, the priest an elderly man in his 80s, insisted on being there that night and asked if I would sit by him. Luke explained that the Bible study had been going on for several months and the priest had never attended.

I went in and sat by the father. He took my hands and placed a rosary in them. He told me that his brother, who was also a priest, had passed away.

"This was my brother's rosary and I want you to have it!" I was so humbled by this precious gift.

"Father, I am not Catholic, and I'm not sure what to do with a rosary. May I wear it?"

He smiled and placed it around my neck.

There was a potluck meal before the study so we had an opportunity to chat with the folks before I shared my testimony. The father asked if he could have one of the crosses. Wendi overheard the question and excused herself to take a short ride down the road

139

to fetch one of the crosses I had planted. The father was thrilled and shared his intent to plant it in his prayer garden.

Luke had been teaching about faith so our testimony fit right in. It was exciting to see my Catholic brothers and sisters enthusiastically searching the Scriptures for references. Many of them had never opened a Bible. Some of them hadn't even owned one before their Bible study group began.

We had been praying for the denominational walls to come down in the Christian community, so it was awesome to see how God was working in a mighty and powerful way around this nation. This was refreshing because I know there are not going to be any Catholics, Methodists, Lutherans, or even Baptists in heaven. God is about relation not affiliation—there are not going to be denominations in heaven—only people—His people!

HEADING HOME

As we were making our way through the islands toward Route 11 where we would begin heading west again, we were contacted by a newspaper reporter who wanted to catch up with us in Mooers Fork, New York. I agreed to an interview. It was November and we were walking in freezing rain when the van pulled up beside us. We were invited into the van for an interview. The reporter had cerebral palsy and was not able to enunciate very well so he had an interpreter. It took almost an hour for the interview, but it was good to get out of the cold, wet weather.

A week had passed and the story was not published so we concluded the article had been rejected by the editor.

The weather was getting worse. I was walking in blizzard conditions and the motor home was using more propane than we could afford in order to keep it heated. We would have headed home, except for the fact that God had given me a vision of a Shell station where I was to end the walk that year, and a knowing that I had to reach my 2,700th mile. So I kept walking.

One blustery, cold day, I walked into a small diner to use the facilities. My glasses fogged up from the warmth of the building when I opened the diner door. The owner pointed to the restroom as if knowing why I was there. Afterward, I thanked her and headed on down the road toward Malone, where I would pick up Highway 37 to head closer to the country's edge along the St. Lawrence River.

On November 11, 2004, I planted cross #2,700 at a Shell station on Route 37 in Westfield, New York. The manager just happened to be an amputee.

The next morning we secured our belongings and battened down the hatches as we prepared for our 12-hour trip home. We had less than $50. This was nowhere near what we needed to travel over 500 miles with two vehicles, one being a 31-foot motor home.

We prayed then discussed what we thought God would have us do. Wendi revealed that she believed God would provide the money from right where we were. We were parked about 30 miles east of Malone in a campground that had been closed down for the winter. We were the only ones there. I believed God was going to make provision for us as we traveled. Since both of us seem to have a keen ear to God's voice, we concluded that we were going to get some support in that general vicinity and also get some help along the way.

We had no food in the camper so we decided to use some of our money to get breakfast at the diner where the woman had been so kind to let me use the facilities earlier in the week.

We walked into the diner, sat at the counter, and we each ordered a modest breakfast. People began to approach us with donations and thanked us for doing the prayer walk. Puzzled, we looked around to see that people were reading the story—the story that we thought may have been rejected. The article was on the front page of the morning paper. All of the people in the diner had read the story and wanted to help.

I went up to pay for our breakfast and the owner said, "No, breakfast is on me!"

I tucked the money in my jacket pocket with the other donations. We walked out of there with enough money to fill the gas tank in both the car and the motor home. So we headed west.

Around noon we stopped and had a snack. I had remembered that Shirley, a woman we had met at DownEast Christian Church, had wanted me to meet the folks at her home church in Canada, not far from Niagara Falls. This wouldn't be too far out of our way. I shared this with Wendi and we agreed that maybe the people in that church might help us with the trip.

I could not find Shirley's number so I called Pastor Clive. I told him that we were headed home and we were very low on finances. We thought maybe Shirley's church could help and we asked if he could help us get in touch with her. He was astounded that we had no money. He said we should have just called him in the first place.

"Whenever you girls are out of money give me a call!" he scolded.

"Pastor Clive, most of the time we are out of money—this is a faith walk!" I replied.

He chuckled and told me to give him a few minutes and he would call back.

Pastor Clive called back and gave me the name of Mr. Stanley Jordan. He told me that we should have enough gas to make it to the Jordan home in Palmyra, New York.

"Stanley is a good friend of mine!" he exclaimed.

"He and his wife Marsha will have dinner ready for you and they'll fill both tanks with gas. That will get you home. Give Stanley and Marsha a hug for me!"

We arrived at the Jordan home about 8:30. Stanley was standing outside to direct us into his drive. As we walked into the house we could smell the freshly baked chocolate chip cookies Marsha had just taken out of the oven.

We felt instant kinship with this young family and them with us. Stanley was a tall lanky man with red hair and a beard reminding me of the backwoods men of northern Maine, which happens to be where he is from. Marsha was a young wholesome looking woman, tall and slender with long brown hair and big blue eyes. She was a bit more refined than her husband, yet definitely a country girl.

Stanley and Marsha were about my daughter's age. I instantly had a grandma kind of love for their three beautiful children. Wesley, 8, was tall and lanky like dad with a round happy face, and like his father, he wore glasses. Aleesha was 6, tall and slender like her mom, with the same brown hair and beautiful blue eyes. Ethan, the youngest, was only 3, a tall lanky toddler, who had difficulty pronouncing some of his words. He called me Tarol!

Wendi and Stanley took a liking to each other in a brother and sister kind of way. Wendi has two sisters so it was fun for her to have a brother.

Marsha fixed us something to eat and we shared stories about the walk and how we had lived in the parking lot at Clive's church. They told us that they had met Clive when they were both students at Zion Bible College, where Clive and his wife, Anna, were on staff.

We talked long into the night. We calculated when we would be walking near Palmyra. The Jordans invited us to park the motor home in their drive for a couple weeks when we passed through.

Stanley had just finished writing a book and gave us a copy of a couple of chapters to read. He asked us to let him know what we thought.

The next morning after breakfast, Stanley followed us to a gas station and topped off both vehicles. He said that Pastor Clive and the DownEast Church would be reimbursing him for the cost. We gave Stanley a hug and headed for home.

DIVINE PLACEMENT

As we traveled home, we discussed the ups and downs of the year and rejoiced in the fact that God had met all of our needs throughout the year right down to the details of our trip home, with the newspaper article being delayed for two weeks and the connection with DownEast Christian Church.

Sometimes we do not understand why or how we are in a certain place at a certain time. Let me rephrase that—most of the time we lack understanding of the appointed time of our circumstances. But one thing we can know for sure is that we are not placed by chance. Doors open and close for us throughout our lives which direct us, or cause us, to be just where we are at any appointed time. I like to refer to this as divine appointments by divine intervention.

There are two situations like this that happened in 2004. The first occasion we were in Ohio for an appointment at The Cleveland Clinic.

In May of 2004, Wendi's ex, Terry, and the girls moved into a different home, closer to their schools. The girls could either walk to school or ride a bus. Courtney, a freshman in high school, planned to walk to and from school with her friend James. On the other hand, Molly was going to ride a bus to the middle school— she was in sixth grade. Molly got a little confused about her bus route for her ride home so she asked Courtney if she could walk home from school with her and James. Courtney agreed to walk to the middle school and meet Molly so they could all walk home together.

Courtney and James were used to crossing Lincoln Way, a busy four-lane highway. Because of the steady flow of traffic, the two would wait until the eastbound lane would clear, walk to the center turning lane and wait for the westbound traffic to clear. Molly had never crossed a four-lane highway and when the three got to the center lane, Molly took off running to cross the other two lanes and was hit by a minivan.

Wendi and I were in Cleveland, Ohio, at my daughter and son-in-law's house. I was working on their pool when I was prompted to check my phone for missed calls. I had a message from Terry about Molly's tragedy. He left word that she had been taken by ambulance to Doctor's Hospital in Massillon, but they were considering transferring her to Akron Children's Hospital. Terry did not know the extent of Molly's injuries.

I grabbed Wendi and shared the bad news with her as we headed for the car. I drove as Wendi directed me to go a certain way—she knows the area better than I do so I relied on her for directions. Right before I was ready to make a turn, Wendi changed her mind and asked me to go a different way.

As we arrived at Doctor's Hospital, they were loading Molly on a gurney for the transport. Molly was struggling with memory loss. Wendi was the only person she recognized. She could not remember words to communicate her needs or her pain.

We drove up to Akron Children's Hospital where Molly had been placed in a private room with a serious head injury. Wendi and Terry stood at each side of her bed as Molly seemed to be reprogramming. Terry kissed one cheek and Molly counted, "10, 20, 30, 40, 50, 60, 70, 80!" Wendi kissed the other cheek, Molly counted, "5, 10, 15, 20, 25, 30!" She counted by fives and by tens, backward and forward.

Terry left the hospital to check on Courtney who was too traumatized to see her sister like this. Molly fell asleep, probably from the pain medication. Wendi and I sat quietly in her room and prayed she would be all right.

When she woke up, I was standing next to her.

"Do you know who I am?" I asked.

"Of course I do. You're Carol!" she replied.

Wendi and I smiled at each other. Molly was going to be fine.

After a couple of days, the doctor was ready to discharge Molly, when she complained that her leg was hurting. The leg was x-rayed to find she had broken her femur. She was fitted with a full leg cast and was not discharged for another day.

Wendi was home to help with Molly's care until she was able to manage on her crutches.

The other occasion of divine appointment by divine intervention was in August of 2004. We had caught up with my friend, Jerry, and my former pilot car driver, Deb, in Pittsburgh, Pennsylvania, where we all had attended a Christian conference. Wendi received a call that her grandpa was not doing well and not expected to live much longer. We were only about a two-hour drive from home.

Wendi lived with her grandparents her senior year of high school. She was very close to her father's side of the family and this

146

was an extremely difficult time for her. We arrived back in Canton in time for Wendi to visit her grandfather in the hospital and say good-bye to him before he passed away.

Again, divine appointment! I do not believe we could have made it home before he passed if we were out walking in Maine. After missing so much time on the walk in 2003, while I was waiting for pilot car drivers, I was really reluctant to take time off, so I had seriously thought about not attending that conference.

Wendi's cousin Jenny delivered her grandfather's eulogy. I was so impressed and affected by what she had to say about her grandfather that I have used it as an example in many of my sermons. I can't remember the exact wording, but I remember that she described her grandfather as someone full of love, joy, peace, patience, kindness, goodness, faithfulness, gentleness, and self-control. She so eloquently depicted a living example of the fruit of God's Spirit, as portrayed by the Apostle Paul in Galatians 5:27. It became my personal goal, from that moment, to work toward living such a Spirit-filled life that I would leave such a legacy. I think this should be every Christian's goal!

A LIFE OR DEATH SITUATION

My dad did not seem to have many years left. He had suffered with stage-3 hypertension for years which had advanced to congestive heart failure and kidney failure. He was also suffering with COPD and not expected to live much longer. I prayed that God would place me in the right places at the right times.

Since we were concerned my dad would not be around long, for the first time in decades, my siblings and I all planned to be at my parent's home in Lake Wales, Florida, for Thanksgiving in 2004. Wendi traveled down to Florida with me and all of my

147

siblings were there except Ken and his wife, Deb, who could not make it.

We had a wonderful time of catching up with each other's lives, playing table games, and sharing some childhood memories. Though Dad seemed to enjoy having so much of his family there, Mom was the one who was really taking it all in. She seemed to be savoring each minute with her kids.

After everyone else had headed home, Wendi and I stayed on a while to visit with Mom and Dad. On our way back to Ohio, we dropped Mom off in Tennessee to spend Christmas with Margie's family. Margie had agreed to take Mom back in January. Andy and his wife, Bonnie, checked in on Dad while Mom was away.

Wendi joined me as I set out for a series of several speaking engagements in Kentucky, Tennessee, Louisiana, Texas, California, and Kansas. While we were in Arizona, we stayed with some friends, Lisa and Dee in Phoenix. We left there to head to Freemont, California. A few hours into our trip as we were crossing the state line, I got a call from Andy. He informed me that Mom had been diagnosed with terminal cancer and he suggested I get to Florida as quickly as possible.

I called my friend Cherie in Freemont, and informed her that I had to cancel my speaking engagement at the church where she pastors. I explained the situation and how I had to head to Florida.

We called Lisa and Dee and told them that we were turning around and heading for Lake Wales. They suggested we stop at their place to regroup. By the time we got to their apartment, they had purchased two one-way tickets to Orlando. I called my brother and he picked us up at the airport that evening.

Mom was in the hospital in Lake Wales. She was suffering with lung cancer which had spread to bone cancer throughout her body. She had lost a significant amount of weight and was extremely ill. Her oncologist gave her two months to two years to live.

I canceled all of my speaking engagements except for one in Kansas and another in Missouri. After a few days, Wendi and I flew back to Arizona to pick up the car. We drove to Kansas where I put Wendi on a plane to Ohio so she could spend the rest of the winter break with her family. I spoke in Wichita, Kansas, and Joplin, Missouri, then I headed to Florida where I planned to spend the rest of the winter.

In mid-February, I moved in with Dad. For the next couple of months, I fixed his meals, kept the house in order, managed his meds, and took him to the hospital every day to see Mom.

Mom was going downhill fast. She asked to see a minister and came to terms with Christ as her Lord and Savior. A week later she was sent home to spend the last week of her life with in-home hospice care.

Her hospital bed was set up in the Florida room where she was surrounded by all of her kids and grandkids. The home was filled with the aroma of her favorite meals as we cooked recipes from her cookbook in memory of our childhood. We played her favorite movies and we took turns sitting by her side. All five of her surviving children were with her when she passed on March 10, 2005.

Laurie had traveled to Florida for Mom's funeral. She was not only grieving the loss of her grandma, but the idea that she had not yet conceived, so her grandmother would never get to meet her children. I took Laurie for a drive so we could offer support to each other during this time of loss.

I spent the next month with Dad. I helped him organize his prescriptions so he could manage them. I showed him shortcuts to housekeeping and stocked the cupboards, freezer, and refrigerator with healthy, easy-to-prepare foods.

I took him to his doctor appointments to monitor his progress. His general practitioner said he was very depressed and if that didn't change he would not make it more than a few months. If he could get the depression under control he may be around a year or two. She suggested I encourage him to look forward to something. Dad loved to cruise so I suggested he plan a cruise.

"Will you and Wendi go with me?" he asked.

I told him we could, if the cruise was scheduled during the winter months. He got excited and got online to look for cruises. He scheduled one leaving out of Tampa on December 11th and returning on the 18th.

I encouraged him to phone people he and Mom had been close to throughout the years. He called their friend, Agnes, and informed her of Mom's passing. They began to converse several times a week.

I had to head back to Ohio. Sharlie was not doing well. I made it back in time to say good-bye to her, before she slipped away into a coma. She passed away on April 24th, just days after her ninetieth birthday.

Not long after Sharlie's funeral, my daughter called and invited me to her house. When I got there, I noticed that Mike's parents were there too. My daughter handed me and her mother-in-law identical packages. We simultaneously opened boxes containing pregnancy test strips showing positive and a due date of December 18th, 2005.

My mouth dropped. I was ecstatic about becoming a grandparent, yet heartbroken about the due date. December 18th is the date I would be arriving back to Tampa from the cruise with my father. I could not be two places at the same time.

I congratulated my daughter and son-in-law and explained my predicament about the due date. My daughter had the answer: "just cancel the cruise." That would have been easy, and I would have done that in a heartbeat if it were not for the promise I had made to my very ill widowed father, whom I was told had little time to live.

I pondered and pondered the situation. I called my father and explained my dilemma, and how I really wanted to be with my daughter when my grandchild was born. He wouldn't bend.

"You are not going to cancel on me are you?"

"No, Dad, I gave you my word!"

I tried to get some understanding from my daughter. She could not understand why I did not cancel. I tried to explain what the doctor had told me, and how if I canceled and something happened to my dad, I would feel awful. She would not give.

I asked Wendi if she would go on the cruise with Dad. She refused to go without me. I was in a real emotional predicament that I did not know how to get out of. The possibility of contributing to depression that could cause premature death for my father was unbearably sorrowful to me. The idea of not being there when my grandchild was born was equally excruciating.

"Please, Wendi, please just go so Dad won't be so upset in my absence!"

"I am not comfortable going without you!"

"I understand!" and I did.

No mercy! I was going through hell on earth!

There was nothing I could do about it now. I trusted God with the circumstances. Laurie and I both came into this life a month earlier than our expected due date and I thought maybe my granddaughter would do the same.

MOHAWK INDIAN RESERVATION

Wendi and I headed back to the field in early May. We left the motor home back in Ohio, parked in Terry's driveway until after Mother's Day, when we would return to Ohio, to each spend the day with our daughters.

We had about $200. and I was hoping we could find a small motel that would give us a really good weekly rate.

Deciding to drive out the route we would eventually hike, we saw a small motel just over 20 miles from where I would resume the walk. We stopped and Wendi went inside to ask the owner if he could help us with a reasonable weekly rate. He said he would have to discuss it with his wife. We decided I would walk and stop back later.

Wendi drove me to the Shell station on 37 in Westville, New York. I walked seven miles and we returned to the motel where Wendi was given a run-around by the same person who was there earlier.

As she was heading back toward our vehicle, a woman called out to her from the parking lot. She asked about the magnet on the side of our vehicle.

"What is Faith Walk Ministries?" she asked.

Wendi told her about the mission and mentioned that we were hoping to get a fair weekly rate at the motel. The woman told us that her daughter, Annette, is a Christian and would be thrilled to help us out. She gave us her daughter's phone number and told us to give her a call.

I gave Annette a call and she invited Wendi and I to come and stay with her family for the period we would be walking before heading home for Mother's Day.

When we arrived at the Samblanet home, Matthew, Annette's husband, who happened to be a Mohawk Indian, was making

Indian Hash and steak for us. We shared our testimony with the family over dinner. We were told to make ourselves at home and we could see they really meant it. Their five-year-old daughter, Angel, temporarily moved out of her room so I could have a room of my own for the duration of the stay, and their seven-year-old son, Jacob, gave up his room for Wendi.

I went to put a few items in the fridge to find that it was almost empty. It didn't seem like there was much food in the house, yet we were served steak. I was very touched by this, how a family that seemed to have so little was giving us their best.

That evening as I was going to sleep I was thanking God for the Samblanet family for providing such a comfortable place for us to stay after each walking day. I thought about the motel and how the man had given Wendi the run-around and how we were willing to pay for the room. I thought about the money we had and how much this family could use the funds for groceries and I decided to give the money to Annette and Matthew in the morning.

As I was waking up the following morning, a still small voice whispered, "I will take care of them; keep the money!"

By then, I knew the voice of God, so I kept the funds stashed away. As Wendi was taking me out to walk, I shared with her that I had wanted to give the family the money, but God stopped me.

We returned to the home that evening to find the counter full of groceries. I opened the refrigerator to see that it had been filled. As I stood in the kitchen, Annette came up from her beauty shop, which she ran in the lower level of their home, and told me that while she was styling a customer's hair an anonymous person came into her home and filled her refrigerator and left the counters full of the groceries. There was much more than $200 worth of food.

I looked up toward heaven and said, "Thank you!"

Matthew's sister, who worked for the reservation's news-paper, came out to the Samblanet's home to interview us before we went home for Mother's Day. We ended up needing every bit of the $200 for gas and other travel expenses to make the trip. God always knows what He is doing, and we need to pay attention to Him when He speaks to us!

The Samblanets invited us to park our motor home in their drive as we returned to the field. The family and their little Pomeranian, Chewy, joined us on the walk as we walked through the reservation.

Wendi took a real liking to Chewy.

"Look, Carol! We could have a dog like this out here!" she excitedly exclaimed as she placed Chewy in her bike basket.

I smiled at Wendi, who had such a liking for Pomeranians, and I jokingly replied, "If God wants me to have a dog, He will send me a three-legged dog!"

Wendi and I joined hands with the Samblanets and we prayed for unity in the hearts of the people in that area, where there were so many territorial boundaries. The reservation has its own set of laws and regulations, apart from New York state government. Part of the reservation is in Canada, while the rest of it is in the United States.

Sunday we attended a small full-Gospel church on the reservation with the Samblanets. After the service, I felt compelled to speak to Matthew. I asked him if I could pray for him. After we prayed, I shared with him that I thought a prayer walk should take place around the perimeter of the reservation because there was so much division among the people in that area.

Matthew was born on the Canadian side of the reservation to Mohawk parents, then reared on the United States side of the reservation, later marrying a woman from the state of New York. He and his family were now living on the outskirts of the reservation in the United States, raising three children who were part native and part European descent.

"You are the perfect person for this quest!" I told Mathew, who had lost his job, and was trying to make ends meet for the family with a small landscape business, and was looking for some purpose in his walk with God. He smiled and nodded!

By the time we moved on from the Samblanet's, Annette's beauty shop business was booming and Matthew had more lawn-care jobs than he could handle. God was truly blessing this family for their generous hearts and their obedience to His call. Matthew was making plans to walk the reservation in prayer for reconciliation of differences among the local residents.

BLOW IT

As we were walking through the farm country, just east of the Thousand Islands area of the St. Lawrence, I needed a place to rest and dry my leg. We sat down on some big rocks we had spotted in a field. The farmer stopped to check on us. I told him what we were doing and apologized for trespassing.

He shook his head and said, "Not a concern!"

He told us to stop in at the farmhouse ahead and his wife would give us something cold to drink. We were at the house within a few minutes and the farmer met us at the side door as we walked up on the porch. The family was pleasant. We were each served a glass of cold water and sent on our way with well wishes.

We walked through a quaint little farm town and once again found ourselves in the midst of fields and barnyards, when we heard a dog barking and saw a woman motioning for us to come up to her farmhouse. Lilly came to meet us halfway down her drive, she introduced us to her dog, Nerf, and invited us to have lunch with her. She said she had been at the farm down the road when we were invited in for a glass of water and she really wanted to know more about our walk.

"I put Nerf out because I knew he would let me know when you were close by!" she exclaimed.

We had such a nice lunch with Lilly. She invited us to park our motor home in her drive for the next week or so. Each evening we toted what food we had and combined it with Lilly's food and I made dinner for the three of us.

Lilly taught us to play a dice game called "Blow It." It is a game I had learned back in Ohio, only we called it "Greedy," and when playing with friends in Michigan, it was called "Farkle." It is a game of rolling dice and scoring, if you roll and don't score, your turn is over. Sometimes there is a tendency to keep rolling, even when the chances of getting the right number are slim, and that is when you "blow it" in New York, you are "greedy" in Ohio, or you "farkled" in Michigan.

Lilly invited her neighbors and friends over in the evenings to meet us and to play Blow It. Lilly was in her eighties, but you couldn't tell by the way she got around. She certainly had her share of trials, having recently lost her husband, survived a bout of cancer, and lost vision in one of her eyes. Lilly, a devout Catholic, got her strength from the Lord.

She let us know that she did not believe in praying for luck. "You either win or lose at Blow It. It is not God's concern!"

Lilly looked a lot like Sharlie and her personality was a lot like hers too. Sharlie always had words of wisdom and inspiration.

Time with Lilly in her farmhouse brought back fond memories of time spent with Sharlie on the Cruise farm.

Sharlie had a toy drawer in her pantry. The drawer was full of drawing paper, scissors, construction paper, colored pencils, Lincoln Logs, and Tinkertoys, useful items to enhance the creativity of my youth. I enjoyed the fond memories of sitting at Sharlie's feet in creative play with the items from the pantry drawer.

I had not seen Sharlie much in the few years before she died and I missed spending time and sharing my dreams with her. She always listened so intently.

Leaving Lilly's farm was difficult in more ways than one. We made plans to keep in touch with Lilly and to visit when I traveled back and forth to Promis Prosthetics for new legs. In fact, we spent the following Easter with her.

GOD IS IN THE BAR

At times while walking, I thought hard about what the other perimeter-walker, Steve, had shared, about the church not being much help to him on his walk. We were supported by many churches along the way but we had also experienced much disappointment in the church. There were times we visited churches with congregations of one or two hundred people, small enough that we certainly would have been noticed as strangers in the building. We would take a seat somewhere between the front of the building to somewhere in the middle, where we could be noticed. There were times when not one person would acknowledge our presence. This concerned me because we might have been attending a church service for the first time.

A couple of different occasions, I sat down in a church, and was informed that the seat belonged to someone else. I couldn't sit there. People actually had assigned seats in some of the churches.

I remember times when a person would come into a congregation, eager to share talents and time, to be told there really was not a place for them. All of the spaces were filled with certain folks who always did certain jobs. We had noticed congregations so set in their ways they had no interest or tolerance for change and sharing positions.

There was a time when I needed a restroom as we were walking through a small city and I went up to a church building to find the door locked. I knocked and two women came to the door.

"I am doing a prayer walk around our nation. I need to use a restroom. May I please come in?" I shouted.

One of the women reached out, grabbed my arm, pulled me into the building, and locked the door behind me. I used the facilities and was escorted, and practically pushed out of the building. I could hear the door being locked as I walked away in bewilderment.

One hot summer day in 2005, we were walking in a rural area of upstate New York. We had finished all of our water, were dehydrated, and desperately needed to use a restroom. We came upon a small church building. There were two entrances to the drive and each had a chain across it to prevent cars from entering the parking lot.

It was about 2:00 in the afternoon, midweek. There was a car in the drive and we could see shadows of movement in the building. We climbed under a chain and walked up to the door, which had a no-firearms sign on it. We knocked and called out to whoever might be inside. Nobody came to the door. I knocked harder and called out, "Can anybody help us?" No response.

We walked across the street. There was a small country bar. We walked up to the door. I pulled it open and we walked inside. I told the bartender what we were doing and asked if we could use the restroom. She smiled and pointed across the room. We walked out of the ladies room to find the bartender holding two glasses of cold water. There were six or eight people there, who took up a collection over $70 and sent us on our way.

Where was God that day? He certainly was not in the church building!

Wendi and I discussed the situation and our hearts grieved for the church in general. I felt so sad that people can often get their needs met better in the local bar than in the church buildings. I remembered the theme song from *Cheers*: "Where everybody knows your name…"

I prayed for the church. I prayed for the doors to be open for passersby, for the lost, the lonely, the widows and the orphans, and, at least, for fellow believers. I prayed for the church to get it right. The only true religion that God our Father accepts as pure and faultless is this: "To look after orphans and widows in their distress and to keep oneself from being polluted by the world" (James 1:27 NIV).

My thoughts went back to Steve. How sad! He was a fellow believer, on a sorrowful mission of grief. I thought of how, in desperation, not knowing what else to do, this brother took off walking to have his needs met by strangers of our world and the church turned their back on him. I prayed for Steve and asked God to keep him safe and heal his heart. I felt so sad, yet had such an understanding of why he did not want to be associated with the Christian community.

Don't get me wrong here—Wendi and I have met a lot of wonderful Christian brothers and sisters and we are blessed to be called Christians and to be part of the Christian community, yet there is a lot that goes on in the name of Christ or in God's name that makes me quiver and it grieves my spirit. All I can do about this is to represent the name of Christ in love, forgiveness, and compassion for others. The only way to make a change in the world is to make a change in one's self.

Before we judge a place or the people in the place, we need to ask ourselves, where is God? God may be in the bar! Wendi and I have found Him there and around a Texas Holdem' table too!

BACK TO THE JORDANS

By midsummer, we had made it back to the Jordans. We parked our motor home in their drive, but they insisted we stay in the house with them and be a part of their family for a couple of weeks.

The first week there, it was just Wendi and me. We covered 10 miles a day as we got closer and closer to their home.

In the evenings we had dinner with the Jordans and we all got to know each other. I became an instant surrogate grandmother to Wesley, Aleesha, and Ethan.

I became especially close to nine-year-old Wesley, who was fascinated by the prosthesis, and enjoyed sitting in the driver's seat of the RV, where he pretended to be a truck driver. He said he was praying for God to grow my leg back. I told him I believed God could grow my leg back, but He was using me as an amputee and I was certainly okay with that.

While Wesley and I chatted one evening, he told me that he believed God called him to be a drummer. He had been drumming since he was a baby and he had totally pounded through a beginner drum set. He asked me why God had not provided him with a better set of drums. I told him that if God had, indeed, called him to be a drummer, He would provide drums. Wesley asked me if I would pray for God to send him drums. I said I would.

Stanley's book had been published and he gave us autographed copies for ourselves and extra copies to give to others. Once again, we were provided with gifts to give others.

Over the next few days, as we approached Rochester, Stanley came out and walked with us and took some photos for our scrapbook. We had contacted the Rochester police to inquire about the safest route through the city. We were informed about the high crime rate in the city and it was suggested we have a police escort through one particular area.

Stan's neighbor, Jim, arranged for the escort. I was given the details regarding the escort and made arrangements to meet the police officer at a designated spot where he would walk with us through the worst part of the city.

Other than one occasion when the officer had to call for backup because he had to break up a domestic dispute, the escort went well. We had one officer on foot by our side and another, following in a squad car.

Our friend, Pepper, from Wichita, Kansas, had planned to join us on the walk, so we asked the Jordans if it was okay if she joined us the second half of our second week with them. They agreed.

Pepper showed up in her red Volkswagen Bug. She opened her trunk and it was full of crosses she had made for the walk. Pepper would have moments when she would forget what she was going to say or do. I have those moments, too, and I am sure most middle-aged people do—but when Pepper had these moments we referred to them as, "Pepper moments." I told her

I was going to mention this in the book one day, if I didn't have a *Pepper moment* and forget! Pepper was a short, thin, middle-aged woman with salt and pepper hair and a big smile. She has been on several mission trips and loved doing mission work. It was good to see her.

We met Pepper in downtown Palmyra and she followed us to the Jordans, where she would stay for the next four nights. After a few days of walking and sharing, it became obvious that Pepper was not called to this walk. Her call to mission work was in Bolivia. We thanked her for the crosses and her support, hugged her, and waved as she drove off to meet a friend in D.C.

PRODUCE, PRODUCE, PRODUCE

We have never had to miss a meal on the faith walk. God's faithful have fed us all the way around the nation. We didn't always get to eat what we would really prefer to eat, but we always ate. I believe we would have eaten better and more to our liking if we had discussed our preferences with God!

We went through several weeks as we walked through Pennsylvania and Ohio when we ate very little produce. We were eating off dollar menus and from food pantries with no apples, oranges, bananas, beans, carrots, or broccoli. I really like fruits and veggies and I was missing them.

I walked by vineyards and fruit stands, large gardens, and one produce stand after another. I would look at all of the melons, grapes, cherries, cauliflower, peaches, red potatoes, and fresh sweet corn.

Finally, I looked up and said, "God, it would be so nice to have $5 to buy some produce."

Not even an hour later, I was walking toward Wendi who was waiting for me in the pilot car, when I ran into a woman standing at the end of her drive retrieving her mail from the mailbox. She said hello and asked me where I was heading. I told her about the walk and she asked if there was anything she could do for us. I thought for a second then I noticed the big tree in her front yard.

"See that blue Cavalier down the road? That is my pilot car. We are about to break for lunch and if we could sit under the shade of that big tree it would be a huge blessing. It is really hot out here," I blurted.

"Sure you can have your lunch under that tree!" she answered.

By the time I walked to the car, discussed the situation with Wendi, and we arrived back to the location, this kind woman had set up an umbrella over a patio table and had filled the table with watermelon, cantaloupe, cherries, sliced tomatoes, and fresh-picked lettuce—much more produce than $5 could buy!

I could not believe my eyes! I told the woman that I had just asked God for produce. We put lettuce and tomatoes on the sandwiches we had packed for lunch and we savored the fresh fruit.

The woman sent us off with what we didn't eat for lunch, and some cabbage rolls and chicken Cordon Bleu she had taken out of her freezer.

The next day we moved the motor home to an RV park in Perry, Ohio. Some of the campers had heard we would be residing there and they applauded as we pulled into our site. We were asked to join the folks for dinner—which included lots of fresh produce!

When we arrived back at the RV after walking the next day, we found a bag of fresh sweet corn on the step by our side door. A few days later, while walking through Perry, I noticed a squishing under my feet. I looked down and saw hundreds of sugar plums on the sidewalk, going to waste. I stopped and picked up as many as I could carry, and took them back to share with our fellow campers.

While walking through Cleveland, Ohio, the following week, I saw that someone had pulled all of their tomato plants, with large green tomatoes hanging from the vines, and put them out at the street for the waste collectors to haul away. I grabbed about six large green tomatoes and took them back to the camper. We had fried green tomatoes for dinner, one of my favorites!

I have never experienced such a variety of fresh produce in such a short period of time, as I did in July of 2005. All it took was letting my desire be known unto God. God wants to give to us, but more than that, He wants us to ask!

"DON'T FORGET THE HAM!"

By the time we got to Vermillion, Ohio, Wendi was coming into the fullness of her PR position. After the produce situation we concluded we have not, because we ask not! "Ask; using my name, and you will receive" (John 16:24 NLT).

Wendi set out one day to let the community know what we were doing and gave the folks every opportunity to help in any way they would or could. She dropped me off to walk and as she pulled away, I shouted, "Don't forget the ham!" It had to be Christian Tourette syndrome, because I would not ask for her to get a ham. I have hypertension and ham is on my "no-no" list.

I had walked most of the 10 miles for the day when she finally caught up with me. She had a voucher for some groceries, some gift certificates for restaurants, three passes for Cedar Point (a local amusement park), two tickets for a safari, and had secured a site at a local campground for a week.

"Oh, and about the ham—the place was all out of hams but we are invited to a Rotary meeting and they want you to be a guest speaker!"

"Wednesday, and there will be lunch!"

Wednesday morning, I had walked six or seven miles when we took a break to have lunch with the Rotary Club. The featured guests were some ophthalmologists from Russia, hosted by two local ophthalmologists. Wendi and I looked at each other in disbelief. Wendi wears disposable contacts and she had been wearing her last pair for about eight months. Her prescription was not that expensive, but she had walked away from her job and her medical coverage and could not afford to get an exam. We had been praying for the means for her to be able to get an eye exam.

After the fabulous lunch and an ophthalmologist presentation, I shared my testimony. The group applauded and passed around a hat to collect money to help us with the mission.

Then a woman came over and handed us a smoked spiral turkey. It was from the German ham store where Wendi inquired about the ham. I can eat a smoked spiral turkey; it has much less salt than a spiral ham. Oh my, that turkey was delicious—we ate it for breakfast, lunch, and dinner. It was so good, we froze some. We did not want any of it to go to waste. Once again, adhering to Christian Tourette syndrome produced great blessings.

As we were heading for our car, after the meeting, we walked right up to the local ophthalmologists. Wendi approached one of them and told him what we were doing, and asked if he could possibly give her an exam or maybe a trial pack of contacts until she was able to get an exam. He told her that he was not going to be in his office and he did not have her contacts on hand.

The other physician said, "I will be in my office today, and I do believe I have your contacts. Stop by in about an hour and I will take care of you."

His office was in Lorain, Ohio so Wendi dropped me off to finish my walking for the day and headed off for her doctor's appointment.

The doctor gave Wendi the most thorough eye exam she has ever had and got on the phone to order a two-year supply of contact lenses. Wendi tried to stop him. "If you would please just write a prescription, I can get them at a department store for much less."

The doctor smiled, "There will be no charge! You can pick them up in a couple of days." He thanked Wendi for letting him bless her with the exam and contacts and made it clear that he would take care of her for the duration of the walk.

Lorain, Ohio, is only about two hours from Wendi's home in Canton, so it was convenient for her to see the eye doctor while we were home for holiday breaks.

OHIO TO MICHIGAN

Our friends, the Merrithew family, came out and walked with us as we were completing the walk in our home state, in Toledo, Ohio. We were invited to stay in their home.

Tracey Merrithew, a former veterinarian assistant, suggested we have a dog out on the walk. Once again, I answered with humor, "If God wants me to have a dog" I began—I was about to say God would send us a three-legged dog—then remembering Wendi's fondness for Pomeranians, I concluded, "If God wants us to have a dog on this walk, He will send us a three-legged Pomeranian!"

Tracey and Laura both have foot problems and have much difficulty walking, but they were each able to walk a 10-mile day on this walk. Their children, Matthew and Molly, walked with us as well.

We were asked to park the motor home and stay at their home while we finished our walk in Ohio and headed into Michigan.

The first evening we were at the Merrithew's home, Laura got a call in the middle of the night that her mother had passed away. It was a Godsend that we were there, as we were able to watch the children that night. The following day we walked the kids to school before we headed out to walk, and picked them up at the end of the school day. This freed up our friends to make funeral arrangements.

We thanked God for our timely placement in Toledo, so we could be of help and support for our friends during their time of loss.

We stayed in Toledo as we finished walking our home state and crossed into Michigan.

We were given a connection to Tracey's mother, Ida, who was a widow living on the outskirts of Monroe, Michigan. She was expecting us to stay with her for a couple of weeks as we worked our way up toward Detroit. She had a home in the country with a long driveway where we would park our motor home. Our stay with Ida was full of the blessings of home-cooked meals and motherly love.

I know a couple of ministers in the Detroit area and we began to spend time in prayer with them as we walked toward the city. One of our minister friends walked into the city with us. As we headed toward Hart Plaza, which is located right on the water in downtown Detroit, God began to speak to my heart about ministering to the homeless population in the area. I had ministered to homeless people on the walk, but it had always been a one-on-one encounter.

I remembered back to Daytona Beach where I met Homer. He was pushing a grocery cart on the sidewalk where I was walking when I approached him and asked if he needed anything.

"Well, maybe a few more cans would be nice!" he chuckled.

Seeing the cart was filled with aluminum cans, I nodded and told him that I would see what I could do.

Over the next couple of weeks I picked up cans as I walked, and we made trips back to Daytona where we were able to find Homer near a local convenient store. He was always happy to see us and thanked us for the donations. Some of the local folks caught on and began to make deliveries to Homer. After we got over 150 miles north of Daytona, I told him we would not be coming back that way because we were walking too far north to make the trip back.

"You'll be back when it gets cold!" he exclaimed. "People always come back when it gets cold!"

I explained again that I did not think we would be able to make it back.

"Well, then," he said, "I'll have to get some new employees then, won't I?"

"I guess so, Homer!" I answered.

Homer was one of many homeless people we connected with along the way. Connecting with a *community* of the homeless was going to be a whole new experience.

CHURCH IN THE PARK

As we approached the park, God spoke to me about lunch, "Feed the homeless!" All we had in the pilot car was peanut butter and jelly. I asked Wendi to go purchase a couple of loaves of bread. She found a local Salvation Army food bank. We didn't qualify for the grocery handout because we weren't on their list. However, they *just happened* to have a surplus of baked goods, including bread, from a local bakery and Wendi was told that she could help herself.

When we got to the park, our pastor friend, Jade, knelt down on the ground by a bench and began making peanut butter and jelly sandwiches, as Wendi and I visited with those in the park. God really urged me to connect with the people and let me know I would be ministering to them for the next three weeks.

I got a tablet and pen from the car and took down their names and I asked each what I could bring them when I came back to the park. I pointed to the little Cavalier that was loaded and had a rack on the trunk piled with camping gear and a bicycle. I explained our mission and shared with them that we were operating entirely by faith for our provision.

"I have great faith that God can provide for you folks the same way He provides for us. So, what are you trusting God for?" I began to make my list.

- Calvin: pants size 34" × 32"
- Michelle: bologna sandwich
- Troy: peanut butter crackers
- Mary: coat
- Mike: hot plate (the homeless had access to electrical outlets that were used for concerts in the park)
- Dale: size 14 boots
- Louis: job and home

- Jessie: feminine hygiene supplies
- Fred: sleeping bag
- Davis: tent
- Floyd: Bible

Sleeping bags, coats, Bibles, tooth brushes, jobs, homes, tents, jeans, shoes, boots, etc. We had a list of about 30 people and 50 needs. I explained that we had no means of supplying the items on the list but we would pray and walk in great faith for each need to be met. I told the group I would be back the next three Sundays with a sermon and we would have a meal afterward.

As Wendi and I drove away, we discussed the needs and began to pray for God to supply.

"We have tithe money?" I reminded Wendi.

We gave away 10% of any money received for our support. Our tithing was nontraditional because we were on the road. Sometimes we gave within the communities we passed through as God led us. I counted our tithe money and it was almost $100.

We went to the Salvation Army and purchased coats, sleeping bags, cots, shoes, and blankets. Then we went to a dollar store and bought cans of soup (the kind with the pull tabs), pudding snacks, nuts, a can of Pringles, and other nonperishables.

We went back to the park with a portion of what was on the list. Wendi opened the can of Pringles and gave a small stack to each of the outstretched hands. We passed out the rest of the food and wares, and bid them farewell until Sunday.

During the week we appealed to pastors in the area about the needs in the park. We also put out the word to friends and family.

I informed the pastors, "There is a congregation in the park in need of a pastor." But the local clergy did not feel called to minister there. I prayed for the homeless each day as I walked. My heart was so burdened for the needs of the community at Hart Plaza.

When we arrived on Sunday, the folks were all waiting in the center of the park on concrete benches that were laid out in a circle. A couple of men were waiting for us near the parking lot. One of them called out "They're here, the pastor and Pringle lady are here!" The greeters led us to the congregation that anxiously waited for the message I was bringing that day.

Wendi was the self-appointed worship leader. She handed out song sheets to all who were gathered. Some friends at a local church had joined us. They brought hot dogs and other food to feed the homeless after the meeting.

Most of the homeless represented at the park had already shared that they were followers of Jesus.

I preached about God and His redemption story. I shared that after the fall of man in the Garden of Eden, God, being perfect, was no longer able to have fellowship with man who was now imperfect. So man communed with God through the blood of an innocent animal without blemish. I shared how God grieved the loss of the more intimate fellowship, so he sent His only Son, Jesus, to live a sinless life and be the ultimate sacrifice for our sins—for all of eternity. I explained how each of us can have a personal relationship with God through Jesus, and that He is just waiting for us to turn our lives over to Him and His care.

We had an altar call.

Everyone there made a personal decision to follow Christ before the service was over. One of the men, Louis, asked me if I would baptize him. It was late October and very cold at the Detroit River on Lake St. Clair. I silently prayed about the situation.

Wendi looked shocked as I asked for her assistance in the baptism and dragged her to a fountain in the park.

Afterward, Wendi collected the song sheets as people got in line to eat. As we fed the 36 who were at the church meeting, a few more strangers approached. We had plenty of food to feed the crowd.

After the meal we handed out sleeping bags, blankets, Bibles, and hygiene supplies. Needs were being met. As we were leaving the park, more and more people shared their need for various items. Our list was getting bigger, but we knew God would supply.

The following Saturday we met again with our friends and a meal was planned. We packed lunch bags with bottles of water, apples, snacks, and left room for sandwiches that would be prepared the following morning. I shared that I believed God wanted me to speak on the principles of tithing. I felt very strongly about this and very concerned about how I would be able to pull it off. I asked our friends if they had 30 lunch bags leftover. They did. I asked them if they would fill each bag with 10 of the same item. My request was granted.

One of our friends, Lynn, told us about a skit that she and a few members of her church had performed. We practiced the skit and planned to meet at Hart Plaza at 11:00 the next morning.

Once again, the congregation awaited us with great expectation. The welcoming committee escorted us to the sanctuary in the middle of the park. Wendi handed out the song sheets to be collected at the meal line after the service.

"People with song sheets will be first to be served lunch!" she explained.

We handed out the paper sacks which had been stapled at the top, so the content was hidden. I asked the group to hold onto their bags and not to open them until after the message had been delivered.

You could have heard a pin drop in that park that morning as the small crowd watched our skit. Wendi and two of our friends sat together in the circle. Each was dressed for church in their finest "Sunday go-to-meeting" attire. They whispered to each other and held their noses as I enter dressed very much like the other homeless people. Once I sat down, they physically moved their chairs away from me.

Jan, who was dressed in a man's suit, was the first to pick up a very large wicker basket and place it on the floor in front of her. She pulled out a very large fake check and unfolded it. She flashed the check which was probably 30" long and 12" wide. The words were large and bold enough for everyone to see the amount which read A LOT OF MONEY. The check was signed MR. SOMEBODY. She folded the check back up and tucked it away. Then she dropped a few cents into the basket and passed it to Lynn at her right.

Lynn looked in the basket and searched in her purse for a few seconds, then flipped a coin in the basket as she passed it to Wendi.

Wendi pulled out a bundle of very large fake bills. She fanned out the money so all could see. There were more hundreds than ones. She picked out a one-dollar bill and very proudly put it in the basket. Then she kissed her bills and carefully put them in her purse, shoved the basket toward me, and turned away disgusted.

I looked down at the basket, sighed, checked my pockets to find them empty, and sighed again. I stood there a few seconds; stepped into the basket, knelt down, and lifted my head and hands toward heaven. Then, the congregation sighed.

I explained God's principles about tithing and shared how I tithe and how God has blessed me over and over again. I told them that I truly believe we can live better on 90% of what we have than we could on 100%.

"God blesses those who give!" I explained.

I announced, "Now, open your bags. Everything in the bag is yours. You decide what you want to do with your gift!"

One by one, each person came forward and dropped items in the basket. Most put 90 percent of their gift in the basket. Everyone put at least 10 percent in the offering. I looked down at the collection and considered, *What next?*

I silently prayed for God to lead me. I picked up the basket and announced, "How many of you would like a granola bar?"

There were exactly enough granola bars for hands that went up. I did the same for apples, then cups, then forks, then dimes, and dollar bills. Every time, I had the exact amount in the basket for each hand that went up, until I asked how many people would like some M&M'S. About 30 hands went up and I only had nine bags of M&M'S, so I gave them until I ran out.

Each person who received a bag of M&M'S, opened their bag, and began to pour into the hands of those who still had their hand raised.

I sure learned a lot about God's principles on giving that Sunday morning!

We grabbed the bagged lunches and emptied our trunk, which was packed full of the items we had collected throughout the week. The people were so appreciative of the gifts. Lynn had a pair of shoes sized 14 for the individual who had been walking in faith for them. She said she was at her office the week before and noticed a coworker's very large feet. She asked him what size shoe he wore. He answered 14 then she told him about

Dale's need for a pair of shoes. He actually took his shoes off and gave them to her. One miracle after another—needs were being met.

We fed over 50 people that day and our list was growing.

The following Sunday, several vehicles hauled in bags of loot, some with individual's names on them. We had everything on our list and much more. Ida, whom we had stayed with in Monroe, had prepared barbeque pork. Barbara, a friend from Toledo who owned a restaurant, brought gallon containers full of various salads and pastas. Tracey and Laura from Toledo brought desserts.

That morning, I shared my testimony about the walk and how God had provided for us every mile of our way.

Each week I had been serving communion. This week, I handed the juice and bread to two of the men who had been ministering to the others throughout the weeks, and asked them to serve.

Wendi had noticed that one of the men seemed to know all of the songs so she asked him to lead in the singing.

After the service we feasted. It was a blessing to serve the homeless one of the most delicious meals I have ever had. Wendi was standing next to me and was serving pasta salad out of a gallon bag. There were over 50 people in the food line and everyone got pasta salad, which seemed to be their favorite food. We opened the lines again for seconds and Wendi was still serving pasta salad out of the same bag. I remember looking over in amazement time and time again and wondering how this was happening.

After we served seconds, a man came up for more pasta salad and Wendi handed him the bag which was still half full. I believe we may have witnessed a fishes-and-loaves kind of miracle that Sunday morning.

We called out names and handed out sacks full of personal items for over 30 individuals. Everyone got everything that was on our list and then some. Over 10 people got homes that week. Some got jobs. The man who was baptized the first Sunday had found a home, and he was playing drums on two different praise teams in the city. He was coming back to the park on a regular basis to minister to the homeless.

We praised God for the congregation that rose up in Hart Plaza, in downtown Detroit, Michigan. We said our good-byes and felt confident the church would grow.

On November 14, 2005, we planted cross #3,525 in St. Clair, Michigan, then we headed back to Ohio. On our way through Detroit, we stopped off in Hart Plaza to visit our friends. The homeless community was still working together and ministering to each other. We thanked God for His work in Hart Plaza as we drove home to spend the holidays with our families.

BITTERSWEET SURRENDER

We drove the RV back to Ida's house in Monroe, Michigan, where she had agreed to let us store it for the winter. We barely got the motor home winterized and covered with tarps when it began to rain—real icy rain. And then it began to snow! My hands were numb as I fastened the last bungee cord and headed for the house. Winter was here!

We were very concerned about whether or not we were going to be able to keep the motor home because the money was not coming for the $370 payment each month. We were almost two payments behind. Wendi and I began to pray about the situation.

I thought back to October of 2001 when I purchased the vehicle. Deb said she would be my advance person under one condition:

I had to get a camper. We went looking at different RV dealerships, when we saw this 31-foot motor home. We were actually looking for a tent camper or much smaller tow camper. We only looked at this one, to see what it looked like inside. There were two others like it on the lot, one for $41,000 and the other one for $43,000.

As we were walking through the motor home, a salesman informed us that they had taken this one in on trade and he would be able to sell it for $31,000. It already had $10,000 equity. I told the salesman that I was unemployed and was about to do this walk so there was no way I could purchase it. He told me that it would not hurt to try. I filled out an application for a loan with a projected amount of faith pledges, and by faith, I handed the application to the salesman.

I laughed and told Deb it would take a real miracle for that to go through. We began walking over to the car to leave when the salesman called out, "It's yours! You are approved!"

I drove the motor home off the lot and Deb followed with her car.

For four years, we had enough money donated to the ministry to pay the payment, the insurance, and the fuel for the motor home. Now we were in a crunch and I was not sure what to do about it.

Wendi and I came to the conclusion that it was time to go out on greater faith. We both admitted the motor home had been a source of security for us. We had a secure place to stay each day after the walk.

Giving up the RV would mean we would have to trust God for our lodging as well as all of our other needs. We agreed that it was time to step up in our faith and give up the home.

I called the bank and explained our situation. I was told that it was not a problem at all. The woman was really nice about the whole ordeal, stating she would send someone out to Michigan to pick up the motor home and would consider it a voluntary surrender. As miraculously as I was given the home, it was taken away.

SOMEPLACE LIKE HOME

When we arrived back in Ohio, we stayed with Wendi's Grandma Miller. This worked out great for a time, as we enjoyed each other's company. But when I began to travel and speak more frequently, we decided to move to a mutual friend's home. Our friends, Kurt and Joni, had said that their place would always be open to us for the time we spent in Ohio.

They had a room in their basement that was partially finished. It had four walls and an opening for a door. We put a carpet remnant on the floor and I hung a door in the opening so we had someplace to come home to. This would be home and office for Faith Walk Ministries for the duration of the mission.

Hello, Bronwyn Carlee Elizabeth Stewart

On December 9th, I went with my daughter to her ob-gyn. I was extremely sad that Dad would not have an ounce of compassion for my wanting to stay home with my daughter for the last week of her pregnancy. The doctor gave my daughter December 20th as a date to induce her labor if she had not had the baby by then. Laurie had gestational diabetes and the baby was gaining weight rapidly. There was no way the doctor was going to let her have a late delivery. I was excited about the projected date, because I would be back from the cruise by then, however I was concerned about my daughter and wanted her delivery to go well, so I was hoping she would not have to wait.

178

The next day, Wendi and I flew to Tampa, Florida, where we met up with Dad and Agnes one of Agnes' daughter, Alice, and her daughter, Tiffy, and my brother, Andy, and his wife, Bonnie. We all stayed in a condominium that night and set sail the next day.

Heartbroken, I prepared to officiate my dad and Agnes' wedding. If I had known then of the heartache and division this was going to cause our family, I most definitely would had backed down. I had made a promise with my father and I was there in the flesh to keep that promise. My broken heart was with my daughter and son-in-law and the anticipation of my first grandchild!

I cannot put into words how miserable I was on that ship. If I wasn't crying, I was fighting back tears. My father paid for this cruise and I have to say it was one gift I wish I had never received.

Besides grieving the fact I would probably miss my granddaughter's birth, Agnes was already showing her true colors. She was making it very clear to me that she was taking full charge of my father's life and death, and that I and my sisters and brothers were going to have to stay out of all of his affairs. I was glad that my dad was not going to be alone, and I had no concerns about being a part of my dad's affairs—I had a walk to do. I was concerned, though, about how controlling Agnes was, and wondered if she had my dad's best interest in mind.

Little did I know how much my dad's finances would be depleted before Agnes would walk out on him. I had no idea that Dad who had already moved from his beautiful home in a lake community to a double-wide trailer, would end up alone in a little park model camper in a campground. If I had any way of knowing these facts, I would have said no!

As soon as we sailed into Tampa, and I was able to make a call, I checked my messages to find out that my granddaughter, Bronwyn Carlee Elizabeth Stewart, weighed in at nine pounds, six ounces, on the evening of December 16th. There had been complications but mother and daughter were both doing well.

I arrived at the hospital about 7:30 that evening, kissed my daughter on the forehead, and held my baby granddaughter for the first time. In my opinion, Bronwyn tied with her mother for the most beautiful baby girl I have ever held. There is a special place in the heart reserved for grandchildren, and I found that place on December 18th, 2005.

God blessed me in a huge way, by orchestrating my granddaughter's birth while I was on winter break. I spent several nights a week with Laurie and Mike and took shifts with feedings and diaper changing. I was able to bond with my granddaughter the first five months of her life. I gave her little back and feet massages. She still pulls her little shirt up for a back massage and takes her socks off for a foot rub. I think Nana was the fourth word she spoke—Dada, Mama, Geger (for her dog, Edgar Allen No), then Nana.

God at the Card Table

When I was not holding my granddaughter in Cleveland, I spent a lot of time with Wendi's family in Canton. The family gathers together to play cards one evening a week. I know some of you do not believe Christians should play cards, but I have to tell you that God was at that table. There was so much love and unity, and this is the place where Wendi and I shared our stories about the walk with her family. Over the years, the family saw how God was working in our lives and we saw how each of them was growing in their own faith, especially Grandma Miller.

Other than my daughter and granddaughter, I was not really close with my family emotionally, spiritually, or geographically.

I embraced Wendi's family as my own and they treated me as part of their family.

Family members hired us to do odd jobs while we were home. This provided us with the money we needed to make it through the winter months of 2003, 2004, 2005, 2006, and 2007, until we would be on the west coast and walking year round.

A Three-Legged Pomeranian

One day in late December, we were driving back to Kurt and Joni's, after being away for a speaking engagement, I got a phone call from our friend Tracey in Toledo. "We found your three-legged Pomeranian!" I was informed.

"You have got to be kidding!" I gasped. "That was a joke. This walk is no life for a dog!" I continued.

"Well, God has a sense of humor because He has this little three-legged Pomeranian and I know this dog's place is with you on the walk!"

Tracey had mentioned, to someone who works with rescuing dogs, that there was a place for the dog if she ever came across a three-legged Pomeranian. Tracey's friend called back within a couple of weeks with the news—a three-legged Pomeranian had been surrendered to an animal shelter in Zanesville, Ohio. Tracey said they were going to adopt the dog whether we took him or not and asked if we would be willing to drive to Toledo to meet him.

I thought about our crowded home office in the basement at Kurt and Joni's home, and I thought about their six cats. After a few moments of silence, reluctantly, and with much reservation, I said yes.

June 25, 2005

To Carol Cruise,

So sorry to hear of the passing of both your mother and grand-mother. That is always such a difficult thing to experience. We know that God has been faithful to sustain you throughout… how thankful we are for the Comforter who constantly abides in us and with us.

We shared with our DownEast church family where you are in your walk; they were all glad to hear the report and continue to keep you both in their prayers.

Have you seen Stan and Marcia, yet? If and when you do, please give them our regards.

Wherever you may be worshiping tomorrow, may you experience a heavenly day in the presence of our Lord.

In Christ,

Pastor and Anna Meidahl

When I read this letter, I felt so connected to the people in the early church, as they corresponded in letters. They were mutually supportive and referred to each other as sisters and brothers.

I often felt a kinship with the Apostle Paul, when I would call on members of the church throughout our country and plead with the people to keep us in their prayers.

MEETING NEW FRIENDS—2006

WALKER T.

In early January of 2006, we drove to Toledo to meet Rascal, the three-legged Pomeranian. I sat down in a chair and took my prosthetic leg off to give my stump some relief from the pressure of the leg. I laid the prosthesis beside me on the floor and began to visit with our friends and continue with the introduction.

There was an immediate connection with Rascal and Wendi. She looked in his eyes and believed he was trying to tell her his story. After a few moments, he hopped over to me, licked my stump, and lay down on the floor next to me, resting his head on my prosthetic leg. My heart melted as I looked into his eyes.

After some hesitation, I said, "I guess we can take him on a trial run!" He was the first of many new friends we would meet over the next 12 months.

The Merrithews agreed to sponsor the dog, so we would not have an added expense. I had expressed my concerns about housing him with the six cats and they agreed to keep him during the winter months. We decided he would be a dog with extended family.

I had some other concerns about housing arrangements out on the walk and how the little dog would fare with the long days and some of the extreme weather we face. I put all of my concerns aside, and decided to put it all in God's hands.

We all agreed to change his name. I wanted to name him Tripod, but Wendi was not so keen on the idea. She liked the name Walker because he would be doing a lot of walking. I agreed to the name Walker and we added T. for Tripod, so his name became Walker T. Sometimes we just call him T.

Over the winter months, the Merrithews took good care of Walker T. They took him to the vet where he got all of his shots and a checkup. They got him a trainer and he began training to be a service dog. They got his tags, had him groomed, and purchased a supply of food for him to take on the road.

We took Walker to Canton with us for a few days so I could train him to serve me and prepare him for his service dog exam. Walker learned to push items to me when I was not wearing my prosthetic leg. The biggest job he learned was to push my prosthesis to me. This would be helpful in times when I was leaning against a guardrail or some other structure to dry my stump. I lean the prosthesis next to me and sometimes it falls over, away from me, and is difficult to reach.

After a short stay with us, Walker stayed with the Merrithews until May, when we picked him up for his trial period out on the walk. He has been with us ever since!

On our way back to the walk, we stopped to visit Ida in Monroe. While we were there, Wendi decided to see how Walker would fare on the bike. She put him in the bike basket and took off for a ride. The little guy lay down in the basket like he had done this a million times. We were impressed.

All of my concerns about having a dog on the walk were soon in vain. It was not long before we were both convinced that Walker T. was meant to be out there as much as Wendi and I were.

People would stop to talk to us about the dog and we were able to share with them about the walk. He had a ministry of his own.

Wendi had more on her plate, having to secure lodging for us, but it did not seem to matter that we had the little dog. We started the year solely tent-camping. One state park after another provided sites for the three of us.

WALKING THE THUMB

The bottom part of Michigan, the section below the Mackinac Bridge, is shaped like a mitten. People in Michigan actually refer to different parts of the mitten when talking about various regions of the state. If I recall correctly, down-state actually is the palm of the mitten and below. Upstate is where the fingers would be in the mitten. There is a region actually referred to as the thumb of Michigan. The Upper Peninsula is referred to as the U.P.

When I walked the state, we traveled the outer rim of the mitten, along Lake Erie, around the thumb, and along Lake Huron, before we crossed into the U.P.

One day as we were walking into Lexington, just at the base of the outside of the thumb, Wendi took the car ahead and parked it at the north end of town. She rode her bike back to catch up with me as I was walking into the city.

She said, "I saw a sign announcing a pork dinner at one of the churches. I looked back to see which church it was. I think it was the Episcopal church."

When we walked up to the Episcopal church, the pastor was changing the letters on the marquee. We looked at both sides of the sign and could not see evidence of anything that might have read PORK DINNER. Wendi asked the pastor if it mentioned anything about a pork dinner before he began changing it. He told her, "No!"

She looked puzzled.

We shared with the minister about our mission and told him that we like to purchase meals as a contribution to the communities we walk through. He smiled and told us that he thought maybe the Catholic church down the road might be having a pork dinner fundraiser.

The father asked about our needs. I told him that we could use some gasoline for the car and perhaps a few groceries. He said he would be having Mass at 6:00 that evening and if we stopped by he would be able to help with the needs. We informed him we would be walking until after 5:00 and asked if we could come in our walking clothes. He smiled and nodded his head.

We continued our walk. After about five or six blocks, we noticed the Catholic church announcing PORK DINNER SUNDAY NOON. I looked back down the street and asked Wendi, "And how fast were you riding that bike?"

By the time we reached the Catholic church, I had to use the restroom. The door was open so we went inside. We were greeted by a delightful priest who looked to be in his seventies. We chatted a moment and he escorted us to the ladies room. We spent some time with the Father before we took off to complete our walking day. He was very excited to hear about our mission and told us that he had just come back from Europe where he was on a 10-day pilgrimage and had walked 100 miles. We were impressed. We made quite the connection with the father who invited us to come to Sunday Mass.

It was almost 5:30 when I finished walking and we headed back to the Episcopal church for evening Mass. The message was about faith. After the service, the father blessed us with a bag of groceries and some money for gas.

The next morning we attended 10:00 Mass at a fairly large Catholic church. The platform was in the center of the church with several sections of seating around it. There were a couple of hundred people at this service and we were not even sure if the father would notice we were present. A few minutes after we were seated, a man came over and handed me an envelope with two tickets for the pork dinner. He said the father asked him to give us the tickets and to tell us dinner was his treat.

After mass, the father spoke about our walk and asked Wendi and me to come to the platform. He prayed over us and announced that he would continue to pray for us as we walk. He whispered in my ear to let him know when I was done walking so he could quit praying for us. I need to give that father a call!

"These two women will be my guest for dinner today!" he announced. "Please feel free to help them with their mission!"

We joined the crowd in the social hall to be served the delicious homemade pork roast dinner. We found seats next to a wonderful older woman, Marsha and her nephew. They asked questions about the walk and our provisions. We shared testimony of how God had provided for us. Marsha told us that she had a cottage right on Lake Huron in Greenbush. After her husband had passed away, she placed it on the market, but there had not

187

been much activity. She said she would like to open it up for us to stay there for as long as we wanted.

I went out to the car to get an atlas. The four of us studied the Michigan map and saw that we would be walking right through Greenbush in July. We told her it would be great to stay there a week as we walked into Greenbush and another week as we walked away from the town. She was delighted to be able to provide lodging for us for two weeks and asked us to call her once we knew for sure when we would be needing the cottage.

Several people came over to us during dinner and many blessed us with money to help with gas and other financial needs.

A Little Girl with Big *Courage*

One very hot day in midsummer of 2006, as we were winding our way around the tip of the thumb section of the Michigan mitten, I received a phone call from a woman who had seen our story in the newspaper and had shown it to her nine-year-old daughter. She went on to share that her daughter was born with birth defects. Instead of arms she only had two little stumps. She was also missing a leg and part of her jaw. She asked if she could bring her daughter, Kim, out to meet me. I shared with the woman that I was about to complete 10 miles for the day and go to the state park down the road to cool off in the lake. She knew where the park was and agreed to meet us there. I told her that I would be watching for her.

About 10 minutes after I got in the lake I saw the little girl making her way toward me. I immediately got out of the water and headed toward the child. She was walking very well through the sand on her prosthetic leg. She had picked up one of the crosses I had planted and when she saw me, she held it up toward heaven. I hugged the little girl then chatted with her mother. I learned that

188

Kim was one of several challenged children this woman and her husband had adopted.

Kim asked me if she could have my autograph on the newspaper. I agreed to sign the paper if she would give me her autograph on another copy. I handed the girl a newspaper with a message of encouragement written over the print and Kim put a pen between her stumps and wrote a message to me on another copy of the article. This is one of my most cherished souvenirs.

Later that week Kim's mother brought her and two of her brothers out to walk with me. One brother had Down's Syndrome and the other was blind. The blind boy sang *God Bless the USA* as we all walked together along Highway 25.

Kim is one of many physically challenged children I have met and she has inspired me to never give up on my faith and hope. My challenges seem so trivial compared to what my little friend, Kim, faces each day.

Person Whisperer

Two women in a sporty little convertible stopped to inquire about my walking along Highway 25, as I was making my way down the inside of the thumb, near Caseville. When I spoke to them about the walk, the driver offered me her half-empty Pepsi and I kindly accepted it.

"I don't know why I am doing this!" the passenger asserted, as she handed me a piece of paper with her name and phone number. She went on to explain that she was not one to talk to strangers and definitely not one to open her home to people, but she felt strongly that she was supposed to invite us to stay with her. She went on to share that she had a very large home with a lot of space that she was no longer using since her husband passed away and her kids were grown.

189

We accepted her offer, and a couple of days later we moved into her home for a few days. The two women were there along with another friend and the five of us had a great time in fellowship over a lovely spaghetti dinner.

This was the first of many people who would stop along the roads and streets and say; "I don't know why I am doing this!" as they offered us a place to stay in their homes. I know why they were doing it! God is a person whisperer!

LAKE HURON

"What If It Was Jesus?"

On July 9th, my fifty-second birthday, we were walking toward Bay City at the inside pit of the thumb. Wendi left me to walk while she went ahead to the communities to arrange our lodging. Up to this point she had not asked for more than a place to put a tent. She made calls and approached several places of business in an attempt to find lodging, but one door closed after another. After all, July 9th was very close to July 4th and we were walking in a very touristy area on Lake Huron.

Wendi, a very determined person, drove over 30 miles north of where I was walking to Standish. She walked into the office of the Standish Motel and shared our story with owner, Jan Hazelton, who checked with her husband John, then generously provided us with three nights of lodging. This was the first of many businesses that would host us. We didn't get into our room until about 8:00 that evening and we were both very tired—me physically from walking 10 miles in the heat, and Wendi emotionally from so many No's! Regardless, we were both thrilled to be sleeping in a real bed, not just for one night, but for three. We walked over to a drive-in across the way and ordered burgers and fries for ourselves and a dish of doggy ice cream for Walker T.

Later that week, *The Bay City Times* covered our story and the reporter interviewed Jan at Standish Motel.

"I can't believe that someone who is doing something to promote herself as a Christian and an amputee that no one would be kind enough to give them a place to stay," Jan reported. "I feel that it was something that we needed to do. 'What if it was Jesus?'" she was quoted.

Cottage on the Lake

It was nice to have our next home waiting for us. Wendi had called Marsha Mattice who arranged with her realtor to unlock her cottage and leave a key for us on the dining room table.

After our walking day we drove 50 miles ahead to our little place on Lake Huron in Greenbush, Michigan. We walked into the cottage to find a fresh baked apple pie awaiting us. Marsha's husband had begun to remodel the cottage before he passed away. It was a little disheveled but very comfortable. Wendi and I each had our own room. Walker T. slept under Wendi's bed.

It was a very hot July. We got up early, walked 10 miles, headed back to the cottage, changed into our swimming attire, and spent over an hour on rafts in Lake Huron, just 50 feet behind the house. This was one of our most memorable retreats. The lake water was warmer than usual that summer. We didn't even feel a chill when we entered the lake and it felt so good after walking in the heat each day.

Cavalier #2

Our car was beginning to overheat in traffic and the air conditioner was not working. It had close to 200,000 miles on it and was not a vehicle one would want to take across the country. I asked God if He would either provide the means to fix our car or provide one in good repair. It did not bother me much because I was walking most of the time, but Wendi often had to deal with traffic and it was miserable for her to spend hours in a pilot car in the heat of the summer, without air conditioning. Anyway, I let my request be made known to God and left it at that.

R.J. had been calling me and asking me if I wanted to buy his Cavalier. I told him that I was not in any better financial situation than I was a few years earlier when he asked me if I wanted to purchase the one we were driving. He told me that he really thought we should have the car and if I changed my mind to give him a call.

I prayed some more about our car situation. I told God that I would like to give the car to Courtney, Wendi's oldest daughter who had recently gotten her license. Courtney took care of things back at home for us. She checked our post-office box, deposited donation checks into the bank, and managed our website.

One day Courtney called Wendi to let her know she would be making deposits. She listed the donation amounts.

"You got a $25 check, a $75 check, a $4,000 check, and a $100 check!" she reported.

"Wait a minute—what did you say?" Wendi asked.

Courtney read off the amounts again.

"Did you say we got a $4,000 check?" Wendi choked.

"Yes, I sure did!" Courtney answered and told us it was from our friends Joe and Arnita in Tyler, Texas.

Wendi and I both knew what the money was for and who we needed to call for the purchase. I called R.J. and asked him if he still had the car. Yes, he did.

"I have to have four thousand dollars for the car!" he responded. That was a real deal. The car was a 2003, it had a lot of miles on it, but it was still worth about $7,500. We told him we would take the car and made arrangements to drive home that weekend to pick it up.

We called Joe and Arnita and thanked them for the money. We told them how desperately we needed a new vehicle and how we were going to purchase the car from R.J.

On Friday of that week, Wendi took me out to walk then went back to the cottage to clean our Cavalier so it would be nice when we presented it to Courtney.

We drove home Saturday and picked up Cavalier #2 from R.J. and took Cavalier #1 to Courtney. Courtney was out in the driveway washing her car when we got there. Her father had given her his old car. It was rusty and not in very good shape, but it ran. Her father thought she could sell the car for about $300. Courtney told us that she would like to keep her CD player that had been installed in the car her father had given her.

We called a friend of ours, Phil, who does that type of work and he told us to bring the car over and he would switch the CD players. When we got there Phil shared that his mother was homebound because she didn't have a car. When Courtney heard this, she gave the older vehicle to Phil's mom. I love this kind of story—the gift that keeps on giving!

God Said, "Lunch"

Oscoda, Michigan, was an oppressed area to walk through. The people didn't seem friendly, and there seemed to be a spirit of fear throughout the area. The economy was bad and people seemed to be holding on for dear life to what they had.

The support bars on Wendi's bike basket had weakened from Walker's weight. She dropped me off to walk one morning, then went ahead to a bike shop in Oscoda and asked about the best deal they had for a bike basket. The owner seemed insulted that Wendi was looking for a deal and she was very unkind to her.

When I walked up to the bike shop, I found Wendi searching through the car. When I got close to her, I could see that she was frantically looking for something. She turned to me with tears running down her cheeks, and said she was looking for enough money to buy the basket. She told me how the woman had treated her and I suggested she forget buying the basket—we could get one at a department store down the road.

Wiping tears from her eyes she said, "No, I want to get it here. The business is suffering so I want to get the basket here."

There were no deals on bike baskets that day. We spent every penny we had for an overpriced basket, but I know we did what God wanted us to do!

The *Oscoda Press* came out and interviewed us in mid-July.

◊ ◊ ◊

As we had returned from our trip home to get Cavalier #2, we were walking along Highway 23 in Black River on a hot summer day, when a couple, Peter and Helen, stopped along the road and asked if they could take us to lunch. We had been climbing some hills, and with the heat of the day a break was long overdue. We were delighted to join the couple. We climbed into the back seat of their Toyota Highlander as they drove us to a small café in a small town north of where I was walking.

Helen had seen the article in the *Oscoda Press*. She said she saw us walking, then she saw the article, then saw us a second time.

"God said, 'Lunch!' That's all!" she said.

"Lunch!" she repeated.

So there we were, having *lunch*. Peter and Helen asked a lot of questions and we answered. We had no idea how involved this couple was going to be in this ministry but we did know in our hearts that we would see them again.

We told them that we were staying in the little cottage on the lake, but we would be moving ahead soon. We also shared that we would be attending the Little Stone Church in Black River the following Sunday.

The couple invited us to spend the weekend with them in their beautiful home on Lake Huron. We all got along really well and they loved Walker T., so we accepted their invitation as they dropped us back on the road to finish a 10-mile day.

We returned to our cottage that evening to find a case of water waiting for us on the front stoop. We had received the first of many care packages Helen and Peter would deliver or have delivered to us over the next several years. They are still sending packages.

Friday evening we moved out of our little cottage on Lake Huron to go spend the weekend with this dear, sweet couple. Today, they are more than a brother and sister in the Lord—they are family.

MACKINAC

We pressed forward toward the Mackinac Bridge. The bridge is only open for pedestrians one day a year, Labor Day. There are no exceptions. If I could not make it to the bridge by Labor Day, I would have to head back down the mitten along Lake Michigan, follow the lakeshore up through Chicago, and enter Wisconsin from the south. This would add over 800 miles to the walk, which was all I was averaging in a year, as I walked the north. That would have meant another year of walking. I was ahead of schedule though, with great promise of reaching the bridge in time for the Labor Day walk. We were hoping to get there a little early so we could make one last trip to see our families before we got too far away from Ohio.

About halfway between Black River and Mackinaw City is the small town of Roger City. We ended up on a walking path and chatted with other walkers along our way. One of the hikers happened to be the daughter of the grand marshal in an upcoming parade and was real involved in the planning of the event. Taking a liking to Walker T. and moved by our purpose, she asked if we would take part in the small-town parade. We chuckled and agreed. She gave us the meeting place and instructed us how to get a number and a place in line.

Walker T. Working the Crowd

Wendi groomed Walker T. for the event. Sunday afternoon we mounted a number on Wendi's bike basket and took our place right behind the bikers and in front of a team of clowns.

The parade route was about a mile long. Walker T. worked the crowd. He would walk to one side of the street, take a bow, wait for the applause, then walk to the other side and do the same.

"You can do it little buddy!" "Ah, look at him!" "You can do it!" More cheers and more claps. We were in awe. What had this dog done before we got him? Walker T. walked the whole route that day. It was the most he had been asked to walk on a

196

given day. We could see he was meant to do more than ride in the bike basket. He had about 3,000 miles of walking ahead of him.

Mackinac Island

Early the next week Peter and Helen contacted us and asked if they could take us to Mackinac Island. We were happy to see them and glad to have an opportunity to see the island. We drove down to their place to spend the weekend and they took us up to Mackinaw City. We caught a ferry to the island. Other than service vehicles, driving is prohibited on the island.

After treating us to a nice patio lunch, Peter and Helen treated us, all three of us, to a buggy ride. I think there may only be one street around the island. We enjoyed the views of the historical hotel, the famous golf course, the lighthouses, and Lake Huron from several different angles.

After the tour we walked around the small shops. All were pet-friendly and many had water dishes set out for their four-legged friends, or in our case, three-legged friend. Peter and Helen bought us some of the island's famous fudge. Before we boarded the ferry to head back to Mackinaw City, the couple took us to dinner, where Walker lay quietly under the table.

We really enjoyed our day on the island with our new friends and had a great time chatting about the day's events as we headed back to Black River.

Later that week, as we were walking into Cheboygan, I noticed a man riding his bike toward the traffic. This stuck out to me because bikers generally rode with traffic. I also noticed something else, something I had not seen anywhere else on the walk. The small dead-end roads had very *large* signs posted out by the highway, so people would be able to find them easily. These signs

197

were at least four times the size of the road or street signs I had grown accustomed to seeing along the country roads.

By the end of the week we had made it to the Mackinac Bridge—three weeks before Labor Day. I walked right to the base of the bridge then got in the car with Wendi and we headed back to Ohio to spend some time with our families.

My father just happened to be in Ohio when I got there. He had traveled with Agnes, who is also an Ohio native. I picked him up so he could travel with me, to my daughter's house, where he would see my granddaughter, Bronwyn, for the first time. He was distraught and brokenhearted as he explained to me that Agnes was not going back to Florida with him. They had a falling out and she was going to stay in Ohio with her daughter.

Agnes' oldest daughter, Theresa, and I arranged for the two to meet at a food court to try to work things out. This meant Dad was left to drive back to Florida by himself. He really wasn't healthy enough to make such a trip alone, so Wendi and I volunteered to travel back with him since we did not have to be in Mackinaw City for a few weeks.

Wendi drove my dad in his car and I followed in the pilot car. We got Dad all settled in his double-wide and prepared to head back to the walk when Dad told me that he wanted me to stay and take care of him.

"I think God would understand that you had to stop the walk to take care of your father!" he pleaded.

"I know God would understand, Dad, but I am not sure if that is what God would want me to do!" I explained.

Meanwhile, my daughter was putting pressure on me to abandon the walk and take a job as a local pastor or work as a chaplain for hospice. I felt really torn once again by the two family members I loved the most.

I seriously thought about postponing the walk. That would mean it would take at least a year longer to complete. I spent a lot of time in prayer. Then I received the following email:

August 23, 2006

Dear Reverend Carol Cruise,

I would love to tell you a story about one of your crosses. I have a summer home about 15 miles south of Cheboygan, Michigan, off of US 23. I am a teacher so I spend most of my summers up there. My wife and I have been going up there for over 20 years. Almost every day I take about a 10-mile bike ride down US 23. I always ride against the traffic. That way, when I have to cross the road, I can see if there is anyone coming in my lane. If not I pull out into that lane and look down US 23 to see if anyone is coming that way. If not, I cross the road.

On Sunday August 13th I found one of your crosses at mile #3,889. I picked it up to bring home to show my wife. When I got to our Lane 57 which we live on I started to pull out into the road and at the last second I decided to go a little bit further that day. I took this ride HUNDREDS of times and never did this. As I got to Lane 57, I passed it. Just as I passed it, a BIG RV came speeding by in the lane I would have been in. He was passing two other cars. If I took the route I ALWAYS take I would have been a bug on his windshield. It scared me half to death. As I stopped my bike I was clutching your cross in my hand. On Labor Day I will also be walk-ing the bridge. What time are you starting? I would LOVE to meet you!!!!

LOVE,

John

I truly believe this was the answer to my prayer. I had to be in that bridge walk on Labor Day. I have a brother and a sister who live near my father. They were perfectly able to take care of Dad. Laurie, Mike, and the baby were doing fine. I had to finish this walk; this is what God would have me do!

I hit Reply after reading the email. I typed an answer and shared that I believe I saw him riding on the road one day. I also told him that I remember the lanes and seeing the numbers, so I knew about where he lived. I told him that I was planning to be at the north end of the bridge at 11:00 and I would be wearing a red, white, and blue shirt that matched my red, white, and blue prosthesis. I hit Send. I got a reply that the mail could not be delivered. I was puzzled. I did not type in the address; I simply hit Reply. I tried again, and got the same response. I typed out the sender's email address and tried sending it again, and once again, it was not delivered. Could this have been an email angel?

Wendi and I headed back up to Michigan on the Friday be-fore Labor Day. We spent the weekend with Peter and Helen. We showed them our email and I explained how I believe it was the answer to my prayer when I asked God to show me whether or not I should go forth with the walk or take a break from it and share my time back and forth between my dad and my daughter. We were all puzzled as to why I was not able to send a reply.

Wendi and I decided to travel to Mackinaw City early enough to see if we could catch John before he left for the bridge walk.

We turned onto Lane 57. There were only a few houses on the lane. Wendi went to the door of one of the houses and asked if John lived there. "No!" was the reply. She asked if the man at the house knew John and if he lived around there.

"No, I have lived here for quite a while and there is nobody by that name on this lane." Wendi and I could not believe this. I do know, though, God used that email to keep me on track.

We crossed the Mackinac Bridge along with about 40,000 people that day.

THE U.P.

We were a little concerned about how we were going to be received in the U.P. We had heard some stories about the people up there. Supposedly they were a bunch of *bubba* woodsmen who probably were not going to be very nice and definitely were not going to be very helpful.

Wendi left me at the Mackinac Bridge and went on ahead to secure lodging, as I began my long trek across the peninsula. Just three miles beyond the bridge, Wendi felt led to go into the Pointe La Barbe Inn. She thought it was kind of odd because she usually would go 20 or more miles ahead to find lodging. When she went in, she was greeted by Tammy and Al, a wonderful Christian couple who extended an invitation for us to stay at their inn for as long as we needed. We were there for a week and we couldn't have asked for better hospitality.

After about a week we needed to move forward. We stopped in a motel near Route 77 where we would turn north to M-28, which was a more northern route than Highway 2. There seemed to be a lot of property around the motel and we asked the owner if we could put a tent there for a few days while we walked up Route 77. The owner was happy to accommodate us and hooked us up with electricity and water. She mentioned that there was a man named Roman, up in Seney, who she thought would really enjoy meeting us and suggested we stop at his restaurant when we got to the area.

We planted cross #4,000 on Route 77 in Germfask.

When we got to the intersection of Route 77 and M-28, we took a break and went to the restaurant in Seney. We ate lunch and inquired about Roman. We were told that he and his wife were no longer the owners. We were also informed that they had built the restaurant, the grocery store, and the bank. At one time, they pretty much owned Seney. The cashier in the store called Roman and he was very interested in meeting us. We drove to his house and he and his wife invited us in for dessert and coffee.

Roman sat across from us with his Bible open. He read a few scriptures then stared away for several seconds, as if in prayer. He looked at us and asked, "Do you need any crosses?"

I laughed and said, "Roman, we have a few groceries, we know where we are staying tonight, Wendi secured lodging for us for a week in Munising, we have a full tank of gas, and it is rare for us to have extra money, but we have a few extra bucks. The only thing we need is crosses. We are out of crosses!"

He told us that he had a box of scrap wood that he had been holding onto and was not sure what he would do with it. He smiled and motioned for Wendi to follow him. He led the way to a small shop behind the house where he cut the wood for over 100 crosses.

Our next home was at the Hillcrest Motel and Cabins in Munising. Deb, the owner, was very excited to help us and told us we could stay there as long as we needed. She shared with us that she and her husband put a sign out every winter, LODGING FOR STUDENTS. They wanted college students to know they could stay there when the winter road conditions were hazardous. She definitely had a heart to help!

One day when returning back from our walk, I noticed a pickup with kayaks in the parking spot next to ours. Then an attractive young woman with a big friendly smile walked around the other side of the truck, and began to ask questions about the ministry. I shared our story with her. She, Susan, said she believed God led them to that particular motel. She and her husband Scott, who is a physician in Grand Rapids, Minnesota, were on a much needed vacation. When searching online for lodging, this place just stood out to her. Susan believed they were supposed to meet us. She said we would be passing right through Grand Rapids on Highway 2 and they would be glad to host us when we got there. Wendi got her contact information.

That weekend we attended two different churches in the area. One particular church meeting stands out to me. The church was new, and there were about 30 attending. The gentleman speaking was not the pastor, but definitely had a pastor's heart. The folks welcomed us with open arms. I was asked to share my testimony which fit perfectly with the message on stepping out boldly in faith. We met Kate and Bill, who own some cabins in the woods and invited us to stay there when we traveled back to Ohio for our winter break.

We had made such a love connection with the people in Munising, it was sad to think we had to move on. Deb, the Hillcrest's owner, told us there was no hurry—the room was there for us for as long as we needed it.

◊ ◊ ◊

I was walking within a few miles of Marquette, when Wendi went ahead to look for a place for us to stay. She figured we should at least try to secure lodging for the next several days, before she began to look in Neguanee. I saw a sign that had a Bible verse on it and it also said "Jesus loves you!" I suggested to Wendi that she try there.

She went in and talked to a girl at the counter, and asked if they would be willing to give us complimentary lodging for two or three nights while we walked through the area. The manager was not in but the girl was sure she would help us. Meanwhile, Wendi secured lodging for us for Thursday and Friday of the week. We still needed lodging for Monday through Wednesday.

As we were driving into town that evening, she got a call from Nona, the owner of that place. She said she thought it was a bit much to ask for three days, even to ask this of a Christian. Wendi told her if she could just give two nights, it would be a blessing. She told her that the owner of the place we had stayed for the past seven nights was willing to extend our stay and we could just go back there for the night. Nona softened, and said she would be glad to help us with Tuesday and Wednesday. It was a delightful little bed and breakfast. We chatted with Nona in the mornings before we went to walk. By the time we left, she was helping me on with my rain coat and thanked us for staying there.

As we headed away from Neguanee, Highway 2 was like a country road that connected one small community to the next. We were given a campsite at a small campground in Sidnaw for the weekend. On Monday morning, we woke up to find ice in our water bottles. We hoped our tent camping would be over for the year.

We were hosted in a beautiful cabin-type motel for a few days near Covington. One place after another opened up for us as we made our way to the Wisconsin state line.

As we were heading through Bruce Crossing, it was early October and the leaves were changing. I noticed a trail where the railroad used to run. We inquired about the path and were informed that it was used for snow mobiles in the winter and it ran for several miles. I was thrilled to move off the road onto the trail. Wendi parked the car at Bruce Crossing and rode her bike to catch up with me. While she was pushing her bike, the front rim, for no apparent reason, just split down the middle.

She took the bike to a business in Bruce Crossing, drove the car ahead, and walked back to join me. She stopped while talking to a newspaper reporter on her cell phone because the signal was weak. As I strolled on ahead of her, I noticed a couple walking toward me in the corridor. As I got closer, I recognized Peter and Helen. They had driven eight hours to catch up with us, to surprise us on the walk.

I asked how they found us. Helen said she thought maybe they had missed us because they were no longer noticing crosses. She prayed for God to give her a sign.

The couple stopped at a rest area, and as Helen was heading back to the car, she found a cross that I had planted, just outside the ladies room. They then noticed the path, just inside the tree line and guessed we were probably on the trail. A few miles

205

down the road, they saw the Cavalier pulled off the road. Figuring Wendi had parked ahead of me; they pulled in a nearby drive and began walking back on the path—good deduction!

We were glad to see our friends. The couple took Wendi's bike to a shop in Wakefield and purchased a new rim. They caught up with us as I finished walking and took us out to dinner.

"We will get a room at the place that provides lodging for you!" Peter told us. So Peter and Helen followed us as Wendi began to search for lodging. Wendi seemed to be in the office a long time at the first place we stopped. After about 10 minutes, I went over and sat in the back seat of Peter and Helen's vehicle, so we could visit while we waited. It was another 15 or 20 minutes before Wendi came out to tell us we would not be staying there but the owner had referred us to a place down the road. It took so long, because she had been ministering to the owner, who was a widow and had been hit with some difficult times.

The place down the road donated four nights of lodging. Peter purchased a room right next to us and the four of us visited into the night. The next morning, after Peter and Helen took us to breakfast at a local diner, Wendi took me back to the trail to walk, and our friends went sightseeing.

That morning, Diane Montz, from the *Daily Globe* in Ironwood, came out to interview me. Around noon, Jean Nordine, from the Ontonagon paper, came out to take some photos and chat. Just as I was meeting with Jean, Peter and Helen showed up with a lunch for Wendi and me. We waved to our friends as they headed back to Black River.

Both reporters wrote great stories and instant friendships were established with each of them.

A few days later, while walking near Ramsey during my lunch break, I went into a convenient store to purchase some copies of one of the papers. As I was walking out of the store, a precious pastor, Todd, from Cornerstone church, walked up and introduced himself. He had just read one of the articles and prayed that God would let him meet me.

Todd invited me to speak at his church on Sunday. I did, and what a blessing! Both Jean and Diane showed up for the service. Jean took photos and told us she would follow the walk and try to be there as we concluded for the year, when we crossed the Bong Bridge from Wisconsin to Minnesota. A collection was taken up to help us along the way, and we were invited to stop back in the spring when we traveled back from our winter break. Diane invited us to have dinner at her home and opened her home for a place for us to stay.

Walking along the evergreen forests, first on Lake Michigan then near Lake Superior, HOT PASTIES lit the windows of nearly every restaurant. Logging trucks, friendly folks, and maximum hospitality—all in all, our experience in the U.P. was one of the most pleasant of the entire walk. We made friends along the way and lifetime memories. The people there work hard, play hard, and love hard. We had one bad experience in the Upper Peninsula, when an individual put a sign on the back of our vehicle that read DO NOT GIVE TO THESE WOMEN THEY ARE CON ARTISTS. Other than that, it was a good experience for us in the Upper Peninsula. Shame on those who speak poorly of the U.P. people! If what I have just described in this chapter defines "bubba," then I just may be a bubba wannabe! I am looking forward to revisiting the U.P. as many times as I possibly can over the next several years… it's one of my favorite places on earth!

207

PASSING THROUGH WISCONSIN

We were met with blizzard conditions as we walked into Wisconsin. The heavy snow covered my glasses, making it difficult to see. A kind gentleman stopped and gave me an umbrella which had to be shaken frequently to remove the weight of the furiously falling snow. My socks were wet and my hands were freezing. Jean called, saying she would be passing through the area and asked if we needed anything. All I could think of was warm mittens and dry socks.

Jean and a friend showed up with hot pasties for lunch, two pairs of wool socks, and a pair of mittens. Wendi and I sat in Jean's car and visited as we sipped on cokes and enjoyed the beef and root vegetable stuffed pastry smothered in gravy.

After lunch, with dry socks and new mittens, I stepped back out into the blizzard to complete a 10-mile day.

Wendi found lodging at the Hurley Inn where Diane caught up with us to do a follow-up story and to capture a photograph of us covered in snow!

By Wednesday, we were walking through the Bad River Indian Reservation. There were several signs speaking out against meth labs. We guessed there was probably a severe drug problem in that area. It was not a pleasant walk. The people gave us *not so friendly* looks and there were a lot of "keep out" and "private property" signs posted along the road.

The only hotel was at a casino. Wendi went in and asked for lodging for the night. To our surprise, we were hosted at the casino Wednesday night.

Wendi was able to secure lodging in Ashland for the next several nights. A reporter from the Ashland newspaper ran a story about the walk and encouraged the residents to stop and chat with us as we walked through the city on Saturday.

Midweek we were hosted at a small cottage. The owners had a restaurant next to the cottages where we went for dinner. Our dinner was paid for by local residents who had heard about the walk, one of them being a restaurant owner who invited us to his place for a meal.

We had three more walking days left in 2006 when Wendi approached an owner of a small motor lodge for housing. The woman said her place was seasonal and she was closed for the year, but she gave us the keys to a room at the end of the lodge and said we could stay there for the rest of the week. Wendi and I prayed she would be blessed for her kindness (this is something we did everywhere we stayed).

The next morning we looked out and every parking spot, in front of every room, was filled. A family was caravanning to Duluth to see an ailing relative, and chose to pull off at this particular inn which happened to have nine empty rooms next to ours. Overjoyed, we laughed and cried at the same time, as we thanked God for blessing this business.

Saturday, October 21st, 2006, Jean Nordine and her mother Mary Ann treated Wendi and me to lunch before we walked the Bong Bridge from Superior, Wisconsin, to Duluth, Minnesota. We planted cross #4,342 at the west side of the bridge, then began our long drive, back to Ohio for the winter.

October 12, 2005

Hi, my name is Charlotte. I live in Monroe, Michigan. I had read your story in the newspaper yesterday. I am a volunteer for the Monroe cancer connection that my nephew is the director of and he asked me if I would pick up a cancer patient in Newport and bring him to his treatment. As I was on my way to get him, I passed you and beeped and waved. I was telling this man about you because he was too ill to read the paper. Then while bringing him in, we passed you and I thought I would love to find one of her crosses and give it to him. I know he is not going to make it but maybe it will help for him not to suffer so bad. So I went slow back home and I found one and only one where we had passed you, so he begged me to take him to his treatment tomorrow and Friday. Of course, I said yes and I will give him the cross tomorrow then get it back Friday and pass it on for you. The marker says 3429.

Good luck on your journey and I hope this will help him a little too.

Sincerely,

Charlotte

I WILL FINISH
THIS WALK—2007

CHRISTIAN RADIO

Wendi contacted Susan Gerling about staying with them the first week of June, our second week back to the walk in 2007.

We arrived back at the Bong Bridge in late May. Wendi dropped me off at the west end of the bridge where I had planted cross #4,342 and I began to work my way through Duluth. Wendi set out to secure lodging for us. She contacted the largest Christian radio station in three states and talked to station manager, Paul Harkness. Paul asked if he could air the story, so during our lunch break we met Paul at a park near the station for the interview.

Paul showed great interest in the walk and he and his wife, Nola, agreed to house us for a few days. While we were there, Paul grilled a fresh catch of trout and fried some perch—the best grilled fish I had ever tasted.

Paul told us about a man, John Halverson, a pastor in Duluth, who did a prayer walk with his family, covering the length and breadth of our nation. He contacted Paul and told him about our mission. John and his family hosted us for the next several days.

We shared tales about our journey with the Halverson family and they shared tales about their journey with us. John's family traveled with him and supported him in a walk from Canada to the Gulf of Mexico. His route pretty much followed the Mississippi River. His second journey was across the center of the United States from the Atlantic Ocean to the Pacific Ocean. His steps formed a cross over our nation. I was thrilled to hear about his journey because I had a vision of the entire perimeter of the nation being walked with a cross in the center. I was on the perimeter walk and I had hoped I would not be called to walk the cross as well.

Sunday morning, John made pancakes for breakfast then we went to hear him preach.

I felt led to walk the perimeter of Duluth instead of just cutting across. This added a few extra days to our journey, but by Monday evening, we were still close enough to Grand Rapids to begin staying with the Gerling family.

A gentleman from a radio station in Canada contacted Wendi one day as I was walking through Brookston. He said he had an hour-long radio program that was like a fireside chat. He asked if she would arrange for me to interview with him for his program. She agreed to schedule the interview.

When it was time for his show, she picked me up on the road and we traveled to a park in Brookston and I sat under a tree and chatted with the radio host. It was really a good time—the host talked with me as if I were sitting on a sofa in his living room. He asked questions and I answered. The hour passed quickly and then Wendi got me back to the road again.

GRAND RAPIDS, MINNESOTA

We arrived at the Gerling's house early that evening. They live on a private dirt road, in a lovely rustic home, nestled in the woods on one of the 10,000 lakes the state is known for.

Within a few minutes, Scott was online with his youngest son, Tyler, and they were looking at our website. Scott addressed me as "gimp." The ice was broken and we were all one big happy family.

The only concern the Gerlings had was the dog situation. They took a liking to Walker T. right away but their little house dog was not too fond of him, and they had two very large dogs who definitely would not take to our little 15-pound, three-legged companion. They warned us about their larger dogs and said they would only let them out when supervised.

One morning I got up earlier than Wendi, who usually tends to T. I thought I would give her a break and let Walker out. I looked around the yard and did not see any sign of big dogs. I walked outside with Walker and let him go potty. As soon as I put him down, two very large dogs came running toward us. I grabbed Walker T. and yelled at the dogs. One of the dogs grabbed Walker from my arms. I held tight to him and found myself in a tug of war with the canine. I was afraid Walker was going to be ripped in half, so I dropped him, and screamed, "Noooooooooo!"

My scream woke everyone in the house. Scott, his daughter Elizabeth, and son Tyler, came running to the rescue. It took both men to wrestle the dogs off of our dog. By the time Wendi got to the door, Elizabeth was carrying Walker into the house and Scott and Tyler were dragging the big dogs to the pen. Walker's hair protected him. The dog's teeth had barely broken through the skin.

213

Everyone was shook up. Scott had put the dogs out early and thought he would have them back in the cage before we went out with Walker. The Gerlings apologized profusely for the dog attack. It was really nobody's fault. It was just one of those things that happen. We were all thankful Walker T. wasn't killed or injured more seriously than he was.

The next day, Walker seemed bruised and sore, but he was going to be just fine, and he was still brave enough to take potty breaks in the Gerling's yard.

We all got beyond the dog incident and had great times in the evenings. Susan even let me cook in her kitchen which was a real treat. Scott and Tyler grilled on the back deck a couple evenings where we spent time visiting. I have never seen as many mosquitoes as I saw in Minnesota. It must be because of all of the lakes.

I really enjoyed evening talks with Susan. She is one of the few people I have met who really gets this "God talking to me" thing. God had given her some messages in her life. Most of the things had come to pass for her and she was still waiting to see how God was going to manifest the rest. I felt a kinship with Susan and I was sure we would meet again or, at least, keep in touch.

We went to the worship service at the Presbyterian church with the Gerlings on Sunday morning, where I delivered a short children's message. After the service, the Gerlings took us out to eat and we were introduced to some of their friends and Susan's parents.

BOY RIVER

Monday, as I was walking into the Chippewa Indian Reservation, a swarm of bees surrounded the pilot car. I am allergic to bees and we were quite a drive to the nearest emergency room. Wendi tried driving real fast to lose the bees, but when she stopped so I could walk to the car, the bees were back. She called me over the walkie-talkie and told me she would drop the cross at the mile and I could pick it up on the side of the road and plant it.

Wendi drove away from the mile marker and carried the bees away with her while I headed toward the dropped cross.

Just as I was about to plant the cross, Jean Nordine and her husband Jeff surprised us on the side of the road. They had decided to go off on a day of adventure and to find us on the walk. They took us to lunch at a restaurant in Boy River, then Jeff drove us to explore the headwaters of the Mississippi River.

By the time we got back to the walk, there were no bees to be seen. We thanked Jeff and Jean and they headed back to Bruces Crossing, leaving us with a promise to see us again.

As soon as I had walked to the car to dry my stump, a fellow stopped to talk to us. He introduced himself as Doug, said he had heard the one-hour interview, and was wondering if we needed a place to stay. We did. He gave us directions to his house. I asked him how his wife would feel about him inviting two women to stay at their home—he said she would be just fine with it.

We arrived at the house just as it was getting dark. Doug and Brenda were sitting around a table with friends, Steve and Lisa. They were making placemats for a Via de Christo weekend that was coming up. We sat down and began to help with the crafts. I told them that I had never been on an Emmaus walk, but I had heard good things about the experience.

It was a great ice-breaker to sit and chat around the table with four strangers as we made gifts of love for people we had never met. Wendi and I became instant friends with the four and we felt right at home.

Over the next couple of weeks, we spent a lot of time with the two families. I became extra fond of Doug and Brenda's daughter Angie, who was a junior at Bemidji State. She would be attending the Via de Christo weekend the week that her parents and Steve and Lisa would be working.

Angie lives in an apartment in Bemidji with two friends. She said she would love to have us stay with her when we walked through the city.

On Sunday, I spoke at the Lutheran church in Remer, where Brenda and Doug attended. The Gerlings came down to Remer to hear me speak. We sat with them after church as we enjoyed refreshments in the fellowship hall.

Wendi shared a story about a time she had left her camera on her bike after she mounted it to the back of the car. When she began her drive, she heard something fall behind the car. It was the camera. By the time she turned around, it had been crushed by the tires of a car. Susan offered to give us a camera that she no longer used. So after church we drove to the Gerling's house to get the camera. Wendi used it to take most of the photos we have on our website, www.faithwalk.net.

The following week, I shared my testimony at a nondenominational, full-Gospel church where Steve and Lisa were members.

After church, we went boating with Steve, Lisa, one of their twin boys, and Brenda. By the time we got back to Lisa's house, Wendi and I both needed to use the restroom. I shared our need with Lisa, and she asked if we wanted to come in her house and release a butterfly. We thought this was an odd way to say it, but we took her up on the offer. We practically raced to her restroom. After we had both had our turn using the facilities, Lisa asked if we wanted to release a butterfly. We thought we already had. She literally meant butterfly. She had some cocoons that had hatched and she handed Wendi and me each a monarch butterfly to release into the air from her back porch.

From then on, when I needed to use the restroom, I used the code word "butterfly" over the walkie-talkies.

Our next home was in Bemidji with Angie and her two housemates, Randy and Karri.

We laid our sleeping bags on a queen sized air mattress on their living room floor, and made our bed there for the next three nights.

We took the three out to eat at a Chinese restaurant the first night and Brenda helped the three feed us the second night. We had a great time. While we were there, Brenda invited Wendi and me to join them for a 4th of July picnic in the park, and we were also informed that the Dicksons wanted to host Wendi and the Seiferts wanted to host me at the Via de Christo weekend in mid-July, which would be held in a church right there in Bemidji. We accepted both invites.

After a few days, we moved out of Angie's apartment and trusted God to open up something for us down the road. That very day, as we were walking into Shevlin, a van pulled off to the side of the road and the driver, a woman, said "I don't know why I am doing this. This is just so out of character for me, but I just felt compelled to stop and talk to you!" Boy, we had heard that statement before!

MARY

The driver of the van was Mary. She and her husband Fran lived just a few miles south of Highway 2. She invited us to come and stay for as long as we wanted. She gave us directions to her guest house which would be our home for the next week.

Another woman stopped to check on us that day as we were walking into Shevlin. She introduced herself as Julie, and thanked us for doing the prayer walk.

We made it to Shevlin around noon and we stopped in the Village Café to have lunch. Our waitress just happened to be Julie. She was delighted to see us. She told the owner, Geri, and all of the other patrons about the walk. The owner would not receive payment for our meals; she wanted them to be her treat. We stopped in the restaurant several times to chat with Julie and Geri after that and each time Geri treated us to one of her delicious homemade meals.

We enjoyed our time at Mary's guest house. Within days a friendship was sparked between Mary and me. She invited us to attend her daughter's wedding which would be taking place in a park in August, and she agreed to watch Walker T. when we traveled back for the Via de Christo weekend.

It turned out that Mary actually works with Doug Dickson…small world! The two knew each other. When we told the Dicksons we were staying with Mary, they were excited. Mary was invited to join us for the 4th of July gathering.

I was asked to preach at a Baptist church in Bagley on the Sunday after the 4th of July gathering. I had noticed there was a bluegrass band playing at another Baptist church that evening. Wendi and I went to see the band for my birthday celebration. We sat toward the front of the room. I really enjoyed listening to the Haining Family Band. What a hoe-down for Jesus!

After the concert, the pastor asked everyone to stay seated for a few minutes, then he asked me if I would get up and share about five minutes of my testimony. What a shock! I had no idea how this pastor knew me and how he knew I was attending the concert. I spoke at two Baptist churches in one day. I am so thankful for

Christian Tourette syndrome and for having enough courage to attend the Baptist church back in Camden, Maine.

We found out later, when we gathered in the basement, that Julie from Village Café attended this church. She was working in the kitchen.

The following Thursday we dropped Walker T. off to stay with Mary while we took a long weekend off from the walk to attend the Via de Christo weekend. Out of respect for those who have not yet attended this kind of retreat, I am not going to share any details. I do hope you get to have your own experience. For those who have attended, *De Colores!*

We traveled back to Mary's for the weekend of her daughter's wedding. Mary and Fran treated us to breakfast the morning of the ceremony. My heart sank when they pulled in front of a restaurant across the street from the Village Café. I had hoped they would be giving the business to our friends at the Village. I was delighted as we all headed across the street to the café and realized there had been no spaces left in the parking lot.

Mary's family had pretty much adopted Wendi and me. They put us to work to help with the final preparations for the wedding. We helped pack the van, we set up tables, and we were able to help with clean up afterward.

STATE LINE

As we walked into Crookston, we noticed a home that had an assortment of signs in the yard, declaring JESUS LOVES YOU, GOD BLESS AMERICA. and different Bible passages. As I was standing in front of the house reading the signs, a woman came out to the road to get her mail. She was interested in our walk and asked if we would visit the Assemblies of God Church in town. It happened

219

to be Wednesday, so we planned to attend the midweek prayer meeting. Wendi gave the woman a brochure, then drove ahead to find lodging.

After checking into our hotel that evening, we showered and headed off to the prayer meeting. The pastor was happy to meet us and gave me an opportunity to speak. He took up a collection to help us along the way.

It was great to be crossing another state line, yet we were feeling sad about moving farther and farther away from Scott and Susan, Doug and Brenda, Steve and Lisa, and Mary and Fran. We have kept in touch and have remained friends with all four couples.

Wendi made a call to the Grand Forks connection. The gentleman shared with Wendi that they were doing some major remodeling and it would not be a good time to have house guests. He really wanted to help us so he said he would get back with her. Later in the evening, he called back to give Wendi contact info for Lilly who lived alone and had just returned from a mission trip. He said Lilly had a heart for missions and would be glad to hear from us. Wendi called Lilly for directions to her home, where we would be hosted as we crossed into North Dakota and through Grand Forks.

Lilly invited friends to dinner, the first two evenings, to hear our testimony over delicious home-cooked meals. She treated us to a meal out and gave us money to enjoy the state fair which just happened to be going on while we were in the city.

As we made our way into a rural area of the state, God orchestrated divine appointments. Wendi met people in parking lots near the state parks and people would stop and talk with us along the road. As we headed west on Highway 2, one door after another opened up for lodging and speaking engagements, as Christian brothers and sisters opened their homes and hearts in support of the mission.

DEVIL'S LAKE

We had divine appointments all along our way which provided places to stay, meals to eat, and places to speak. Our journey across North Dakota was off to a good start.

As we traveled along Highway 2, I noticed that most of the river beds were dry and many of the lakes were dry as well. I noticed this because, from the beginning of the journey, I stopped at every waterway I crossed, and prayed. I thanked God that we live in a country with plenty of clean, fresh drinking water. I thanked God for the ability to transport along our waterways. I thanked Him for water to bathe and swim in. I prayed for the waters to remain safe and pure. I prayed against crime on the waterways and along the water's edge and I prayed for many baptisms to take place along the shorelines.

As we were walking into Devil's Lake, we noticed that the lake seemed to be spread out and was overtaking the wooded areas and the fields. We also noticed it was flooding out homes. What a phenomenon—how could this be? All of the other lakes and rivers were dried up, yet this body of water was encroaching on homes, farms, and even surrounding communities.

I thought about the name of the lake. Why was Devil's Lake thriving? Did it have something to do with the name? I thought about how evil had spread across our nation like wildfire with; children killing their parents, children being abducted and sold into sex slavery, and youth taking guns to school and shooting teachers and peers. I thought about how metal detectors were being installed in most inner-city schools and how teachers, including my daughter, were working at high-risk jobs. What has this nation come to? Why was the evil spreading like wildfire over our nation? I began to pray over Devil's Lake, for the people in the community, and for the nation at large.

As I entered the city, I came down with a virus—the worst virus I have ever had. The whites of my eyes turned red and my eyes seeped with mucus. I had trouble moving my neck because my glands were swollen. I even had glands protruding on my cheeks—I wasn't even aware that I had glands in my cheeks. I began to experience chills in the 90 degree summer weather as I spiked a fever.

I asked Wendi if she would try to secure lodging for a couple of days so I could rest.

She asked for lodging at an Assemblies of God church camp. The camp director said we could spend one night in the dorm then we would have to move off the grounds because a youth group would be arriving for the weekend.

We found an urgent care facility nearby and I went in to be examined. I was given medication for pink eye.

Then we drove to Taco Bell to get a quick dinner before driving to the camp. We parked in a dirt parking lot near the restaurant so our dog would be in the shade while we purchased our order. When Wendi backed our vehicle up to pull out of the lot, we heard a crash. Apparently she had hit another car with the bike on the rack behind our car. We both got out of the vehicle to see if the impact had caused any damage. We noticed a dent about the size of a large grapefruit on the bumper of a black car that was parked behind us. An angry young woman came running out to us as she frantically pressed buttons on her cell phone.

"That's my car!" she shouted.

Wendi walked toward the girl to apologize. I looked down at the bumper to further examine the damage. To my surprise, the dent had vanished. Wendi and the girl walked over to the car to find me down on my knees, rubbing the fender and curiously looking for damage. There was no sign we had hit the car.

The girl insisted we report the incident to our insurance company, so we did. Our agent asked us to take pictures. We did. We took photos of a bumper that had no apparent damage. I believe we witnessed a miracle that day.

The next day, Wendi secured lodging at a local motel. Again, we were given lodging for just one night. The next night was the same. We were given lodging, but for only one night. For the entire summer we had been housed for several days to a couple of weeks at a time. But there we were in Devil's Lake and I felt sicker than I had ever felt in my life and we had to move every night: Tuesday night at the camp and Wednesday and Thursday night at two different hotels.

Until this time, I had not taken a sick day away from the faith walk. I would just keep walking when I was sick and symptoms would dissipate as I walked forward in faith. This time seemed different. I called two of my prayer warriors from two different parts of the country, who had no contact with one another, to advise me in this situation.

First I called Sylvia, in Michigan. "You need to stay put this time, Carol." She insisted. I called Lisa, in Arizona and she said, "I really believe you need to stay put and get better!" I did not like Devil's Lake, and I did not like what I was hearing. I called a few other people and got the same response. I was really sick, so I yielded to the advice of those who kept us in constant prayer.

Some of the folks we had met at Via de Christo had arranged for me to speak at two different Lutheran churches near Fargo for the weekend. I called both places where we would be staying and explained how sick I had been and asked if I should reschedule. Both families asked me to come ahead. I was concerned I might be contagious, but no one else seemed to be worried. I was especially concerned about the first place we would be staying because our host ran a day-care in her home.

I was able to speak at both churches but I continued to get sicker and sicker. I covered my pillow with T-shirts so the seepage from my eyes would not get on the pillows. I washed my hands often and used a towel to turn door knobs. I prayed I would not spread this somewhat mysterious illness.

On Monday, I was still running a fever so we drove to the emergency room in Fargo where I was referred to an infectious disease specialist across the way. The doctor diagnosed my illness as a rare virus, and not pink eye. I was relieved to hear that I did not have pink eye which is highly contagious. I was given a prescription for a different type of eye drops and told the virus would just have to run its course.

By Wednesday, I knew I had to continue in the walk. Still sick, I walked and prayed. I mostly prayed we would be able to move out of Devil's Lake.

As I walked I noticed a sign for a campground. After I could not walk anymore we decided to check it out. It was a little drive off the road. We were greeted by a charming woman who was more than glad to let us set up camp. As she was showing us to our site, she stopped in front of a shed.

"I am fixing this little shed up for the girls!" she said.

"I don't let the hunters stay in here, but I would like to open it up for you two!" she continued.

We were excited. She opened the door to the little shed and showed us around. She said we could run an extension cord for electricity and we could stay as long as we would like.

We made curtains with sheets, set up beds on the floor, and ran a cord for our light and electric skillet. We were all set and we were no longer in Devil's Lake.

We had planned to go home in a week. The woman offered to store our camping gear and bike in the shed while we traveled back to Ohio.

WALKIE-TALKIE HUMOR

Other than the few and far between metropolitan areas, there is not much traffic on Highway 2 in North Dakota. For the most part, it was relatively safe on the side of the roads and it was great to have Wendi and Walker T. join me as I walked.

We all three enjoyed each other's company and we tried to have a little fun along the way. We used our walkie-talkies to communicate. We were not always able to make out exactly what the other was saying, and sometimes it would turn out to be quite silly.

One day, while Wendi was driving the pilot car ahead, so she could park and ride her bike back to me, I almost got hit by a van. Having to keep a close eye on my footing, so I would not get my prosthesis caught up on something or trip in a hole, I had learned to use my peripheral vision to watch for traffic. I also had developed a keen sense of hearing and was able to quickly detect an unusual pattern in the traffic flow. My acute senses saved my life more times than I care to mention.

In this particular situation, I had noticed a car, with a lawnmower sticking out of the trunk. It was approaching me from

225

the front. The vehicle had its blinker on and was slowing down for the turn. The driver of a van, coming up from the rear of the car, apparently did not notice the turn signal or the brake lights, and failed to slow down. I could see an accident about to happen when the driver of the van locked up the brakes and swerved to miss the car. When the van swerved, it was heading right for me on the side of the road. I jumped in the ditch to avoid being hit.

A bit shook up, I cried out to Wendi, via walkie-talkie, "I just missed getting killed!"

She heard, "I just messed myself!"

She replied, "Do you need me to drive back to you?"

I answered, "No, I'll show you the skid marks later!"

She asked again, "Are you sure you don't want me to come to you?"

"No, I am okay. I will show you the skid marks later, they are about 30 feet long!"

I had calmed down from my near-death experience, by the time Wendi and Walker T. reached me on the bike, but I really had to use the facilities, and there were none in sight.

As Wendi began pushing her bike beside me, she asked again, "Are you okay?"

"Yeah, I'm fine. After we finish walking we can drive back to where I almost got hit, and you can see where the vehicle slid off the road, right where I had been walking."

Wendi began to laugh hysterically. She began to share with me what she thought I had said.

I could not hold back laughter, I began to laugh and scream, "Stop, stop, stop talking. I can't laugh right now—I have to use the restroom!"

I looked at her and saw how much she was struggling to keep from laughing, and I was unable to hold back. I laughed so hard, I wet my pants, right there on the side of the road.

Maybe, just maybe, Wendi heard a prophetic message over the walkie-talkie that day. No, probably not prophetic, but somewhat poetic, and memorable—we will laugh about this chat, hopefully for the rest of our lives.

MINOT, NORTH DAKOTA

"Let's Take a Break!"

Christian Tourette syndrome raised its head again one day as we were walking about 70 miles east of Minot, North Dakota.

Wendi and I both gasped as "Let's take a break!" came out of my mouth.

"We need to go find a place to have lunch!" I blurted.

"I saw a sign for a rest area a few miles down the road. Let's go there," my mouth continued.

We both knew by then not to question these spontaneous outbursts.

I got in the car and Wendi drove us to the rest area, where we sat at a picnic table and tried to enjoy our lunch. It was a windy day—we spent more time chasing napkins, sandwich wrappings, and paper plates, than we spent eating.

After we had decided we were tired of fighting the wind, I took our cooler over to some weeds to empty the water out. All of our ice had melted and the water in the cooler was not even cool anymore. Since bacteria likes to grow in warm water, I took time to dispose of the potential breeding ground. When I tipped the cooler over, to pour the water out, the lid came loose from the hinges and dropped on the ground. I imagined dogs had watered this same patch of weeds, so I grabbed the lid and headed for the ladies room, where I could wash the lid with soap and hot water.

As I was about to leave the restroom, a jolly woman approached me with, "Hi, how are you?"

"I'm blessed!" I replied.

"So am I! So am I!" she repeated. "So I hear you are taking a long walk!" she continued.

Surprised, I answered, "Yes, how did you hear about it?"

"My husband is out there in the parking lot talking to your partner!" she replied.

As I walked back to the car, I noticed Wendi was engaged with an older gentleman who was parked next to the pilot car. When I walked up to the two, Wendi introduced Pastor Henderson to me.

After he prayed over me, he looked in my eyes and said, "This walk is going to be completed. God ordained this walk and He will see to it that it is completed."

Not even halfway through the projected miles, this was music to my ears.

Pastor Henderson told us that he never stops to use the restrooms at this rest area. He and his wife always stopped in Rugby, at a particular place of business, to use the facilities.

"God told me to stop, so I did!" the pastor exclaimed.

"As soon as I pulled up, I noticed the magnet on your car and knew it was a God appointment!" he continued.

We chatted a bit. The Hendersons asked if we would visit their church when we made it to Minot. The pastor handed Wendi his business card and promised to take good care of us. We explained we would be leaving in a couple of days to go home for a short break, so it would be about two weeks before we would actually be walking into the city.

Pastor Henderson handed me a $50 bill to help with our travel expenses and said he was looking forward to seeing us in a couple of weeks.

Wendy's Joy

We walked into Minot on a Tuesday evening and Wendi said, "I was not able to find a place willing to donate a room tonight, but one place offered a good discount!"

We rarely had money for lodging, but that day we had enough cash to get a room for one night. "So, we will go with the place with the discount!" I answered.

The next evening, Wednesday, we were scheduled to be at Pastor Henderson's church. He invited Wendi and me to the front. He introduced us and announced that I would be speaking on Sunday. While he was introducing us, I glanced down and noticed that my sock was hanging through the toe of my shoe on my right foot. *Oh my!* I thought, *Everybody seems to look at my feet when told I am an amputee!*

Pastor Henderson arranged for us to spend the rest of the week at the Vegas Hotel. We were a little puzzled why a church would put us up in the Vegas Hotel, but were excited about the provisions for an extended stay.

On the way to the hotel, I told Wendi about the sock sticking out of my shoe. "We need to find a second-hand store so I can get another pair!" I exclaimed. "I don't want to speak at the church on Sunday with my toes hanging out!"

After we checked into the hotel, I took my leg off and crawled into bed. It had been a long day with walking 10 miles and attending a church service.

Shortly after I had begun to relax, the hotel phone rang. I answered the phone to hear, "Is this Carol?"

"Yes!"

"My name is Wendy and I am the manager here. I am a born-again, Spirit-filled, Christian and I was wondering if I could meet with you."

I explained that I had just taken my prosthesis off and was resting and asked if I could meet her in the morning.

"Sure!" she said. "I will be in around eight o'clock. We have complimentary breakfast here. How about I meet you in the breakfast room at 8:30?"

"Sounds great!" I replied.

The next morning, a bubbly middle-aged woman with a blonde ponytail, dressed in jeans and a casual blouse, came to our table and introduced herself. I introduced Wendi to Wendy and she laughed and said, "Wendy Joy, my name is Wendy Joy!"

I chuckled and said, "Wendy Joy meet Wendi Love!"

Joy was the perfect middle name for this woman; she was definitely full of joy. We had just finished eating so we followed Wendy Joy to a meeting room where we could visit.

Wendy told us that she used to be caught up in sorcery with card readings and palm readings until she turned her life over to God and God's ways. She believed she had the gift of prophesy but had been hesitant about operating in the gift, because of her past. "I just want to be sure it is coming from God!" she exclaimed. "I believe God has given me word for you!" she went on.

She shared some things with us that seemed a little off, but I have to say they all turned out to be right on. But, the biggest thing she wanted to emphasize was, "God showed me that you are going to finish this walk!"

Wendi and I stared at each other as we remembered the prophetic word Pastor Henderson had shared just two weeks earlier.

"There is something else! God keeps saying 'shoes'!" At this point, I was puzzled. She said it again, "God is saying 'shoes'!"

"A woman in Detroit provides all of my shoes!" I told her.

"I am sure I am hearing shoes! God wants me to buy you shoes!" Then it hit me, my dress shoes, not walking shoes—God is letting her know that I need dress shoes. I chuckled and told her about my shoe experience at the church the night before.

"Wendy, I am not sure about everything you have prophesied, but I believe you are right on with my finishing the walk, and my needing some new shoes!"

Wendy opened up a room that was scheduled for minor repairs and said we could stay there as long as we needed and we were welcome to store our bike, camping gear, and anything else we had, while driving home for winter break. She also said she would have the bike lubricated and the brakes adjusted, over the winter so it would be in good shape for the next year. She provided dinners for us in the hotel restaurant, she bought my shoes and bottled water, and she topped off our gas tank. She told us we had a room there anytime we traveled through and she gave us a contact for help down the road.

Terry and Judy, from Pastor Henderson's church, invited us to dinner at their home. I am still trying to make chicken tetrazzini as good as we had that evening. Later in the week, Judy brought care packages for us to the Vegas Hotel.

Sunday morning, we were received well at Pastor Henderson's church, where I delivered the message. Afterward, the pastor and his wife, who by then we referred to as Mama Henderson, as did the congregation, took us to lunch.

We were asked to speak at a couple more churches in the area. Wendy scheduled a room for the next couple of weeks so we could stay at the Vegas when returning for the engagements.

Wendy called some friends in Stanley, Don and Mona (actually they are the other grandparents of her grandson) who happen to have a camper, to see if they were willing to let us stay in it while we walked through Stanley. The couple was more than happy to help. They set the camper up in a park and stocked it with groceries.

As we were walking into Stanley, a van stopped on the road and a tall gentleman with long brown hair got out of the vehicle and approached me. He said he had started a walk around the country on a pilgrimage of his own. He had walked several miles and got shin splits and now was traveling by car. After we chatted a bit, we told him where we were camping. He and his wife planned to camp at the same park and the gentleman planned to walk with me as we entered Stanley.

We stayed in the park for a week then Don and Mona moved the camper 50 miles down the road to a park in Ray, where we were able to use it for another week.

Don gave us a name and phone number of a friend of his, Ron, who had a radio program called *Preacher in the Patch*. Ron and his family live in Williston and Don was sure they would be able to help us.

Wendi contacted Ron and he arranged for us to stay in a very nice suite in Williston. We were invited to the family's house for dinner and were asked to stay with them for a couple of days. Ron interviewed me for his *Preacher in the Patch* radio show and the family arranged for us to be their guests at a crusade they were hosting a few weeks later in Dickinson, North Dakota.

ENTERING MONTANA

As I walked the northern border of our country, I experienced some spiritual anxiety about what was before me. I had been warned about some danger I might encounter in Montana, on the west coast, and along the southern border of the nation.

When we were in Boy River, Minnesota, with the Dicksons, Doug told us that he would cover our backs in prayer when we walked through Montana. He said that some of the natives there were prejudiced against white people. He and his family had traveled through the state a few years back and found themselves in a situation where he was not sure he and his daughters were going to get out alive.

Just a few days before we crossed the Montana state line, a gentleman stopped along the side of the road to visit with us. After we had shared our story with him, he told us that his wife was a waitress at the Copper Kettle, a restaurant in Williston. He said his wife would really enjoy meeting us and if we stopped in he would like treat us to breakfast.

The next morning, we took the car to a Walmart right next door to the Copper Kettle, then we walked to the restaurant to meet the man's wife and order our breakfast.

After we had finished eating, Wendi walked over to pick up the car and met Charleton Burgett, who had gone to the automotive section of Walmart to get a gas cap for his motor home—which he referred to as his mobile prayer unit. He was driving the perimeter of our country on a prayer mission. He would stop to pray as the Holy Spirit directed him. Charleton joined us at the restaurant. We sipped on beverages and enjoyed the fellowship.

The next day, Charleton met us out on the road. He parked his vehicle at a small casino, just over the state line. Wendi drove him to where I was walking so he could join me. She took the car ahead, then rode back to us with Walker T. in her bike basket. The four of us walked together as we entered Montana. The first mile marker, in the state to post mile 666, was missing. We planted a cross in its place.

After we exchanged contact information with Charleton, he went on ahead of us to pray along our borders. He drove the path I would walk. I believe he was sent as a forerunner for our prayer walk around the perimeter of the US.

By the end of the week, we were walking into Culbertson, where we were given a room at the Diamond Willow Motel. The people were friendly and hospitable. The motel owner called the local paper and a reporter met us for an interview. We were invited to share at a local church and afterward the pastor and his wife took us out for lunch. We planted cross #5,000, just west of the town.

Fort Peck

By the end of the following week, we were in the Fort Peck Indian Reservation. We stopped at a church in Poplar and shared our story with the pastor, who happened to be the pastor of three churches, of three different denominations, on the reservation. He and his wife, who was a teacher at the tribal school, invited us to stay in their home.

I was asked to speak about grief at the school on Monday. After I spoke, I was asked to speak to another class. Afterward, the principal asked me to come to the school the following Monday to speak on grief to the entire school at an assembly.

By Saturday, we had made it to Wolf Point, a much bigger town. Wendi and I decided to find a restaurant to celebrate our 5,000 mile milestone. After I finished walking for the day, we drove around the town in search of a restaurant. We found one at a hotel, and went inside to check it out. It looked like a fine place to dine, but we were dressed in walking clothes. We noticed there were no other diners, so we decided to stay and celebrate.

Just after we were seated, a group of folks were seated right next to us. I noticed they all bowed their heads while one of the gentlemen prayed a prayer of thanks for the food. As I was walking back from the salad bar, I found myself face to face with the man who had said grace. I introduced myself and told him that it was nice to have a group of Christians sitting next to us. He just brushed me off.

Saturday night we attended a movie night at one of the churches and on Sunday morning, we went to hear our host preach.

Monday morning as I was being introduced at the assembly, I glanced over at the wall and saw the same gentleman who had shunned me at the restaurant. He seemed to be sliding down the wall when he noticed I was the speaker. After I spoke, he was the first to leave the room.

The principal thanked me for sharing. She had just lost her mother and said she really needed to hear what I had to say. She made a personal donation and told me there was someone she wanted me to meet. She led me down the hall to a classroom and introduced me to the pastor of the Assemblies of God Church. The gentleman seemed embarrassed—it was the same man who was practically sliding down the wall at the assembly—yes, the same man who shunned me at the restaurant.

We really have to be careful how we treat strangers! We never know where we may see them again!

◊ ◊ ◊

The next week, we were hosted at a church that had hotel-like rooms on the upper level of the building. Our host was the caretaker and actually lived at the church. She asked if I would share on Sunday. I said I would.

Sunday morning, I woke up sometime between 2:00 and 3:00 a.m. God told me that I could not speak at the church. He let me know that the pastor was only going to give me a few minutes and I was to decline. He let me know that even though I had given short 5 or 10 minute testimonies at several churches, I had to say "no" this time. I was so uncomfortable with this that I could not go back to sleep. I knew the voice of God, and I could not disobey Him, but how was I going to be able to decline the invitation? I had never done this before.

About 7:00, I woke Wendi up and told her that I was not going to be able to share at the church and I just wanted to pack up and leave.

"No, we can't just leave!" she said. "You have to talk to the pastor!"

I didn't want to, but I knew she was right.

We got ready for church and went down to the sanctuary. I told the caretaker what God had revealed to me during the night. She smiled and said, "Just tell the pastor!" I smiled and thought, *Easier said than done!*

As soon as the pastor arrived, he approached me, "I'll give you five minutes to share your testimony!" he said.

"I am sorry, but I can't do that!" I answered.

"Do you mean you have been staying here and you are not willing to share at my church!" he exhorted.

"No, I am sorry!" I replied.

The pastor appeared to be very angry as he walked away from me. He paced back and forth in the back of the church, then returned to me.

"Are you staying for the service?" he asked.

"Yes, I am looking forward to hearing your message!" I replied.

Wendi and I found seats in the second row from the front. Several of the women came and talked with me. Some of them had been told that I declined the invitation to speak for five minutes and commended me for declining. A couple different women told me they thought the pastor had cut people short when they had shared their testimonies.

The pastor's wife approached us and asked if I would be willing to share with the women of the church that evening. Without hesitation, I said yes!

The pastor took the seat in front of us. I leaned over the pew and told him that I had agreed to speak at the women's meeting that evening. He still seemed to be pretty upset with me.

The service started and the pastor began to pray and as he did, I saw a change of attitude, as he began to pray for Wendi and me to be protected as we continued on the prayer walk around the nation. It was obvious God was doing some work in our dear brother's heart.

The prayer was followed with praise and worship then the pastor delivered a powerful sermon. Before the service was over, he introduced Wendi and me and announced that we would be speaking at the church that evening and all were invited to attend.

Several women from the congregation showed up for a time of fellowship and food before I shared my testimony. Afterward, we were blessed with financial gifts and the group prayed for us.

I am so glad God gave me the courage to stay and talk to the pastor. I really wanted to run, but I am glad I didn't. Sometimes God uses us as instruments to grow others. I can always tell when God is using me in this way—it is not comfortable and I usually want to run.

Glasgow

After walking through Fort Peck, we met Shorty and Carol, who invited us to stay at their home in Glasgow. The couple had three dogs and Shorty took a quick liking to Walker T.

Carol contacted the newspaper and a very young reporter, just a senior in high school, called and arranged for us to meet her at a local café so she could do her very first interview. In the interview, the young reported asked me something about being religious.

I told her, "I do not like to be called religious. I consider myself spiritual, having a relationship with God!"

Somehow the girl equated religious with Christian, and in the article stated "she refuses to be called a Christian…"

There are misprints or typos in most of the hundreds of articles about the walk. Wendi and I usually just chuckle about the mistakes, if we give them any notice at all. One time, my name was spelled Proust, and this didn't even bother me, but I had to do something about this misquote. Even though I am often disheartened about the actions of some Christians and I do not want to be identified with some behavior, I am proud to be called a Christian and to identify myself with Christ.

We had attended several Bible studies in the area with Shorty and Carol. Their cell phones were ringing nonstop. People were questioning our cause. One woman actually told Carol, "This must be true! It was in the paper!" The four of us got a good laugh out of that statement.

There were two other mistakes in the article. It reported I was from Utah, instead of Ohio and it said our dog only had one leg. We laughed off these two misprints but I called the editor and voiced my concern about the report of me refusing to be called a Christian. The editor said that she had received more phone calls, about this story, than she had ever previously received for an article. She apologized to me and told me she would reprint the story, which happened to be on the front page.

I expressed my concern about the young reporter and the editor reassured me she would work with her and the girl would not lose her job over the mistakes. I was glad to hear this and thanked the woman for her willingness to make the corrections.

We shared with Carol about staying with Ron and his family and how they invited us to attend the crusade. We asked if she and Shorty would be able to watch Walker T. for us the next weekend while we traveled to North Dakota. She excitedly asked if she could go with us. We agreed to call Ron and ask if it would be okay; meanwhile, she was going to talk it over with Shorty. Ron thought it would be great to have her attend the crusade and Shorty agreed to watch Walker T. Carol offered to pay for the room and to drive us in her vehicle. The three of us attended the retreat in Dickenson, the following weekend.

MY NAME IS WARREN

I felt led to go on a partial fast for the last 40 walking days in 2007. I shared this with Wendi, and she agreed to join me. We had some concerns about our safety for the journey ahead. We wanted to focus more on God and ministry and pray for God to guide us and direct us in His will and ways, with less concern about food and food preparation.

We began with a three-day total fast. Then for the next 34 days, Monday through Friday, we had honey and peanut butter on whole grain flat bread for breakfast. We did not eat at all during the day while we walked. In the evening, we had a very simple dinner of rice and fish. After dinner, we would each go to our own private corner and read the Bible and pray until dark. Lights off at nightfall and up at the crack of dawn. On the weekends, we ate whatever was provided for us. We ended with another three-day total fast.

One day while I was walking, as Wendi was driving away, I noticed Cavalier #2 was carrying a load way bigger than any little car should have to haul. The trunk was full of camping gear, materials to make crosses, and overflow clothes for the different seasons. A kennel for Walker, all of our luggage, everyday necessities, and a box full of crosses, filled the back seat. The bike rack not only held the bike, but a tent and large bag of crosses.

As I walked, I chatted with God about our load.

"God!" I said. "We could sure use a bigger vehicle!"

I asked God if He would consider providing something bigger for us, "Perhaps an SUV—it wouldn't have to be new or pleasing to look at, just something that would fit our lifestyle a little better!"

I went on to tell God, as if He didn't know, "We gave Courtney Cavalier #1, and now Molly is old enough to drive, it would be nice to be able to give her Cavalier #2."

"And Wendi and I live about 25 miles apart, when we are home, I could drive one vehicle and Wendi could drive the other!" I continued. In my mind's eye, I envisioned, a 1970-some, Ford Bronco or older model inexpensive Geo Metro. Anyway, I knew God had it covered, and I just let it go after that.

As we were ending the year, on the last day of our fast, we were walking in the Fort Belknap Indian Reservation. The very last day, before we took our break for the winter, I had another bout of Christian Tourette syndrome. We had just three miles to walk, before we would begin our long journey to Ohio, when "We are going to take a break!" came barreling out of my mouth.

Wendi and I stared at each other in disbelief. If I just kept walking, we would be heading toward home in just a little over an hour.

We were out in the middle of nowhere, we were fasting, so we would not be looking for a place to eat—what was this all about? We got in the car and drove west for about 30 minutes to a gas station, where we gassed up for the trip home.

By the time Wendi took me back to walk, we would have been on our way home, had we not taken a break. Wendi dropped me off on the side of the road and drove three miles ahead where we would plant cross #5,205, the last cross for 2007. By the time she rode her bike back to me, I had just two miles left to walk.

Wendi got off of her bike and took Walker out of the basket, and the two joined me. Suddenly a car heading west came to a screeching halt on the side of the road. We looked over to see three natives in a compact car. One of them was the tallest man I had ever seen. He was hunched over in the back seat of the car. He barely fit.

That man, the big one, rolled down his window and asked, "What are you doing?"

I thought to myself, *I don't think I know the right answer!*

"I am walking the perimeter of the United States and I am praying for our country!" I nervously answered, as I tightly clutched the two crosses in my hand. "Oh, and I am planting one of these in the ground every mile!" I added.

"When did you start?" he asked.

"2002!" I answered.

241

As soon as I said that, the man got out of the car and headed toward me, the other two, right behind him. I never felt so vulnerable in all of my life. We were walking in the high desert. There were hardly any houses around and that was the first car I remembered seeing all day. There seemed to be no civilization for 20 miles ahead and several miles behind us. Anything could have happened to us and I don't think anyone would have noticed.

I remembered what Doug had said about the problem he had with the natives in Montana, as I stared at the belt buckle of the tallest man I had ever met. Often when I tell this story I say that the other two people were short, but Wendi reminds me, it wasn't that they were short, it was that the man in the middle, the one right in front of me, was so tall!

The man, standing inches in front of me, looked down at me and said, "I had a dream about you! I spent 17 years in the penitentiary and I had a dream about you! I had a dream about you! You are going to finish this walk!"

He pointed to the person to the right of him and said, "This is Saddle Horse!" then he pointed to the person on his left and said, "This is Rattlesnake! My name is Warren!" he added. "I spent 17 years in the penitentiary and I had a dream about you!" he repeated. "You are going to finish this walk!" He went on to tell us that he lives on a mountain alone with his dog. He told us that his dog bites everyone who travels up the mountain. "But that's okay—he doesn't have any teeth!"

Warren prayed for us in his native tongue then he prayed in English, ending his prayer with, "In Jesus name, Amen!" God used the scariest most vulnerable moment of the walk to send me a message! I am going to finish this walk! About an hour later, I planted cross #5,207 and Wendi, Walker T., and I were on our way home for the holidays.

On our way home, we stopped in Black River, Michigan, to visit our friends, Peter and Helen. A few days into our visit, as we all sat at the table, Helen announced that she and Peter both felt led to give us their 2002 Toyota Highlander. Both of our mouths dropped open. I began to tear up as I told them about my prayer.

God is so good! Not only did we have a bigger vehicle, a car for Molly, and a vehicle for both Wendi and me to drive while we were home for the winter, but it was only five years old and in excellent condition. It was beautiful! God really knows how to show Himself, when He answers our prayers.

That winter, Molly was able to practice driving the exact vehicle she would be receiving on her sixteenth birthday.

July 19, 2007

Greetings, dear Carol…I am blessed to tell you that my son, Ben 42 yrs. old, found one of your crosses down by the river here, the Red River, in front of the bench where he sits every morning during his morning walk. He works nights, and stops by here to see Ma and maybe have a bite, and then on home. Now get this…home for Ben right now is at Cornerstone, a half-way house for recovering alcoholic/addicts who have been thru the Texas program at a place called Centre. Ben is a real believer in Christ, and has many problems with alcohol and is doing well at this point. Finding that cross was stunning for him, and I cannot thank God enough for it! You know, of course, how it is decidedly difficult for the devil to get past a mother's prayers, and I continue to pray for God's will in my son's life. I will pray every day of my life for the same in YOUR life and the lives of those in your association. Oh, Carol…

it is decidedly uplifting to hear the footfall our Lord Jesus, as he walks ever so quietly around, looking for whom might be saved. A mighty blessing on your efforts, dear child. We will never forget you.

In His love…a sister in ND, Karen

PS…Ben is one who loves to walk and it makes me wonder… Hmm…? He will soon send you an email and a donation for your organization!

Heading West—2008

Trail Friends

As we headed back to the walk in 2008, we drove the same route we had walked the year before, and stopped to visit many of our friends along the way. Our first stop was in Toledo, where Walker T. had spent the winter with the Merrithews.

Our next stop was a quick visit with Ida in Monroe, Michigan, where I spent some time with her daughter, Torrie, who had been diagnosed with non-Hodgkin's lymphoma. I took a walk with her and asked if she was ready to meet our Lord. She was concerned about leaving her teenaged son, Chad, but ready to meet her Maker. This was a very sad visit because I knew in my heart I would never see her again, in this life and the next time we would see Ida, she would have lost a daughter, and the next time I would see the Merrithews, Tracey would be mourning the loss of a sister.

We stopped off in Wyandotte where our elderly friend, Betty Sykes, was waiting for us with a two new pair of New Balance walking shoes (Betty had insisted on donating our walking shoes). Betty, a widow, lived on limited income and we were concerned about her being able to afford such a generous gift. She couldn't wait to tell us about the fabulous sale the store had on the shoes.

Our next stop was in Black River, to see Peter and Helen, who by then had become more like family than friends. We kept in contact at least once a week. They covered our backs with prayer and blessed us with faithful support and care packages (love packages). It was nice to spend some time together.

Helen is a fabulous cook and seems to enjoy feeding others. We couldn't wait to enjoy her home-cooked meals. We looked forward to spending the evenings at the kitchen table playing board games. This brought back precious childhood memories, meal times and times of playing board games with my siblings over Christmas break. Even though I love my sisters and brothers, we are not close. God filled that void with Peter and Helen.

The couple presented us with a new bike rack and Peter mounted it on the back of the Highlander before we headed back on the road.

Pastor Todd had asked me to speak at the Cornerstone Church in Ramsey, Michigan. Both Jean Nordine and Diane Montz had announced our arrival in the two local papers. We were surprised by a fairly large turnout. Jean and her mother were both there to hear me preach. Afterward, we gathered with the group for a meal and were presented with a cake, decorated with a map of the United States. What a great way to return to the walk!

We spent a night in Shevlin with our friends Mary and Fran and stopped in at the Village Café to see Geri and Julie.

The next day we had made it to Minot where Wendy Joy was waiting for us at the Vegas Motel. She had stored our camping gear for the winter months. It was great to see Wendy again; she had a room waiting for us. The next morning, Wendy topped off our gas tank and gave us the address to the shop where she had taken Wendi's bike for brake work and a lube job. The shop owner had agreed to store the bike for the winter. Yes, we were getting off to an excellent start.

With the Highlander loaded down with all we would need to make it out in the desert, we headed west, and stopped in Williston for lunch. When we traveled to and from the walk, we made a point to give business to the places that supported us along the way, so we stopped for lunch at the Copper Kettle—the restaurant that donated our lunch the year before, the day Wendi met Charleton at Walmart.

After lunch and a friendly visit with the folks in the restaurant, we headed back to our vehicle to continue our trip. We found a newspaper tucked in the door handle of the SUV. I looked around and noticed that our vehicle was the only one in the parking lot that had a paper in the door. Puzzled by this, Wendi, who was driving, tossed the paper over to me, and suggested I scan through it to see if there was an obvious reason for the paper to be put on our car.

I read an article about a man named Donald Stevenson, dubbed the Pacin' Parson, who was doing a walk across America to heighten awareness about Huntington's disease and to raise research money for a cure. He just happened to be walking into Culbertson the next day. Apparently, someone had noticed the magnet on the side of our car and thought we would be interested in reading about his walk.

247

There was a cell number to contact Donald. I called the number and talked with Loretta, his wife, and was told they would be in Culbertson about 3:00 and staying at the Diamond Willow Motel, which was the same place that hosted us when we walked through that area.

We got to Culbertson just before 3:00 and found Loretta in the parking lot of the motel. She was waiting for Donald to meet her there on foot. Loretta told us, with great excitement, that Donald had walked over 40,000 miles for different causes. She was his advance person for the walks and spotted him pretty much the same way Wendi spotted me. We had never met another team like ourselves and were happy to exchange stories and contact information.

After about 45 minutes, Donald had walked up to the car. The newspaper reporter who had written a story about cross #5,000, which was planted just west of the town, showed up to interview Donald. After the interview, Loretta and Wendi took photos of Donald and me together, then Donald decided to get a mile or two more in before he called it a day. Wendi and I continued to visit with Loretta for a while. Wendi and Loretta gave each other lists of places of lodging that had been helpful on each of our journeys. We told Loretta to be sure to stop at the Vegas Motel to see Wendy Joy.

We drove to Glasgow and spent the night with Carol and Shorty. The next day we were not sure what we were going to do about lodging. We drove into Malta, which was the closest town to where we had left off the year before. As Wendi began to pray for God to open doors for us, one contact led to another, and we were donated three nights at the Chinook Motor Inn, by Rhonda, a sister in the Lord who worked at one of the banks in town.

HUTTERITES

A couple of days after I resumed walking, we stopped for lunch at a place called Deb's Diner, near Harlem, Montana. While eating, we discussed the possibilities for future lodging. Our waitress happened to be a Christian and took great interest in our conversation.

After we had finished eating, Wendi went to the car to get a brochure for the waitress. While she was gone, two women, dressed very much like Amish women, began to ask me questions. So, I did not have to talk across the room, I joined them at their table. By the time Wendi returned, one of the women, Anne, had invited us to stay with them. The two women were Hutterites. They lived in the Turner Colony about 14 miles north of the restaurant.

That weekend we experienced colony living with some of the most hospitable people we had ever met. We stayed with Anne, a middle-aged single woman, and her widowed mother Anna. The family embraced us and we became friends. Someone in the colony had picked up one of the crosses and placed it in a flower garden near the chapel.

Dining was like a production. Meals were served in a common area, with the men on one side of the room and the women on the other. Women in the Colony, took turns cooking and cleaning up. Eating was just like another chore to them. No sooner had we sat down, than they began to clear the table.

The people all worked together for the common good of the whole community. I enjoyed learning about how everyone had all things in common. They ate together, worked together, and prayed together. I thought about how wonderful it would be if Christians could work together and live together in one accord like it was in the early church (Acts 4:32–35).

One day while in search of a restroom, I asked Wendi to drive to a community off the beaten path. When we entered the store to use the facilities, the owner, Laura was ecstatic. She had heard about the walk on the local radio and prayed that God would let her meet me.

The Mercantile in Gildford, Montana became our next home base. Laura fixed meals for us in the evenings and gave us water and other food items from the store.

COLORFUL PEOPLE

One time a friend referred to Wendi and me as her most colorful friends. I never forgot that, and I am still trying to figure out what she meant by it. I did not consider myself or Wendi as very colorful. If we had names like Black or White or Brown or Green, at least then it would be a play on words.

Wendi and I did meet some people with colorful names. They brightened up our lives and are probably the most colorful people in our lives, only because their names are Green and Brown.

By the time we got to Chester, we were too far from the Mercantile to keep driving back. There were not many businesses in the area, so we figured we should find a place to camp. We needed to find an air mattress so we stopped at the local hardware. Wendi went inside to price a mattress and I waited in the SUV. It was mid-June and I had the window down to keep cool.

A woman came up to my window and announced, "My name is Bev Green and I am really shy and I never do anything like this, but I am curious about what Faith Walk Ministries is about!"

I figured she had read the magnet on the side of the vehicle and I began to tell her about the walk and how Wendi was inquiring about a price for an air mattress. Bev told me that she and her husband were Christians and said, "I never do anything like this but how would you like to come to have dinner at our house with my husband and me?"

By then, Wendi had returned to the car to report the mattress cost more than we could afford. I shared with Wendi that Bev had invited us to stay with her and she would be fixing dinner for us.

We were delighted to be invited for dinner and to have a place to stay for the night. We followed Bev home where she introduced us to her husband Leroy.

Leroy visited with us while Bev prepared dinner. He prayed for us and had a prophetic word for Wendi.

After dinner, Leroy gave us the name of a friend of his, Fred Brown, who was a pastor of New Life Community Church in Shelby. He told us that, at his word, Fred would take care of us. He gave Wendi Pastor Fred's phone number and said he would call Fred and let him know we were headed that way.

Wendi was able to obtain lodging for us at a motel in Chester the next day, and a place in Shelby donated a room for the weekend and another place for Monday. On Tuesday, Wendi contacted Fred Brown and he reserved a night at a motel in town and made arrangements for us to stay with a family from the church for a few nights.

We attended New Life Community Church on Sunday, where Pastor Fred announced our presence and told about the walk. The pastor and his family took us out to lunch and Fred said he would make sure we were safe and taken care of until we got through Browning which is the west end of the Blackfeet Reservation.

He made arrangements for us to lodge at the Super 8 Motel in Cut Bank for several nights and arranged for Pizza Hut to feed us while we were staying there. He gave Wendi a number for Pastor Joe, who was the pastor of two churches, Community Bible Church in Cut Bank and another church in an upper room of a business in Essex.

While we were lodging at the Super 8 in Cut Bank, we walked the Blackfoot Indian Reservation toward Browning. Each day, as we headed west toward the Rocky Mountains, we were able to appreciate the massiveness of the range. At first, we were only able to see the snow caps peeking through the top of the clouds. Within a couple of days we were standing in awe of the dimensional masterpiece of the rocky formations. By the time we reached the foothills, we were overwhelmed with the majestic wonder of one of the most beautiful mountain ranges in the world.

The beauty of the Rocky Mountains kept our minds off the forewarned danger of walking through the reservation—this was the area where Doug and his daughters had their unfortunate encounter with the natives. Although the people were not very friendly toward us, we made it through the reservation without incident.

Thanks to Leroy Green, connecting us with Fred Brown, which ultimately yielded provision for us through the Blackfoot Reservation, where we ended in the magnitude of colors of the Rocky Mountains, this was one of our most colorful couple of weeks on the walk.

THE ROCKIES

We attended the Community Bible Church and Pastor Joe gave us the name of a woman, Penny, in Essex, who had been a missionary in Naples for a while. Penny lived alone and Joe felt confident she would be willing to house us as we walked through the mountains.

We stayed at a small inn in East Glacier then moved in with Penny who was glad to put us up at her house.

It was the first of July when I began climbing the mountains. I would have to climb Marias Pass before I would reach Essex. The pass reached an elevation of 5,220 feet. It was closed in the winter due to hazardous conditions from excessive snow, and it had only been open a couple of weeks when we got there.

We enjoyed our scenic walk through the Rockies and we especially enjoyed the people. Penny, who attended the Upper Room Church, was a wonderful host. We attended a service with Penny and met some great folks who wanted to be a part of the walk and help with meals. One couple owned a restaurant and motel. They provided several dinners for us. Another couple, who owned a bed and breakfast, invited us to have breakfast in their dining area each morning.

Penny came out and joined me on the walk one day as did the children of the family that owned the bed and breakfast.

We were staying at Penny's house on the day of my fifty-fourth birthday. She invited her neighbors over for dinner and a birthday celebration. At the party, Penny presented me with a scrapbook of our Rocky Mountain experience. Later, she blessed us with a white-water rafting trip in West Glacier.

A couple of days later, Wendi and I enjoyed the adventure in the evening, after I had finished walking. The trip included a dinner. We rafted on some level-2 and level-3 rapids for about an hour, then we pulled ashore and enjoyed the scenery while our guide prepared trout and steak on an open fire. We visited with the other rafters while we enjoyed our dinner on the bank of the river. The second half of our trip was more of a leisurely ride on smoother water. It was nice to relax and enjoy the beauty.

BIBLE CAMP

Our next two homes were at Bible camps. The first camp was a little challenging because Walker T. was not permitted in the building provided for our lodging. We walked until almost dark, had dinner out, and took Walker for a long walk. We had to leave him in the car until morning.

The second camp, Thompson Lake Bible Camp, was much better for all three of us. We were given a campsite on the grounds. Youth camp was taking place at the time and we were invited to take part in all of the meals and to mingle with the camp leaders and the youth.

One evening, I was asked to speak. I was received well, and after I spoke I was approached by several of the young people and the directors who wanted to hear more about the walk. By the end of the week, we had made several connections for future lodging. We met the pastor and his wife, from the Hungry Horse Baptist Church, who invited us to stay with them the next weekend and to share at their service. We met Amy from Bonners Ferry, Idaho, who invited us to stay with her once we reached the state line.

We also met a young girl, about 10 years old, who asked if we would be walking through Coeur d'Alene, Idaho. When we told her we would be walking right through Coeur d'Alene, she gave us a phone number for her mother and asked us to call her because she believed housing would be available for us there.

We became friends with Tom, the cook, and helped him with some kitchen chores. Tom was from the Baptist church in Hungry Horse.

That weekend, we went to Hungry Horse and stayed at the church with the pastor and his family. The church was made up of two families who came there from Tennessee, to help build the church, and a congregation of about 40 people—most of them under the age of 12. I enjoyed speaking to the children. I had never experienced a congregation quite so young.

Hungry Horse was an oppressed area with a high crime rate. It once had more murders per capita than any other place in the nation. The youth in that small church were a light to the community.

I was warned about a bridge on Highway 2, just west of Hungry Horse, that had no shoulder and a steady flow of high-speed traffic. It was suggested I have an escort over the bridge or perhaps have the state officials close off traffic for my crossing. I asked about the length of the structure—when I was told that it really wasn't very long, just dangerous, I decided to take a chance on it without coordinating an escort.

When I approached the bridge, Wendi sat at the west end of the bridge with a walkie-talkie and announced there was no traffic and it was okay to cross. I began a brisk walk across the structure and realized the westbound traffic was very steady but there was no eastbound traffic, which would be the traffic facing me. By the time I got to the car, both Wendi and I were puzzled that there had been no eastbound traffic.

I walked around the mountain on Highway 2 to find a big truck holding back the traffic while lines were being painted on the highway. What perfect timing!

The next week, we stopped off at Thompson Lake Bible Camp, to say hello to Tom, the cook. He was somewhat in despair because his kitchen help was not going to be there that week. We told Tom we would be glad to help. He was delighted and gave us a cottage for the week.

Each morning, we would get up at 5:30 and help prepare breakfast. After the meal, we helped with clean-up then we did all of the prep work for lunch and dinner. We then went out and I walked 10 miles. We were back to the grounds in time to help prepare dinner, serve, and help with clean-up in the evenings.

WEST OF THE ROCKIES

We continued to have an adventuresome walk as we headed toward Idaho, west of the Rockies.

On our way back to the walk in 2008, after our winter break, Wendi told me that if she ever were blessed to go to a concert, while we were doing this walk, she hoped it would be a Casting Crowns concert! One day while listening to Christian radio, we heard about a contest to win tickets to a Casting Crowns concert. To win, you would have to call in and answer a question about a particular song. Wendi called, her call was received, but she did not know the correct answer.

I called the station and shared our story. I told them about Wendi's desire to see Casting Crowns in concert. I asked them where and when the concert was being held and if they knew where I could purchase some tickets. I was told the concert was being held in Bozeman on the 25th of July and the DJ said he had two extra tickets for us—all we had to do was drive down to the station and pick them up. Wendi and I attended the concert with great joy!

"Delight yourself in the Lord; And He will give you the desires of your heart." Psalm 37:4 NASB

We went to a Cowboy Church in Kalispell and the pastor gave us a name of a pastor in Libby. When we got to Libby, we got

256

in touch with the pastor and met him at his church. He told us that we were welcome to stay as long as we needed. When we got to the house, we felt we were being interrogated by this man's wife. This made us both uncomfortable. This was actually the first time either of us experienced such awkwardness with a host family. We had told the pastor we needed a place for a week, but we were not sure we wanted to stay that long. We had no place to go, so we stuck it out. By the end of our week, we believe God had removed any doubts this woman may have had about our integrity and this walk. I'm glad we stayed!

Also while in Libby, we were able to take part in a Relay for Life walk. This was so meaningful to both Wendi and me. I had lost my great grandmother, my mother, and an aunt to cancer and Wendi had lost an aunt.

◊ ◊ ◊

One beautiful summer day, we finished walking a little early and explored some trails along the Kootenai River, and came upon a swinging bridge. Another day, we took a drive after the walk to visit Ross Creek and the giant cedars.

A few days later, as I was walking about 20 miles from the Idaho state line, it seemed like Wendi should have caught up with me, and I began to be concerned. About a half hour later, I could see Wendi up ahead standing by a car. As I got closer, I could sense that something was wrong. I saw several young college-aged people walking around with their heads down. Wendi was cradling a young woman in her arms. By the time I reached her, most of the young people had left. Wendi shared with me that she had been informed that a couple of college boys had been diving a few days earlier and one of them had been missing. They had just found his body. Wendi had not made it to me because she was about doing her Father's business!

IDAHO

Both state lines in Montana had definite changes of scenery. On the east side, we left the well groomed landscape of North Dakota to high weeds along the road in Montana. Now on the west side of the state, we left the beauty of the Rocky Mountains. The scenery was still nice, but when we walked into Idaho, the landscape was breathtaking. The grass along the road side, recently mowed, was bright green and the foliage was rich in color. The mountains displayed various shades of green, and the rivers ran through the valleys below with contrasting blues.

Wendi took out her list from the Thompson Lake Bible Camp and contacted Amy in Bonners Ferry. Amy, who had studied our brochure, was expecting our call and had arranged for our every need to be filled while we walked to, through, and beyond Bonners Ferry. She had made appointments for Wendi and me to have haircuts and massages; she made an appointment for Walker T. to be groomed. She bought dog food for Walker T. and bottled water and food for Wendi and me. She arranged lodging for us with some of the people from the church. She and her family had us over for dinner and she took us out to lunch one day. She prayed for us and arranged for me to speak at the First Baptist Church. She got a cushioned bike seat for Wendi. She even invited us to spend an evening with her family at the local fair.

As we walked down toward Sandpoint we were given a connection to MaryJim, who took us in without hesitation. She was a widow with a nice big home. MaryJim embraced us and asked what she could do to help. We needed an oil change so she met us at a garage and paid for the service.

While we were there, I received a phone call from my daughter, Laurie; she was going through a traumatic time. She had lost total hearing in her right ear. She would be going through a series of tests to diagnosis the cause of the sudden deafness. Understandably, she was scared and wanted her mom close by.

I was pretty shook up by the time I got off the phone. It was so hard for me to be so far away when my daughter was going through such a difficult time. I shared the sad news about Laurie's hearing loss with Wendi and MaryJim. Both women prayed with me. MaryJim had a one-way airline ticket that she wasn't going to be able to use. She said she would arrange for me to fly to Ohio so I could be with my daughter during this trying time.

MaryJim was not able to book the flight for a few days, so I continued the walk. In Bonners Ferry, Highway 2 merged with Highway 95. The two roads separated in Sandpoint. There were a lot of switchbacks ahead on Highway 2, as the road meandered around a mountain range. I stayed on 95 and headed south toward Coeur d'Alene.

Coeur d'Alene

Wendi contacted the mother of the little girl from the Bible camp. The woman was excited to hear from us. She said when her daughter returned from camp she could not wait to share our story. Wendi inquired about lodging in Coeur d'Alene. The woman told us that the North Star Church had an annex for lodging ministers, and it happened to be empty. She made the necessary phone calls and connected us with the interim pastor of the church.

We met with the music minister, Tom, and his wife, Fondra, and became instant friends. We were offered a place to stay at the annex for as long as we needed. I explained to them that I would be leaving the walk for a period, to fly to Ohio to be with my daughter at her time of crisis. I asked if Wendi and Walker T. would be able to stay there while I went home, and if we could continue the stay after my return, while I walk through Coeur d'Alene and into Spokane. They said they were blessed to have us and asked if I would preach at the church upon my return. I was delighted to once again be preaching at a Baptist church.

The next day, Wendi drove me to Spokane International Airport to catch my Northwestern flight to Cleveland, Ohio. She then returned to her living quarters at the church, where she had plans to spend some downtime and to take a bicycle trip with Fondra.

It was good to know Wendi and Walker T. had a safe and comfortable place to reside while I went home to console my daughter. While I was home, the worst-case scenarios were ruled out. Laurie did not have a tumor, nor did she have M.S., or any other debilitating disease; instead, she was diagnosed with some rare form of virus that sometimes caused hearing loss. She also was informed that the damage was irreversible and could not be corrected with conventional hearing aids. I was glad to be with my daughter as she had to come to terms with being permanently deaf in one ear.

After a week with my daughter and her family, I had to get back to the walk. I flew back to Spokane where Wendi and Walker T. awaited me. Wendi was anxious to share about all of her little adventures, especially her 46-mile bike ride down the Hiawatha Trail. The ride took her along the mountainous countryside, over old railroad trestles, and through long dark tunnels. Walker T. was the only dog ever permitted to go on the ride. He was only allowed because he is a service dog. It was a good thing, because he happened to be with her and it was too hot to leave him in the vehicle. I was glad to hear the two had some fun on their break from the tedious walk.

It was great to be back and walking into Coeur d'Alene. A reporter from *Coeur d'Alene Press* asked to meet with me as I walked to North Star Church. I got caught in a terrible thunderstorm that day. I was walking along Lincoln Way and Wendi was having a hard time spotting me. The traffic was thick through the area and there were a lot of traffic lights.

We kept losing track of each other. I found myself walking in a hail storm and unable to take cover because I was concerned Wendi would not be able to find me. I was not able to use the walkie-talkie because it would get ruined in the rain. By the time Wendi found me, I was drenched and had less than a mile to make it to the church so I just stayed out in the weather and made my way to the reporter.

The storm had ceased by the time I walked to the church parking lot. I went inside and changed clothes then met with the reporter.

CANINE ABDUCTION

During the summer we would leave Walker T. in his kennel in a shady place while we would have lunch or run a couple of errands. We would usually find a tree, bush, or awning right outside the door of the business. This had not been a problem in the small communities. The dog was never bothered and he seemed to enjoy sniffing the outside air and watching people pass by.

261

One very hot August day, we had to pick up a prescription, and a few groceries and other items for the road. We decided to go to Walmart where we could tackle both tasks at the same time. Wendi would shop while I got the prescription filled.

We pulled into the department store parking lot about 2:30 in the afternoon. There was no shade in the parking lot. We were concerned about what to do with the dog. We thought about one of us staying in the car with him. That was not an option because it was too hot and we did not think it would be a good idea to run the air conditioner in an idle car.

I noticed there was a shaded area by the store near the door. We discussed the situation and decided to chance leaving the dog, in his kennel, tucked up in the shady area. It was kind of a hidden corner so we trusted all would be fine. I rushed off to the pharmacy and Wendi ran to get the groceries.

By the time the prescription was filled, Wendi had come through the checkout and we headed out to get Walker T., and discovered he was gone. We both panicked. I asked a boy pushing shopping carts if he had seen anyone take him. He said he had seen the animal protective officials take the dog. We both sighed with relief. We knew he was okay. We asked for directions to the animal shelter and I called the agency while Wendi drove in that direction.

I explained to the woman who answered the phone who I was and what we were doing, and why we left the dog. She chuckled and said she was glad to hear from us. She told me the dog was fine and she knew he was not abandoned because he was well groomed and had a freshly laundered blanket in his kennel. She told me I could come and get the dog. We walked into the shelter to find Walker T. running around the building like he owned the place. He had certainly captured the hearts of the folks who worked there.

One of the workers told us that there would be no fine and thanked us for caring for the dog so well and for trying to do what was best for him. She told us to take him in the store the next time. They explained that animal abduction was common in that part of the country, especially smaller dogs. We thanked them for taking such good care of our little dog, Walker said good-bye to his new friends, and the three of us went on our way.

Spokane

As we walked from Coeur d'Alene, we enjoyed miles and miles of the scenic Idaho Centennial Trail, which then connected to the equally scenic Washington Centennial Trail. Wendi and Walker T. were able to join me as I crossed the state line. This was the most enjoyable state line crossing I had experienced on the walk. It was such a peaceful and serene walk on a beautiful August day.

I walked into Spokane on August 26th. As I walked through the city, I noticed a house of prayer. We went inside to see if anyone there would know of someone who would be able to house us down the road. We were given a number for Alna, who lived west of the city.

Wendi made the call and, sure enough, Alna, who lived near Medical Lake, was glad to have us stay with her. She could not do enough for us. She made dinners for us, provided breakfast foods, and provided food for our lunches. She invited her pastor and his wife over for dinner so they could meet us. I was invited to share at his church service and we were asked to help with a homeless feeding in Spokane, where I was asked to deliver a 10-minute message to the folks before they were served.

I was so impressed by this homeless outreach. After I spoke, Wendi and I waited on tables where the folks had been seated.

It was a restaurant type meal. There were about 20 tables set up that could seat four to eight people. Each table had a centerpiece and a salt and pepper shaker. This really touched my heart. How often do homeless people have a restaurant experience? We carried plates filled with a delicious roast beef dinner, took beverage orders, and kept the beverages topped off. As the folks finished their dinners, we gave them choices of several different desserts.

People waited in line for their turn to be seated. We served about 40 people at a time. As a table cleared out, we would clean the table for more guests. It gave me great joy to serve the less fortunate. I will never forget this experience and would love to be a part of this type of service again one day.

We picked up Highway 2 again in Spokane and I began the long and desolate walk toward Seattle. I stayed steadfast in the walk to try to make up for time lost when I was home. I had to clear Stevens Pass in the Cascade Mountains before the first big snow fall. This particular pass was sometimes closed off to traffic for six months or more after the first major snow storm.

COWBOY CAMP CONNECTIONS

By the time I was walking into Creston, we were too far west to keep driving back to Alna's house. As I walked toward the small town, I noticed a sign that said CHRISTIAN COWBOY CAMP. I, being the country girl that I am, was ecstatic about the possibilities of camping with the cowboys. One of my biggest childhood fantasies was to be able to cook at a dude ranch.

Wendi was parked by the sign and could tell by the look on my face as I approached the vehicle that I had already had my heart set on camping there. She got out of the Highlander and the two of us approached some of the campers to see if it would be okay to set up a tent for the weekend. The cowboys and their wives were kind and pointed to the gentleman in charge of the event.

"That's some dog you have there!" one of them chuckled as he pointed to Walker.

"Not sure if he could really pass as a cowboy dog!" he continued.

The cowboy in charge pointed to a place by the barn where we could set up our tent and gave Wendi a rake and me a pitch fork, so we could clear the horse manure off our site. He supplied us with an extension cord so we could have some power. All of the other cowboys had self-contained campers.

We cleared off a patch in the pasture, set up our tent, and there we were, the three of us, cowboys for the weekend. There would be some meals provided throughout the weekend, but everyone was on their own for dinner that night. We had a little bit of money—not enough to buy groceries or eat at a restaurant. I knew we were going to have to be creative for dinner. I found some noodles, some canned chicken, and a package of chicken seasoning, in a care package from Peter and Helen. I tossed it all in an electric skillet and dinner was served 20 minutes later. Not the best dinner I ever ate, but it had to do.

After dinner, we attended a service in a big barn. There were probably 100 cowboys and their families. I know because there were at least 100 cowboy hats. They had country Christian music followed by some preaching. After the service, an offering was collected to help pay for the expenses of the weekend. I felt sad that I had no money to put in the hat—the 10-gallon hat.

We were invited to have breakfast with the folks Saturday morning. There were about six tall muscular cowboys serving coffee, biscuits, gravy, taters, and eggs. I figured they got to be so

265

muscular from throwing bales of hay and straw and perhaps from lassoing cattle.

I chatted with one of the cowboy cooks and told him that I had always wanted to cook at a dude ranch. He told me that if I showed up the next morning, he would let me flip pancakes.

He said, "This is a real working ranch! That is better than a dude ranch!"

"Yes sir! I will be here!" I replied.

After breakfast, Wendi took me out to walk 10 miles. We returned to the camp and began to mingle with the folks. There were some booths set up for vendors. I noticed one of the booths had Christian books. As I was looking through the books, I struck up a conversation with the vendor, Lauretta. She was a pleasant woman who shared that she and her husband made a living selling the books.

We talked a while and I told her how God had called us to the walk. She was excited to hear about our journey and how we walked by faith and not by sight (2 Corinthians 5:7). Lauretta was impressed with the fact that we did not have prearranged housing. She told me that she and her husband Irwin lived in Hartline, Washington, which was right on our path and invited us to stay with them. Wendi had arranged for us to stay in a motel for a few nights after the weekend camp but we said it would be a blessing to stay with them after that.

Barbeque was served for dinner before the evening service. We noticed cans were placed on the counter for donations. We figured they had switched from passing the hat to a more anonymous way to give a donation. After dinner, Wendi and I went out to the car and looked for any money we might have to put in the offering. I had two $1 bills, Wendi had some coins in the bottom of her purse, and we found some loose change under the seat and in the glove box. All in all, we found about $5. Not much, but this was all we had. I handed the money to Wendi so she could put it in the offering can.

When we went back in the barn for the service, there was an open mic for testimonies. My heart pounded as we sat and listened to several testimonies. I felt prompted by God to testify, but I felt uncomfortable about going forward. My heart pounded even harder and I knew I had to share. My hands shook as I took the mic and gave a very short testimony of my call to this walk. As I began to walk away, a very tall strong cowboy grabbed hold of my jacket and pulled me back.

"You see this red jacket? It has pockets on each side! I want you to fill these pockets with cash to help these women on this mission!" the cowboy announced as he flashed a $20 bill, before he tucked it in my pocket.

All through the service and even up until we walked out away from the barn, people came and tucked bills in my pockets. There was so much cash in my pockets that I had to hold my hands on them to keep from losing the money. Wendi and I were in tears as we counted over $200. We talked about how there is no way you can out-give God. We were prompted to give all we had in the offering and God saw to it we got 40 times back in our pocket. We knew where we would tithe this money. It gave us great pleasure to have a $20 bill to put in the offering plate Sunday morning at the cowboy camp.

We enjoyed the cool mornings of early autumn, as we made our way to Hartline. Lauretta and Irwin live in a modest farm house at the east end of the small farm town. They had reared a large family there and four of their grown children still lived close by. The family was well-known and respected. Their oldest son was mayor of the town.

Because the family was so large, eight grown children and several grandchildren, the family had seasonal birthday parties where they celebrated all of the birthdays in a particular season. We happened to be there for one of these birthday parties. I think there were six individuals who celebrated a birthday. We got to meet several of Lauretta and Irwin's children and grandchildren at this event. The family embraced us as part of their family. We felt right at home!

Gloria, one of the younger children, was visiting there with her husband, Derrick, and their four children. They live in Monroe, which is the city where we would change directions on the walk, and began heading southwest into Seattle. When Gloria heard we would be walking right through Monroe, she asked if we would stay with her and her family.

Gloria said her sister, Grace, lived in Newburg, Oregon, which was right on our path between Portland and the west coast. We would be walking right through there when we returned from the holiday break.

Two of the sons made us enough crosses to make it to Portland, where we planned to take a break for the holidays. Jim, the mayor, told us he would make more crosses and somehow get them to his sister in Newburg.

I was invited to speak to Lauretta's Sunday school class that week. Her pastor extended an invitation to share my testimony with the congregation.

We met the Black family at the church. They live in Mansfield and invited us to come and stay with them next. Mansfield was a bit off our path, over 20 miles north of Highway 2. We were not sure we should spend the gas money to travel that far, but Wendi and I both felt prompted to accept the invitation. The

Blacks became our next host family. We stayed in a small apartment attached to their daughter's beauty shop.

The Blacks arranged for us to share at two different churches the following Sunday. Between the two small congregations we received over $1,000 in free-will offerings. We were invited to the Black's house for dinner and the family gave us a GPS system. It never ceases to amaze us how God blesses us for our obedience to Him. Even though it was against our better judgment to travel 20-plus miles off the beaten path, God said go. We went. He blessed!

It was mid-October by the time we made it to Stevens Pass in the Cascade Mountain Range. I had to climb to an elevation of 4,055 feet. I climbed 1,000 feet in the last mile of the climb. We planted cross #6,000 at the peak. As I began coming down off the west side of the mountain, there was an entourage of dump trucks and snow plows heading up the mountain. We just beat the snow!

By then, we had moved in with Irwin and Lauretta's daughter Gloria and her family, the Philps. We had arranged to stay with them for a week as we walked into Monroe and for another week after we turned off of Highway 2 onto Highway 522 toward Seattle.

I enjoyed spoiling the Philps children by making breakfast for them each morning. They especially enjoyed it when I made pancakes or French toast. Most of the time, Gloria had dinner for us when we got home, but a couple of times we cooked for the family. Wendi treated the family to seafood nachos one evening—one of her specialties!

Derrick's grandmother passed away while we were staying with the family. Wendi and I helped care for the children while Derrick and Gloria spent time with other family members and made the necessary plans to attend calling hours and the funeral. We were glad to be able to help and grateful for God's impeccable timing.

SEATTLE TO PORTLAND

By the time we made the turn in Monroe, we had less than 100 miles to complete our trek across the North. On Saturday, October 25, 2008, as we were walking the last mile before we hit the coastline, I had a very hard fall as I stepped onto a sidewalk after crossing the road at an intersection. Somehow, I miscalculated my step up and I did not lift my prosthetic leg high enough. The foot caught the sidewalk and I tripped. I fell straight down like a rock. My elbows and forearms were scuffed and bleeding. My face hit the concrete and I had a scrape under my eye. I laid there a moment hoping I was okay and that I had not broken any bones.

Wendi saw the fall and was at my side within minutes.

"I'm afraid to move!" I gasped. "I think I may have broken something!" I said while I examined my cracked glasses (they'd been knocked off my face in the fall).

After a few minutes, I reached my hand out to Wendi and she helped me up. I was sore and beat up a little, but I was very determined to make it to the coast.

"I think the devil is trying to trip me up, but I am not going to stop. In fact, I am going to make it to the water, then I am going to turn and start down the coast!" I insisted.

About 20 minutes after the fall, I planted cross #6,093 at West Point Light House at South Beach Park. I sounded a shofar (a ram's horn) and Wendi and I celebrated having completed our northern walk across the United States. I limped away from the cross and insisted on walking at least two more miles just to prove nothing was going to trip me up.

◊ ◊ ◊

Donald, the Pacin' Parson, came out to join me as I walked through Seattle. He enjoyed our walk so much he decided he would walk with me every day for the next week. Each day he would meet me in the morning. We walked the city streets together while his wife, Loretta, joined Wendi in spotting us through the metropolitan area.

Donald made a sign and attached it to a reflective vest for me to wear. He thought more people would become aware of the walk if they could see what I was doing. The sign read WALKING AND PRAYING FOR AMERICA. I was not too keen about wearing a sign, but God had a purpose for it in the greater Seattle area. The only one-on-one encounters I had with people in that area were with people who saw that I was doing a prayer walk. Many stopped along the way and thanked me for praying for the country. Some confessed that they do not pray enough for the nation and seeing the sign was encouragement for their own prayer lives. For this point and time, God had a plan for the sign.

One cool autumn Monday morning, as I was walking along Highway 507, I heard a joyful shout from a passing car, "God bless you, sister!" The driver turned around and came back to inquire about my journey. She introduced herself as Emma, a sister in the Lord, and invited us to stay with her for the next three nights.

Emma was from Chile and blessed us by cooking us meals the way they were prepared in Chile. We spent the evenings sharing our testimonies with one another and developed a great friendship.

Tuesday morning, she invited us to meet a local pastor who asked me to speak at his church the following Wednesday.

Emma extended her invitation and opened up her home for several more days. As we visited in the evenings, she told us that she had a lesbian daughter in Texas and a son in Texas who had a tattoo of the devil on his arm. She suspected her son who lived with her was gay and she forbade any of his gay friends to come near the house. She had a lot of unloving things to say about her lesbian daughter and her friends. This mother was in great distress about the decisions her three children were making and she was dealing with it in anger and rejection.

The morning we moved on from Emma's, Wendi and I spent some time with Emma and ministered to her about the importance of loving her children and trying to lead them, and their friends, to Christ through love. I shared with her that I did not think that anyone would come to Christ through hate or abuse; this kind of behavior would cause people to run away from Christians and Christ. Wendi encouraged her to embrace her children and love them into the Kingdom of God. I told her that she did not have to agree with her children's decisions, but it was important to treat them with love. Jesus would!

We left there believing we may have made a difference in how Emma would deal with her children. Instead, she cut off all contact with us. I received a voicemail from the pastor she had introduced us to, he canceled my speaking engagement at his church saying: "You are no longer welcome to share at my church! I know for a fact that you are promoting something that God hates!"

I tried to call Emma several times and she would not answer my calls. I also tried to reach the pastor and he would not receive or answer my requests for a return call. Wendi and I felt so sad that a sister and a brother, in Christ, would treat us in such a matter.

We shook the dust off of our feet and took our peace with us as we headed on down the road.

God-Given Mother

My spiritual mother, Naomi, lives in Hoquiam, Washington. I had met her at a conference in 1989 and she stayed with me in 1991 when she came to speak in Akron, Ohio. A motherly person, a few years younger than my biological parents, she became the Christian mother I had always prayed for. She was one of the few people who believed in me and my call to do the walk, right from the time I went public with it. She was there to encourage me when I spoke to over 200 ministers in Phoenix, Arizona, in 2002. She prayed for me and was always there to encourage me.

We traveled to see Naomi several times while we walked from Seattle to Portland. We happened to be at her house for the weekend on Wendi's birthday in November. Naomi invited some of her friends and relatives to her home for a birthday celebration for Wendi. Two of the guests were her sister, Nina, and Nina's husband, Herb, who happened to be in very poor health. Herb and Walker T. became great pals. Herb, who enjoyed working on projects, made a box of crosses for us.

One day, north of Centralia, I was being interviewed by a newspaper reporter, when a woman pulled off to the side of the road, got out of her car and came running toward me.

"My Dad made those crosses!" she shouted as she approached us and pointed to a cross that I was handing to the reporter. "I am Naomi's niece and my dad made those crosses!"

"I want one of those crosses!" she continued.

I told her she could pick up a cross—they are meant to be picked up. I told her she could find one in front of the Assemblies of God Church.

273

A few days later, Naomi called me and told me that her niece had gone out that very evening to find the cross. A few miles before she got to the church, she reported she had seen a 10-foot illumination of a cross on the side of the road. She stopped, got out of her car, and walked toward the illumination to see one of the little crosses her father had made at the foot of the light. She believed God showed her where the cross was with a ray from heaven. Naomi shared that her niece, who had not been attending a church, was showing great interest in getting right with God. Naomi also told us that Herb had taken a turn for the worse and they did not expect him to recover. Making the crosses was the last project Herb completed before he went to be with the Lord.

◊ ◊ ◊

The Astoria Bridge, which connects Washington to Oregon on the west coast, is only open for pedestrians one day a year in October. Since I did not make it to western Washington until late October, I was denied permission to cross the bridge. I had to stay inland a bit and cross the waterway at the Longview Bridge which was about 50 miles north of Portland.

We finally made it to Portland, Oregon, on Monday, November 20th, 2008. I walked to mile marker #9 on Highway 30 and planted cross #6,294 before we headed home to spend the holidays with our families.

SHEEP'S REST

Sometime back, I had received an email from a double amputee, Judy, who had read about the walk in *inMOTION* Magazine. She and her husband, David, had bought a place in Grant's Pass, Oregon. They

274

created an environment of rest and relaxation at this country home and called the place Sheep's Rest. Judy invited us to stay there when we made it to Oregon. This sounded like a place to refresh and retreat before a long trip across the country. I contacted her and let her know that I would not be walking through Grants Pass, but we would like to stay with them on our way home for the holidays. Judy was excited to meet us and invited us to stay with them for a couple of days.

So we went to stay with the couple, the night after I planted the last cross in 2008. The couple had named the place well. It was a place of rest. They offered storage space for us to leave the bike and camping gear for the winter. David helped us unload our car and carry our things to the pool house. This lightened our load for the trip home.

On our way to Ohio, we stopped off in Phoenix to visit our friend, Dee, who was very ill and on hospice care. Wendi and I both spent a few minutes with her and were able to say good-bye. We knew she was heaven bound.

We spent Thanksgiving in Mesa with Wendi's dad, Bobby, and her step-mom, Vernice, and Vernice's mother, Elizabeth. It was nice for Wendi to have a Thanksgiving meal with her father. She had not spent a holiday with him since she was a child. We had stayed there a couple of times when we were traveling across the country in the winter months from one speaking engagement to another. I had grown fond of Bobby and Vernice and I enjoyed getting to know Elizabeth. Vernice showed great interest in the walk and encouraged us on the journey. Bobby may have thought I could provide better for his daughter's well-being, but it was not my call on her life, it was God's and He was our sole provider. I understood; he was just being Dad! We were able to rest a little before our long drive home, where we spent Christmas and welcomed in the New Year with family.

While home in Ohio, we got news that Dee had passed quickly. We did not make it back to Phoenix before she passed away, but we got there in time for the memorial service.

We drove back to Sheep's Rest to spend some time with David and Judy and to have one more night of relaxation before getting back to six-day-a-week workload. David helped us load our car with the camping gear and the bike. Judy had arranged for Walker T. to be groomed by a local groomer, who was delighted to meet Walker T. The local paper came out and did a story about our ministry and the generosity of the dog groomer.

December 10, 2008

Cross #6,199

God bless you as you walk and pray for our country! I'm sure you could write a book about your experiences. (So, when DOES your book come out ☺?). I recall reading an article in our local paper some time ago about your mission and that you were passing through our area. I found this cross about 200 yards from our Christian school just off the side of a sidewalk in a commercial area. I picked it up and took it with me to a local hardware store where I gave it to Bob and told him Jesus loves him. He said he would give the cross to his Mom! (Is SHE a believer? He didn't respond to my words…but he heard them). I will see him again. I will go to your website to keep track of your progress.

Godspeed.

Denny

Centralia Christian School

THE WEST
COAST—2009

WELCOMED IN OREGON

By the time we got back to Portland, we were three well-rested sheep and ready for the walk. Wendi had prearranged for us to stay with Gloria Philp's sister, Grace, and her family in Newburg, Oregon. We were on our way out to the coast and Newburg was right on our path. Grace and her family embraced us with open arms.

I was walking on Highway 18. It seemed like it took forever to make it to the ocean. Once we got within 15 miles of the shoreline, I hit switchbacks for the first time. The curves were so sharp and so frequent, I had to walk over two miles to gain one mile in a westward direction. I was thrilled when I began to hear the waves of the Pacific Ocean pounding on the western shoreline. Even then, I was still over three miles from actually arriving at the coast.

Once we hit Highway 101, we were southbound. Well, sort of! Highway 101 is a very winding highway! We had completed the east coast, the trek across the north from east to west, and now we were heading south to San Diego, where we planned to turn to begin our last leg on the perimeter walk. All of this would be happening over the next several months.

After staying with Grace and her family, we went to stay with Bambi in Newport. Bambi is a daughter of our friends, the Horns. I met the Horns at a conference years earlier. Judy Horn gave me a pair of socks that had *walk by faith* embroidered on the sides of them. I wore those socks completely out on this walk.

Bambi and her husband set up their fifth-wheel camper for us in front of their home. We stayed with them for two weeks while we walked to and away from Newport.

Bambi was in charge of the after-school program in the area and invited me to speak at the high school one evening. Walter, her husband, was a fisherman by trade. He was a captain of a fishing rig and would sometimes go out to sea for days with a crew of fisherman. He wanted to take us out on the boat but was not able to, in the timeframe of our stay, so we took a rain-check.

It was nice to be in one place for a while and to be a part of another family. We enjoyed playing games at the kitchen table in the evenings with Bambi's two teenage children. We bought pizza for the kids one night and made dinner for them on another occasion. Walter was quiet but seemed to like our company. He smiled a lot and enjoyed eating our cooking. The hardest part about stays like this is moving on. We had to keep moving.

Moving on down the coastline we stayed at a campground near Lakeside. One day I was walking up to the SUV in a desolate area about halfway between North Bend and Lakeside. Wendi was parked on the side of the road. I got in the car and asked her to drive me to a state park so I could use the facilities. When she put the car in drive, it wouldn't move. The shifting cable had either become disconnected or it had snapped.

I said, "Praise God, I can't wait to see how He works this one out!"

We were about 15 miles south from where we were camping and about 25 miles north of the next town south of us. We sat there a few minutes and prayed for wisdom. I remembered we had AAA so I took out my card and made a call. The tow truck driver drove us back to the campground where two nights of lodging had been donated to us and took our vehicle to a small garage in town.

It was Saturday and the garage was closed. It was apparent we could not have any work done on our car until Monday morning. It rained all weekend. On Sunday morning, Wendi put a poncho on and rode her bike to an Assemblies of God church. After the service, she explained our situation and our needs. The pastor went to the campground and paid for us to continue our stay there.

On Monday, it was still raining. Later in the day, Fox News out of Coos Bay came out and did a story about the walk. Meanwhile, the mechanic at the small garage fixed our shifting cable and we were back on the road by Tuesday.

In the middle of all of this, a woman, Madeleine, from Bandon, Oregon, called and left a message on Wendi's phone. Her husband, Bob, had seen us on Fox News and the two invited us to stay with them at their beach house. Wendi returned the call and made arrangements for us to stay with them as we walked to and from Bandon.

Madeleine worked with senior citizens and was taking one of her clients to run errands when she saw me walking along Highway 101. She stopped to meet us and introduced herself as the woman who would be hosting us. She was a tall, cheerful woman from South Africa and spoke with a strong accent. It was a blessing to get to meet Madeleine before moving into her home.

She and Bob were awesome hosts. We each had a room on the second floor of the beach house. Madeleine fell in love with Walker T. and we had to almost pry him away from her each day as we headed out the door.

Bob was a little hesitant about our faith and beliefs. Madeleine was a Christian and he was okay with that, but he was not sure what he thought about all that he had seen on television about the Christian faith. Madeleine attended church and Bob supported her walk with the Lord even though he did not necessarily agree with all of the hoopla he saw on television. He watched Wendi and me very carefully.

One day he commented, "My wife walks a walk of faith and I see that the two of you do as well!" He seemed to approve of our testimonies.

Each morning Bob would fix us coffee with his French press and we would discuss our walk with him over breakfast. Bob, an excellent cook, prepared dinner for the four of us each evening and we kept our conversations light with friendly jokes and laughter.

By the end of our second week with the couple, Bob had watched us closely enough to trust us in our faith. The couple invited neighbors in to hear our testimony. He said he was going to park his chair by the door so he could escape if he had to. Instead, he leaned in to hear every word I had to share about how God was carrying us along each mile.

Madeleine packed lunches for us and on several occasions, she joined us on the walk. One day she caught up with us with a packed lunch and treated us to a trip—an adventure at a game park. As we strolled through the park, Madeleine cuddled baby cougars, panthers, and possums. She had this little expression,

"Maaaa" she would say, each time she picked up one of her furry friends.

Eventually we had to move out of the beach house. Even Bob cried when we had to say our good-byes and head on down the road.

Walking the Oregon coastline was an awesome experience with most of our lodging provided by families, for the first half of the state. Then, heading south, we were provided with lodging in guest houses and resorts in rooms that rented for hundreds of dollars a night—the managers would thank us for staying with them.

One of these fabulous places was in Gold Beach, where one evening, after a long day on 101, we took a short walk to a Jacuzzi that was halfway between our beach house and the ocean, with a privacy shield on one side and an ocean view on the other. God had opened doors for us in places we could not even imagine staying.

NOT SO "WELCOME TO CALIFORNIA"

Walking into northern California was like entering a whole new world. We felt like foreigners and we were treated as such. We didn't run into many Christians and people seemed to be suspicious of us when we spoke of our faith. Needless to say, the walk didn't get much news coverage. Once in a while we were given a room for a night or two but most of the time we camped as we headed down the coastline.

The first bigger city we walked into was Eureka. Wendi drove into the city as I was walking toward it. She inquired about lodging at every place of business and was turned away. As we were about to head to a homeless shelter, a woman, from a very exclusive bed and breakfast called and asked Wendi if we found a place yet. When Wendi told her that we had not, she offered us a voucher for a room. God is good and was watching over us! We stayed in one of the most exclusive places in the city, right downtown!

Even though it looked pretty grim, as far as having lodging donated to us, we knew God would come through. As I was walking out of the city, I noticed a place up on a hill to the left of me, overlooking the ocean. Wendi had noticed this place as well and drove up to inquire about a donation. A very sweet girl gave us two nights lodging but her father, who owned the place, retracted one of the nights.

The next day, Wendi drove down to Fortuna and one place after another turned her away. At one particular place, a young girl who was working the desk was excited to hear about our walk and told us we should contact her pastor at a local church, as she was sure he would help us. Wendi called the pastor as we drove up to the church building. There was a car parked in the designated pastor's parking space. The pastor answered the phone, and told us he did not have time and he did not seem the least bit interested in meeting us. There definitely was no room at the inn in this town and, if there was, it was not open to us.

We shook the dust off of our feet and Wendi drove to Rio Del Scotia. One man who said, "I have never done this before!" gave us a room for one night.

We were not sure what all of the suspicion or rejection was about, but it sure seemed high.

THE REDWOOD GIANTS

Just about 100 miles after crossing the California state line, we entered one of the most breathtaking, massive forests one could ever imagine. We were walking in one of nature's wonders, the Redwood Forest on the Avenue of the Giants. This is a place to go if you really want a glimpse of God's handiwork. I remember looking up at the giants and thinking, *How big God is and how small I am!* How humbled I felt in the presence of all of His wonder.

The people seemed a little more accommodating in the forest. It helped that we had a connection to a place in Phillipsville. Loretta, the wife and pilot car driver of the Pacin' Parson, had given Wendi the name and number of a place she and Donald had stayed when he did a walk up the coast from Mexico to Vancouver a few years before. Wendi made the call to find that the business had changed hands.

The new owner, Dotti, wanted to help us and invited us to stay at the lodge while we walked through the forest. She and her husband, Graham, were very accommodating and invited us over to their place for dinner. Dotti invited us to a town meeting in Garberville, where we met some nice folks. One woman invited us to dinner at her house and another woman offered to let us stay at a recovery center that she owned and operated.

Dotti came out and walked with us. We shared our faith with her and she shared hers with us. She was practicing Christian Science and she invited us to go to a reading with her. We agreed to go to the reading if she would attend a service with us at a nondenominational church in Garberville. She agreed to go and seemed to enjoy the full-Gospel service—we got an education about some of the Christian Science beliefs.

Wendi contacted Patti, the woman at the recovery center, to arrange housing for us as we finished our walk on 101 and connected with Highway 1 on the Pacific Coast. Patti told us the place that was available was open because of a unique situation. It was a camper that was reserved for her night help. She had recently hired a new night person and was not sure if he was going to work out so she did not offer to let him stay in the unit. Once again, I believe this was divine timing. God continued to pave the way for us.

GOING TO SAN FRANCISCO

We didn't have any flowers in our hair as we headed south to San Francisco, but I had many briars in my britches and thorns in my shoes. The California coast was, by far, the most challenging stretch of terrain in the entire walk. In fact, I had gotten word that right after I walked through Montana, a man from there had begun a walk around the US. I looked up his website, where he had recorded being mauled by a mountain lion and hit by a truck on the California coast. I would never attempt walking that route without the leading of God and His protection.

Highway 1 may be one of the most scenic routes in our nation, but it is also one of the most treacherous. It is a winding, narrow highway that meanders along the seacoast with a multitude of switchbacks. Some of the switchbacks switched back so much that the ocean would be on the left side when southbound. On a good part of the road, there are mountains on the east side with a guard rail on the west, to prevent vehicles from dropping off a steep cliff into the ocean or a valley.

I walked with traffic to prevent being pinned between a northbound vehicle and a mountain. Wendi would sit in the pilot car behind me, walkie-talkie in hand; she would watch my back as I disappeared out of sight around the many curves.

She announced the traffic that approached me from behind, "Carol, there are eleven cars, the last one's a black Civic!" she warned. I would quickly climb over the guard rail and hold on for dear life as I counted the vehicles and took note of the last one mentioned. Then I would climb back over the rail and scurry down the highway until the next alert.

I carried a walking stick to ward off snakes, because I often had to step into high weeds to keep from being hit by a car. If I had not had the stick, I would have stepped on or near a snake on numerous occasions.

One time when I was hanging onto a guard rail, counting vehicles, when the mirror of a bus would have clipped my head if I had not seen it in time. I swung back as the bus came around a curve.

Our days would start at sun up and I had to walk until dusk, just to get 10 tiring miles in each day. By the end of the day, my socks and shorts were covered with briars, my face was covered with soot, and my hair was drenched in perspiration. I picked thorns out of the soles of my shoes and nursed scratches, cuts, and bruises from climbing in and out of brush and climbing and hanging over the guard rails.

I planted cross #7,000 in Bodega Bay on June 12, 2009. We had difficulty finding lodging in that area. Wendi tried to get a place for us to put up a tent but we could not afford the cost of the site. So Wendi called a local church where a woman named Judy answered. Wendi explained our predicament and she met us out on the road with a donation to pay for the campsite. Judy attended a church in Guerneville where she invited us to attend the following Sunday. The folks at the church encouraged us in the walk and helped us out financially.

For the most part, people were still suspicious as we headed down the coast. A woman in Dillon Beach, asked Wendi, "You are not one of those Christians who hate people, are you?" as she handed her a small donation. Wendi assured her that we do not hate anyone and neither does God.

Wendi called a bed and breakfast in Inverness for a place to stay. The woman directed her to another place down the road. By the time Wendi checked out the other place and they refused help, I had walked to the front of the bed and breakfast. I had a strong feeling we would be staying there. Wendi pulled up to me and I shared this with her.

Wendi told me that she had already approached the owner on the phone and she was going to go tell her that another place she had suggested fell through. When Wendi and I met her face to face, the woman thanked us with tears in her eyes and told Wendi that she knew without a doubt that she was supposed to help us. Then she began to cry and asked, "Are you Christians who hate people?"

With tears in my eyes, I said, "No, we do not hate people!" She smiled and showed us to our room.

We stayed with our friends Cherie and Sandy and their third housemate, Matthew, in Fremont for the next several days. It was nice to be with friends. I enjoyed sharing with the three about all that was going on out on the walk. I told them how my heart was broken as I thought about the two different women, from two different towns, who somehow got the impression that Christians hate people or, at least, that some Christians hate some people. If I believed that, I would not serve the God of love, Who called me to this walk to spread the message of *His love* for all people!

Cherie, a pastor, arranged for some of her congregation to make crosses. That weekend we had a cross-making assembly line on the back patio. This was not the first time crosses were made for us on that patio, and would not be the last.

Cherie came out to meet me on the north end of the Golden Gate Bridge so she could walk the bridge into San Francisco. We stopped midway on the bridge and prayed for the Bay Area as we looked out over the cities. We prayed that God's love would be known by the people on the west coast and that Christians would not operate in hate or perpetrate hate crimes. No one has ever come to God through hate or anger.

Wendi's cousin Lisa, who lived nearby, picked Wendi up and treated her to dinner, a movie, a massage, and a shopping spree for sweet smelling bath products. We actually got to spend quite a bit of time with Lisa and her family, which included her oldest son's graduation party. It had been years since Wendi and Lisa had seen each other, so they had a lot of catching up to do. Soon we were too far south to continue with our visits, but Lisa was planning to fly to Ohio for their family reunion, so the two were able to see each other again soon enough.

GOD IS IN THE CAMPGROUNDS

Big Sur

The coastline between the Bay Area and the greater Los Angeles area is breathtaking and a popular area for tourists and camping. Camping became a way of life as we ventured south along the shore.

Camping in Big Sur is one of the most memorable adventures we had on this walk. I noticed the campground to my right along a river bend, as we were entering the park. Wendi asked about a campsite and there were none available. The manager believed in what we were doing, so she created a site for us right behind the store, about 30 feet from the river. We were given permission to run an extension cord from the store to our tent for cooking and lights at night.

Each evening, we would shower then I would sit near the tent and cook dinner for the two of us in an electric skillet. We both enjoyed camping and enjoyed talking with the folks who were there from all parts of the world. The family camping behind us was from England. They seemed exceptionally interested in the walk and before they left they tucked a roll of quarters for laundry and a note inside our tent.

On Saturday, we took a rafting trip down the river on our pool floats. It was an adventuresome ride with mild rapids and a swift slide through a culvert. It was kind of embarrassing when I slipped into the water and my raft took off downstream! A young boy about 12 years old ran along the shore and was able to fetch it for me. We thanked the boy and had a nice visit with his mother. They were from Huntington Beach and were out for one last adventure before the school year started. We still keep in touch with the family.

One evening while I was attempting to make macaroni and cheese in the electric skillet, two women stopped by our tent. Their names were KK and Cathy. They were two single women who often traveled together. They invited us to their campsite for dinner the next night and friendships were sparked. They blessed us with help for provision in so many ways.

God was definitely in that campground!

San Simeon

One Saturday evening, while camping in a state park in San Simeon just south of Hearst Castle, we were given a flyer about a worship service that would be held on the grounds the following morning at 8:30. It was about 9:00 and I was really tired from a long day on the road. I was so tired I chose to wait until morning to shower.

The next morning, it was almost 8:00 when I climbed out of the tent—not enough time to shower before walking down to the meeting place. I began to talk myself out of attending the service when I felt a strong prompting to get dressed and go. It was kind of embarrassing, but we were camping and I didn't guess anyone would really notice how rough I looked.

Wendi and I went to the shower room, splashed some water on our faces, brushed our teeth and rushed down to the meeting. It was great to see that this was available for the campers. There was a turnout of about a dozen people. After the service, we visited with the pastor and his wife and we met the Watkins family—Jeff, Donna, Jacob, and Lexi, and a man named Fred. Donna and Jeff shared that they would not have attended the service if it had not been insisted on by their 14-year-old son, Jacob, who was on fire for Jesus and hoping to be a youth pastor one day.

We had only been donated one night's stay at this park. The Watkins invited us to put our tent up on their site. They were going to be there for several more days and the park permitted two tents as well as a camper per site. They had a trailer and one tent. Some friends of theirs had left the day before, leaving the second tent site available. It was great. We had meals together and began a friendship and connection that would be vital to this walk.

One evening while Donna, Jeff, Wendi, and I were talking, we thought it would be nice to see if Fred was still on the grounds and if he would like to join us for our evening meal. We knew where his site was because he was camping right next to where Wendi and I had been camping before we moved onto the Watkins' site.

Fred was still there. He was camping by himself and was delighted to be invited for a meal and fellowship.

Over dinner, I shared with the Watkins and Fred that I was hoping to be able to fly Wendi home for a couple of weeks. Her oldest daughter had a lead part in a play, her younger daughter was getting ready to go back to school and needed to go clothes shopping, and her family was having their very first family reunion. I shared some concerns about trying to make it out on the walk alone with the dog. The Watkins offered to let us leave Walker T. with them in San Clarita and told us there was a shuttle to the airport not too far from where they lived, which would be convenient if Wendi was flying out of Los Angeles.

Later on in conversation, Fred told us that he was a veteran and was able to get campsites in the state parks for free. He told us that he was newly single and waiting for an apartment to open up. Meanwhile he was enjoying some of the state parks. He offered for us to put our tent up on his site after the Watkins left and said he was willing to move his camping down the road to parks further south, in order to help us out with lodging for a while. We were grateful to have the offer.

We enjoyed the next several nights with the Watkins. Donna came out and walked with us on the last day of their camping in San Simeon.

It certainly seemed like God was in that campground too!

Pismo Beach

That evening we set up camp on Fred's site. We were getting pretty far south and we needed to move on, so Fred said he would get a site down near Pismo Beach. The next day, we moved our home base there.

Fred seemed nice enough. After we walked, he took us to a place where we could get online to schedule Wendi's flight. That evening we sat at a picnic table and Fred helped me work on my prosthesis which needed parts and repairs. I took a foot off an old prosthetic leg, which seemed to have more life left on it, and put it on the leg I was wearing.

As I was trying to convince Fred that I knew what I was doing and I did not need his duct tape, a couple from the campsite next to us came over to visit. They had noticed the magnetic sign on our SUV and inquired about the ministry. It was a pastor and his wife, Caesar and Helen, who were on their honeymoon, both older than most newlyweds, and were already grandparents from previous marriages. Helen was from Mexico and Caesar was second generation American also from Mexico. Helen, a very large woman with a fair complexion compared to most of the Mexicans we had met, spoke fluent English and was often used as an interpreter. Caesar was very short, with a much darker complexion, and spoke with a stronger accent. The two were fun to visit with. We sat by the campfire for several hours. Caesar sang some songs he had written. We were blessed by their company.

The next night while visiting around the campfire, Caesar sang, we all sang, and Caesar sang some more. People began to gather at our site to be a part of our fellowship. Many approached us for prayer. It quickly became known as a "the Christian" site. People would come out of their way to meet us and spend some time in prayer and fellowship with the five of us. Some were healed and many were encouraged.

God was definitely at that campground!

Fred had been insisting on walking with us each day. He had committed to being my pilot car driver while Wendi was in Ohio for a couple of weeks, but we began to notice some red flags. He was separated from his wife who had some serious health issues. He was talking about finding another wife and he was not even legally divorced. He said he had been a Christian for 40 years and also admitted he had no friends. This seemed very odd that a Christian would have no friends.

Fred misrepresented himself on the walk by indicating to people we met along the way that he had been a part of this ministry from the start with statements like, "We started this walk in South Beach, Miami!" which is true except for the fact that he was not part of "we."

Fred became controlling with me on the walk and told Wendi and me that we would leave the pilot car someplace while she was home because we would operate out of his truck. He seemed to have some strange obsession with duct tape. He carried it with him and often suggested we fix or fasten something with the tape. Both Wendi and I became very uneasy about Fred. Wendi was having some anxiety about leaving me out on the walk with the man. I was concerned too and was not sure how we were going to get rid of him.

One evening, Caesar began to pray for each of us and he prayed to God that if there was anything that was coming up against us, it would have to leave in the name of Jesus. That night, while tucked away in the tent, I could hear Fred conversing with Caesar about wanting to find another wife. I thought to myself, *he may be looking for another victim.* He had definitely sent off perpetrator vibes. I silently prayed as I drifted off to sleep.

The next morning, Wendi approached me as I was coming out of the tent and told me Fred had been inappropriate with her. I was irate, to say the least.

Wendi is a strong, beautiful woman, of a medium build. She is full figured and has a thick head of brilliantly highlighted brunette hair. She has a round face and big beautiful blue eyes. She is like a big heart walking around on sturdy legs with outstretched arms. With her boisterous personality, she makes her presence known when she enters a room with a cheerful greeting. You seldom hear a negative word come out of her mouth—she is the first to edify a person in love and good works. She is living testimony to 1 Thessalonians 5:11 (NASB), "encourage one another and build up one another."

Wendi told me that her uncle used to say she made a better door than a window, when she would be in the way of him viewing the television. In my opinion, Wendi makes an excellent window. I believe a person could be extremely empowered and enlightened if they were to look through the window of Wendi's heart and just see what she is made of. I have met many wonderful Christians, but not one who walks their talk as steadfastly as Wendi does. My life has been greatly enriched and I have grown tremendously having her in my life and by peering through the window of her heart. Now I was flabbergasted that someone attempted to violate this most precious vessel of God's light and love.

I knew I had to confront Fred so I walked over to him and told him I needed to address some issues. He would not look me in the eyes. It was like the darkness in him could not face the light of the truth. As soon as the words come out of my mouth, he scurried over to his truck, took out a Christian book we had given him, threw it in the window of our SUV and backed out of our campsite.

Wendi called out to him as he drove away, "Fred, please, we just want to talk! We want to clarify some things!" she cried out, as he drove off in a huff, leaving his camping gear behind.

It was apparent that Fred had been up to no good and God was removing him from our lives.

We drove down Highway 1 to where I had left off the day before, just south of Oceano. I began walking my 10 miles while

Wendi looked for housing in the area. She stopped in a thrift store where she met Sherrell, the manager. Kim, another woman who was working there that day, invited us to stay with her family for a night and Sherrell opened up her home for the next night.

We finished the walking day near Guadalupe and headed back to the campground. Fred had not returned to get his camping gear. He had told us that he had spent a couple hundred dollars on the items. He had also left his Bible. Wendi has a good memory for numbers. Fred rode with her one day and pointed out where his apartment building was and told her the number. Wendi shared this information with Caesar. We all thought the Christian thing would be to try to get his items to him.

The next morning his stuff was still there, so Caesar and Wendi took the gear to the apartment. He was not there, so his things were left on his front stoop. Otherwise, the campground officials would put them in the dumpster once we left the site. Wendi left a note saying that we apologize if we offended him in any way and she thanked him for helping us with campsites.

Now that Fred was gone, we were going to be sure that God was still in the campground. After all, it was our job to let His light shine. "Let your light shine before men in such a way that they may see your good works, and glorify your Father who is in heaven" (Matthew 5:16).

"WENDI, GO HOME"

We tore down camp the next morning. After a 10-mile walking day, we stayed with the woman from the thrift store and the next night with Sherrell. She and I became quick friends and she invited me to spend the weekends with her while Wendi was in Ohio.

The next morning was Wednesday and Wendi would be flying home. She had never left me out on the walk alone and was not happy about doing it this time. I knew it was important for her to be with her family so I said, "Wendi, go home! God has it covered! I am going to be all right!"

Just north of Lompoc, we were advised by a highway patrolman that I should turn onto Highway 246 and work my way out to 101. Even though it was interstate through that section of the mountains, it was safer than what I would face if I stayed on Highway 1. The patrolman said he would let the other officials know he had advised this detour and ask them to keep an eye on me.

We discovered a road that cut over from Highway 1 to Highway 246 that would cut off a few miles of the detour. I walked the road and ended up at the intersection of the country road and Highway 246. We called it a walking day and drove to Santa Clarita where I would leave Walker T.

The next morning Donna took Wendi to catch a shuttle to the airport, and I drove back to walk.

It was already after noon when I parked the SUV at the intersection where I had left off walking before the trip to Santa Clarita. Not sure how it was all going to work out, I packed a bag with crosses and a bottle of water, and I took off walking toward Buellton where I would pick up Interstate 101.

I had about 18 miles to reach my destination. I walked eight miles and began to be concerned about how I was going to get back to the vehicle. Usually drivers stop each day to check on me. Not this day! I knew if I turned around then, I could make it back to the car before dark. I hesitated a moment, turned around, and began walking back toward the Highlander. A mile into my walk back to the car, a state highway patrolman stopped to check on me. I explained my situation and he gladly drove me to the vehicle.

I paid for a camping site at a campground in Buellton for two nights and set up camp. I missed Wendi's help but I was glad she was able to be with her family.

The next day, I went back to where I had completed the eight miles and, once again, I walked away from the pilot car. This time I walked seven miles and came to a nursery. Entering the parking lot, I noticed a man loading some plants into the back of his truck. I assumed he was about to leave so I asked him if he would be heading in the direction where I had left the SUV. He said he was. I asked if he would please give me a ride to my vehicle. He said he would. He was a nice Christian man who seemed to enjoy hearing about my quest.

The next day was Saturday. I had three miles to walk to be at the on ramp of Interstate 101. I decided I would walk to a Taco Bell that was across the street from the ramp, then pick up from there on Monday.

I drove to the nursery and parked the car. I took off walking with three crosses in my hand. About a mile and a half into my walk, I came to an Assemblies of God church. There was a carwash fundraiser taking place in the parking lot. I walked up to one of the teen volunteers and shared what I was doing. I told the young man that I had $7 and some change and I would be glad to donate the money for a carwash if someone would take me back to get my vehicle. He was glad to drive me to the SUV.

After the car was washed, I explained to the workers that I had another one and a half miles to walk that day. I asked if I could leave the car in the parking lot. I was given permission.

296

I then asked if anyone would be willing to pick me up at the Taco Bell in about an hour and a half, to bring me back to the car. There were about a dozen people there, but no volunteers. I left the vehicle in the parking lot and walked to the Taco Bell—then I turned around and walked back to the church. There were several of the workers standing around in the parking lot. I smiled and waved to them as I walked to my vehicle and drove away.

This is going to be quite interesting out here without Wendi! I thought as I drove to spend the weekend with Sherrell and her husband Eddy near Oceano.

HARASSED ON INTERSTATE 101

I shared my interesting trials with Sherrell and Eddy over dinner that evening. It turned out that Eddy works for the railroad and the tracks which he patrolled ran along 101. Eddy said he could pick me up each day after he finished working and drive me back to my car. What a relief.

I went to a church picnic with Eddy and Sherrell that weekend and met some of the folks from her church. A couple of young gentlemen volunteered to help me get back to my car once I was out of Eddy's jurisdiction. Things were looking up!

Monday morning I drove to the Taco Bell and walked onto Interstate 101 planting crosses every mile along the way. I received a call on my cell phone from a man from Cal-Tran, which is the California Department of Transportation.

"Are you planting crosses along the highway?" he inquired.

"Yes!" I replied.

"*You have to stop!*" he continued with a raised voice.

"Excuse me?" I asked.

"You are costing the state of California thousands of dollars by putting your crosses on the side of the road!" he continued!

"Excuse me?" I repeated.

"I have to send my men out to pick up those crosses you leave and it is costing the state of California thousands of dollars. You may very well be fined for each cross we pick up!"

I tried to explain to the man that the crosses were not meant to be left in the ground and that people were picking them up. I told him there was no need for him to send men out to get the crosses.

"Stop putting them in the ground!" he insisted.

I told the man that I would look for private property to plant the crosses.

I continued to plant the crosses but I was very deliberate and discreet about where I planted them. Later I shared the phone call conversation with Eddy as he was driving me back to Taco Bell.

"Not a problem! I will pick the crosses up and pass them on!" he said.

The next day as I was walking up to a mile post I saw one of my crosses laying on the ground beside the post. As I approached the post I noticed the tag was not hanging from the cross; instead, the tag was duct taped to the cross. I picked the cross up and looked at the number. It was a cross I had planted about 100 miles back in the San Simeon area. *Fred!* I thought.

I called Wendi and told her about finding the cross and how the tag was duct taped to the cross.

"Fred!" she screeched.

"How does he know where I am? How does he know I took a detour? He must be stalking me!" I babbled.

"I don't know! Maybe he is following your website!" Wendi answered. Every week, Wendi posts my location on my website so people can follow my progress. The two of us decided she would not post my whereabouts for a while, just in case Fred was stalking me.

By the end of the day, I was walking along the ocean where Highway 1 and Interstate 1 run together. I was still walking along the tracks and I was planting the crosses on property managed by the railroad officials.

I was averaging almost 10 miles a day; I was making headway. Eddy picked me up about 14 miles north of Goleta. I told him about finding the cross. He told me he would keep an eye on me and tell the other workers to do the same. I would be walking out of his jurisdiction in a couple of days so he was going to call ahead and ask the officials south of him to watch over me. He gave me his cell phone number and told me to call him if I saw any sign of Fred.

The next day I received two calls. The first was from a dear friend of mine, Cecelia, who lives in Attalla, Alabama. It was always good to her from Cecelia. I met her in 2002 when I was walking the east coast. She and I had become close over the years. We had kindred spirits and similar backgrounds. I would often spend a day or two with her in the winters when I traveled from Ohio to Florida. Cecelia was one of my prayer warriors and always had words of wisdom when I needed council. She has been a constant with financial support.

Cecelia asked me where I was walking. I told her I was about halfway between Buellton and Goleta. She asked how far I was from Santa Barbara. I told her it was about 25 miles. Excited, she shared with me that she has a niece, Teia, who is a traveling nurse and was currently working in Santa Barbara. She said she was sure Teia would love to host me and help me out. She gave me her niece's phone number and told me she would call ahead.

The second call was not so pleasant.

"Hello!" I answered.

"You must stop planting your crosses!" I was informed by someone who did not bother introducing himself.

"I am no longer planting crosses on interstate property!" I answered.

"Yes, you are! I saw one of your people plant one today near Lompoc!"

"Well, that is not possible because there is only one of me and I am walking 40 miles south of Lompoc!"

"I saw one of your people plant the cross today. You have to tell your people to quit planting crosses along the highway!" he scolded before he hung up on me.

"He must have seen someone retrieving a cross I had planted!" I thought. Tired of being harassed, I remembered a verse in the Bible, "Blessed are those who are persecuted because of righteousness" (Matthew 5:10) and I figured I was going to be blessed, as I planted another cross on railroad property!

GOD PROVIDES HELP

I called Teia and she told me that she would love to have me stay with her. She was renting a condo in Carpinteria, less than 30 miles south of where I was. I drove down to meet Teia after I finished walking and planned to begin staying with her on the following Monday night. I had secured a site at one of the state parks through Friday night and I had plans to spend the weekend with Sherrell and Eddy.

By Friday, I had walked out of the area where Eddy was working. I called one of the young men I had met at the church picnic and he drove over an hour to where I was to drive me back to my car. I was very touched by his willingness to do this. I walked to the airport just south of Santa Barbara the next day. The young man and his friend drove an hour and a half to drive me eight miles to retrieve my vehicle. I was so thankful to have the help.

I spent an enjoyable weekend with Sherrell and Eddy. Sherrell had turned 50 and Eddy threw a barbeque birthday party for her. I got to meet many of the couple's family and friends and I got to see some of the people from the church again. One of Eddy's brothers, Ben, and his wife, Alicia, lived in the Los Angeles area. They offered to give us lodging down the road and gave me their phone number.

On Monday, I parked at the airport and walked about eight miles through Santa Barbara. Teia drove out to meet me on the road and drove me back to pick up the pilot car. Teia was like an extension of Cecelia and so was the newfound friendship. It was like I had known her for years. Even though Teia was very shy and usually quiet, she had no trouble engaging in conversation with me. She said I could stay as long as I needed, so I planned to stay with her for the week. I ended up staying for almost two.

She brought lunches to me on the road, she took me sightseeing in the evenings, and she was there to pick me up for the next several days. I eventually got too far away and I had to move on. I really was sad about moving on. My times with Teia in Carpinteria are some of the most memorable times on the walk.

I got a campsite on the north side of Ventura for the last few nights that I was out there without Wendi. Judy, who had somehow heard about the walk, gave me a call and asked if I needed anything. I sure did! I needed rides back to the car for the next few nights. Judy said she and her husband, Floyd, would see to it that I made it back to my car. Even though they had to drive over an hour to do so, they were there each day to be of service. The couple invited us to attend their church in Simi Valley. I told them that I would be there the following Sunday, and I was!

It was tough being out there without Wendi, but God provided help!

"THIS WALK IS FOR THE *ALL* THE WORLD!"

Wendi, Walker T., and I were back on the road together and the walk seemed easier. We had one contact after another with provision being provided to us as we walked through the greater Los Angeles area. For the most part it was a joyful uneventful walk with weekends spent with old friends we knew in the area and new friends God had placed on our path.

Earlier, at a conference, I had met a pastor, Linda, from the San Bernardino area, who had invited me to speak at her church. Her friend Laverne had a home in Long Beach. She opened her home for us to stay there while we walked through the city. Linda has a heart for this ministry and came out to walk with me on numerous occasions. Her congregation made crosses. Linda, also a teacher, asked me to share with her class about walking the perimeter. It was a public school, so I was not at liberty to speak about my faith. She taught in a primary school. Walker T. was invited to visit and demonstrate some of his service-dog tricks.

The next week, we visited the church again, this time to hear Linda preach. During the praise and worship portion of the service, God spoke to me about the walk. This time he let me know the walk was not just for our nation but for *all* the world. I had to take this walk to all of the nations, and He would not tolerate my waiting nine years to do so. I kept feeling nudged to "speak it out!" "To speak it out now! Then! And there!" Yes, it was God's voice, I knew it well. It was the same voice I had ignored for nine years when He was calling me to do this walk! I knew the voice and I knew it well!

I began to lament. I leaned over and through sobs I shared this call on my life with Wendi. She began to weep. The two of us were a mess. I was so looking forward to making it back to South Beach, Miami, Florida, and going back to Ohio to pursue a life as a chaplain or pastor or some other type of clergy. I remembered the revelation I had back on the east coast when the policewoman had called me. I cried even harder because I knew I had surrendered my life to God. It was His to do with as He chose. I stumbled to the front of the church and announced the call from God to the best of my understanding.

Lottie, one of the congregants, a quiet person who rarely speaks and tries to act invisible, jumped up, pointed her finger in my face and said that I was not the one who would be doing the walking. I would be sharing my experience with others and they would do the walking.

People began to rise up out of their seats and speak.

"My name is Marcy and I am a faith walker!"

"My name is Rick and I am a faith walker!"

"My name is Laverne and I am a faith walker!"

"My name is Rachel and I am a faith walker!"

"My name is Donny and I am a faith walker!"

"My name is Melinda and I am a faith walker!"

One by one, each person stood up and announced their name, declaring themselves as faith walkers.

I prayed about all of this as I walked down the west coast. The more I prayed the more God made it clearer to me that I was not being called to walk the entire world. I was being called to go

303

into all of the world and share what God had done on this walk and encourage others to walk their nation for God.

I am called to encourage others in their faith walks. Everybody has a faith walk—they do not all look the same, but we each have one. I have a friend who is an obstetrician in Florida. His faith walk is, every time he delivers a baby, he holds the little child up to the heavens and prays for God to love and protect the infant. I have another friend whose faith walk is to sit with people in the last days of their lives and love them into eternity. Some are called to walk, some are called to talk, some are called to go, others are called to be still—whatever the call, if it takes faith, it is a faith walk!

HOSTILE ESCORT

There were a few places in the walk that I began to pray about and prepare for weeks, months, and sometimes years in advance. The James River Bridge, the York River Bridge, New York City, and the Mackinac Bridge are a few of those places that I have already mentioned.

Camp Pendleton, which is located on the coast north of San Diego between San Clemente and Oceanside, was one of those places. I began inquiring about regulations in that area, two years in advance. The only route through Camp Pendleton is Interstate 5. The freeway runs right through the base. I was told by the state highway patrolman, Cal-Tran officials, and officers on base that pedestrians are permitted to walk on the freeway through Camp Pendleton, but were not permitted to walk through the base.

The most recent time I talked with an official was two weeks before I arrived on foot at the base. I had been given specific instructions to walk through a campground, then follow a tow path that would come up behind a rest area where I could enter the interstate with the pilot car behind me.

My pastor friend, Linda, from the San Bernardino area came out to walk with me through the park and on the tow path. We walked and prayed for God's safety for this walk and for God to bless each cross we planted along the way.

The next day, I proceeded in great faith, out of the rest area and down Interstate 5. I got a few miles down the road and a state highway patrolwoman stopped and told me I was not allowed to walk along the interstate and I must get off immediately. I began to tell her about the many phone calls I had made and the instructions I had been given a few weeks prior. She told me that I had been misinformed and asked if there was a pilot car. I told her Wendi was parked at the rest area. She saw that I had a walkie-talkie in my hand and told me to contact the pilot car driver and tell her to come and get me now. I told her that I had connected every step and I would have to back track and walk well over 100 miles to detour around the government property. I only had about six more miles to walk to Oceanside where I would have other options besides the freeway. She told me I could try to get permission to walk through the base or get a permit from Cal-Tran, otherwise I was not to be on the freeway.

I contacted Wendi and she came and picked me up. She drove me to a base entrance where I tried to get permission to walk through the base. There was active training going on at the time and permission was denied.

I was not sure where the nearest Cal-Tran office was located so we went to the Visitor's Center in Oceanside to see if someone could assist us. The manager at the Visitor's Center was very helpful. She actually knew the Cal-Tran supervisor who had jurisdiction over that area, so she gave him a call. He said the officer must be a rookie who had not been informed that pedestrians were permitted to walk that portion of Interstate 5. She said I did not need a written permit. In fact, I did not need permission to walk that section because it was not prohibited. He told her to give me his phone number and if anyone gave me any trouble to ask them to call him. She wrote the number on a piece of paper, handed it to me, and explained to me what the official had said.

Wendi took me back to Interstate 5 where she had picked me up. I proceeded down the road. I walked a little over two and a half miles when the same patrolwoman showed up. She was irate, to say the least. She began to speak very harshly to me and asked for a written permit. I told her everything that had transpired and handed her the slip of paper with the official's phone number. She yanked the piece of paper out of my hand and contacted her supervisor on her cell phone. She informed her superior that I was back on the road and I did not have a written permit, then she handed her cell phone to me.

I said hello to the man on the phone and he began to pretty much read me my rights. Every time I tried to explain the situation he told me to be quiet. He accused me of being dishonest with his patrolwoman, telling me that no Cal-Tran person would give me permission to walk that freeway. After verbally abusing me for several minutes, he told me he only had two choices. One was to haul me in to jail. The other was to risk his patrolwoman's life by asking her to escort me to the nearest exit. He said he was concerned about how the media would handle it if he had me put in jail, so he had no other choice than to risk his patrolwoman's life. I could think of other choices, but I was glad he didn't. I kept my mouth shut and listened.

"Now, I want you to know that everything that has been said in this conversation is my word against yours. Now give the phone back to my patrolwoman."

I spent the next two hours walking along Interstate 5 with a very disgruntled patrolwoman at my tail. When we got to the end of the ramp, which would have been the exact place I would have exited the freeway had she left me alone, I walked up to the car to thank the woman for the escort. She would not look at me as she gave me verbal warning that if I ever stepped foot on a freeway in California again, I would be incarcerated for breaking the law. She drove away. I wiped my brow and gave a sigh of relief. It was not a friendly escort, but at least I did not have to do the 100-mile-plus detour.

I was interviewed by the Oceanside newspaper the next day. I did not mention my hostile encounter. I told the reporter that I appreciated the help of the local officials and left it at that. I thought that was the Christian way of leaving it. I pray God shows mercy to the two patrol people who were so adamant about making this walk difficult.

On October 10, 2009, about 15 of our west coast friends joined Wendi, Walker T., and me as we made our way along the beach to Ocean Beach where I planted cross #7,695, which was the last cross planted on the west coast before I turned, walked through the city of San Diego, and we began our trek east toward Miami, Florida.

EASTBOUND

Heading east had a new set of trials. I had walked away from the ocean and headed for mountains and deserts. It took a few days to get through the metropolitan area. Faced with a whole new kind of wilderness. I found myself walking right along the Mexican border on 94.

Anxiety rose as I scoped the so-called wall that separated the two countries. It was more like a fence and it had several breaks in it. I was very much aware that a lot of people crossed the wall to escape poverty but I was also aware that many crossed over to run from the law. I have to admit, I felt pretty vulnerable.

We were invited to visit our friends Camille and Mary in Apple Valley for the weekend. I was asked to share my testimony at a Friday night service where we met Dennis and Gloria who invited us over for dinner the following evening. Gloria provided me with an iPod to listen to as I walked through the desolate southern route of the nation.

By Sunday morning I had begun feeling ill, achy all over, feverish, with cold-like symptoms. Camille, Mary, Wendi, and I were playing a board game when I excused myself early to go to bed. We were headed back to the walk the next morning and I wanted to get as much rest as possible.

By morning, I could hardly move. Wendi had also become very ill overnight. I stumbled to the kitchen. No one was up. I wrote a note explaining we were both very ill and I hoped it would be okay if we could stay a little longer. I went back to bed and fell fast asleep. I woke up a few hours later to use the bathroom and to get some water. Mary was sitting in the living room and reported that she too, had become very ill overnight. She said it was okay for us to stay on and went back to bed. Camille got up and made a big pot of soup for the three of us. By evening, all four of us were sicker than I ever remember being, even sicker than I was in Devil's Lake.

All four of us slept all night and all day the next day. Mary called some of her friends from church to find that most of the people who were at the Friday night service had become ill. A couple of the people went to the doctor. The diagnosis was swine flu. This was not surprising—there seemed to be an epidemic of swine flu in the southwest region of our country at the time.

Wednesday morning, I awoke early for my morning prayer time. I told God that if his Son could rise from the dead in three days, I certainly could raise up from swine flu in three days! I told Wendi that I really needed to go back to the walk. She still was not feeling well either but she knew we had to move forward. Not sure where we would be that night, we hugged our very ill friends, thanked them for allowing us to stay with them and drove back toward the border.

When we got as far south as El Cajon, Wendi felt led to seek lodging for us. She went into a hotel to ask. The manager had a room that was closed for repairs. It did not have a working television and there were a couple of outlets that were shorting out. We could live with the problems and were blessed to have the room for the next couple of nights.

Wendi drove me back to the walk. My next mile was straight up a mountain. I climbed, I perspired, I climbed some more, and I perspired some more. I made it to the top of the mountain and said, "Okay, I'm done!"

Wendi drove us back to the hotel and we got some rest. I walked 10 miles the next day and another 10 miles the day after.

On October 25th, we returned to San Diego, where we walked a 5K benefit walk for challenged athletes. All three of us, me, Wendi, and Walker T. walked for the cause. Walker T. wore a little T-shirt with his number pinned to the back. As we crossed the finish line, it was announced that he was the first challenged animal ever to compete in the event. The crowd roared and applauded for the little fellow.

I was very touched by the whole event. I had never been in the presence of so many amputees. There were thousands of amputees proudly sporting all types of prosthetics. It was a day to be proud to be different. I was especially touched to see so many young challenged athletes. Sometimes it is difficult to stand out in a crowd because of a prosthetic leg. This particular day, the two-legged competitors were the ones who looked different. I thought about the kids there, and what a great day it was for them.

The Watkins drove down from Santa Clarita to see us. They offered to take Walker T. for the winter. It was hard to part with him so soon, but we knew he would be in a familiar place with people he knows and loves. So we agreed to let him go. The Watkins said they would arrange to return him to us in January when we traveled back to the walk after our Christmas break.

Caesar and Helen came down to walk with us for a while as we headed along the Mexican border. Caesar walked with me. Helen drove their car, following Wendi's lead. The two visited as Caesar and I made it up and down one hill after another. We walked along a long stretch of nothingness on 98 as we trudged toward Calexico, the place where we would plant the last cross for 2009.

I was invited to speak at a church in Westmorland on Tuesday night. Our friend Moe who lives in Salton City attends there. We would be staying with her until we left on winter break. Caesar and Helen went on ahead of us and found lodging in Westmorland. We met them at the service. Wendi and Caesar each shared special music. I gave my testimony and was invited to share with the children the next day.

Later that evening, after we were all settled in at Moe's house, Moe got a call from her pastor's wife, who said she had received a phone call from the mother of one of the little boys who had attended the service that evening. The mother said her son came home in much excitement to report that a one legged prostitute was at church that evening and she would be at their school the next day. The pastor's wife assured the mother that apparently the boy must have mistaken the word prosthesis for prostitute. We all got a chuckle out of this. The wide-eyed little boy anxiously and innocently awaited my appearance at the school the next day. He wanted to touch my prosthesis.

We planted cross #7,805 just outside of Calexico before we headed home for a holiday break. We stopped to see Bobby, Vernice, and Elizabeth on our way back to Ohio. Wendi got to have breakfast with her father on her forty-third birthday.

February 20, 2009

Message from Scotland

Hi Carol,

I read about your walk when looking for stories online. The description of your inspiration in the Siuslaw News *(thesiuslawnews.com) was just what I was looking for help to convince my parishioners that I haven't lost my mind. If you can walk round the US—we can pray in every street. Having prayer-walked my parish before now I had a dream of prayer walking every street in my town, Clydebank near Glasgow in Scotland.*

On Sunday they will hear something of your story and they won't be left with an excuse to not join in.

May God bless you in your journey and in your witness to Him.

Gregor

CROSS WALK

No need to reply

Rev Gregor

Fairfley Parish Church

Clydebank

Scotland

COMING IN—2010

ARIZONA TRIALS

After a wonderful holiday break with our families, we returned to southern California for a long year of walking. I had more than 2,600 miles to reach the goal God had set before me. God spoke to me years earlier and let me know that I was going to finish this walk on December 31, 2010. Knowing it was going to be miraculous, I set forth from just west of Calexico with great expectation and excitement to see how God was going to carry me all of those miles. I only covered 1,451 miles when I walked eleven months in 2002, and I only covered 1,511 miles in 2009, when I walked fulltime. Now I would be covering over 2,600 miles in one year.

We stayed with Moe while we finished walking the southern route in California and made our way to Yuma, Arizona.

Arizona was, by far, the most difficult state on our journey. As I walked into Yuma, on January 19th, it seemed like a force was trying to keep me from crossing the state line. I pressed forward and pushed across the state line in the biggest rainstorm I had endured on this walk. Yes, the biggest rainstorm I had ever encountered was in the desert. I planted cross #7,880 just over the state line.

The next day, both a television reporter and a newspaper reporter waded through mud to cover the story, as I walked the mud covered country roads east of Yuma. Soil had washed off the fields by the torrential downpour from the previous day, which made for a difficult and tiring walk. My shoes became weighted down as mud from the road caked on the soles.

A few weeks later, I planted cross #8,000 in Gila Bend, Arizona, on February 3rd, as I headed along Interstate 8 about a quarter of the way across the state. We drove up to Phoenix to make our home with our friend Lisa. We planned to stay with her while we walked the metropolitan district of Phoenix. I spoke at a small church in town, that had been faithful in donating to this walk for the past several years, and we enjoyed great fellowship with some of the members.

Lisa, a blind woman, walked with me on several occasions.

One morning while Lisa, Wendi, and I were traveling on I-10, a car almost ran us off the road as the driver frantically motioned for us to pull over. Wendi swerved our car onto the median between the eastbound and the on ramp traffic. The frantic driver pulled his car off the road, just right of the on ramp. He got out of his car, crossed in front of traffic, and ran up to the driver's window.

He was a young Mexican man. He said his name was Freddy in broken English and asked if we would pray for him and his wife, Laticia. He went on to share with us that he had lost his job and his wife was expecting their first child. Lisa, also Hispanic, prayed with him in Spanish. I handed him a Spanish edition of the *Upper Room Daily Devotion* book, *Dios*, the plan of salvation in

Spanish, a business card, and cross #8,036, a cross Lisa had picked up and planned to pass on.

Months later this young man called me while I was walking and I gave him Lisa's phone number so she could minister to him is Spanish.

One morning Wendi went out to the locked garage area of Lisa's apartment building to find that her bike had been stolen off the back of the Highlander. We couldn't figure out why or how this happened, but someone got into the garage, stole the bike, and apparently was able to get it out of the supposedly secured garage without being seen by the security officer who patrolled the complex. This was the first of many Arizona trials.

Each trial was followed by a blessing. The next Sunday we attended church with Lisa, and our friend Deanna. Deanna took the three of us to lunch after the service and blessed the ministry with a sizable donation to help with Wendi's travel expenses. Wendi's youngest daughter, Molly, was the female lead in her high school play, and was graduating from high school. She was to be honored at several different banquets. Wendi would be traveling home for these events and Deanna's gift was timely, to say the least.

Deanna also gave us money to purchase new lenses for my glasses. My glasses had taken a beating over the past few years and I could hardly see out of them. New lenses were greatly needed and appreciated.

Even though the bike had been stolen, we were walking away from the situation greatly blessed.

Mesa

Our next stay was in Mesa with Bobby, Vernice, and Elizabeth. We had gotten word soon after we returned to the walk in January

315

that Wendi's Grandma Miller, Bobby's mother, was diagnosed with cancer. The cancer had been surgically removed but she had experienced post-operative complications. She remained in the hospital in intensive care. Bobby was planning to drive to Ohio to see his mother. Wendi and I discussed the circumstances and concluded that Wendi should ride to Ohio with her father.

Meanwhile, we had an issue with the Highlander. It would jerk several times when we put it in reverse, like something was catching in the transmission. We called our friend Peter, who had given us the car. He is like a brother to us and the only one we knew to consult. We explained the problem to him and he insisted we take the vehicle to a garage and have it checked out. He was concerned about the miles we would be driving in the desert over the summer and did not want us to be stranded. He instructed us to take it to a shop in Mesa and he would pay for the work.

We took the vehicle to a popular transmission chain to have it checked out. After a mechanic ran a diagnostic test on the Highlander, we were informed that our transmission had serious problems and that it should be replaced. Peter gave the manager permission for work to be done and gave the info from his credit card to cover the expenses. The morning Wendi and her dad left for Ohio, we took the car to the garage and I picked up a rental.

I called my friend Lisa to see if she knew of anyone who might be able to spot me while Wendi was in Ohio. She called back with a phone number for her friend Julie, who was willing to help me out in Wendi's absence. For the next week, Julie drove the rental car and spotted me as I walked away from Mesa toward Tucson. She greatly encouraged me and she picked up crosses to give to her friends. She sent one of them to Joyce Meyer, and another one to Billye Brim, who later passed her cross on to Gloria

Copeland on national television. Joyce Meyer Ministries sent me a letter to inform me that the cross they had received had been placed in their prayer room.

Every day the manager at the transmission shop told me the car would be ready by the time the shop closed for the day. Each day I stopped walking shy of 10 miles to drive back up to Mesa, in case I needed to go to the shop to pick up the Highlander. Each day, I had to call the rental company and let them know I needed the car for another day. And each day, I was walking farther and farther away from Mesa.

Finally, after eight days, I was told that the car was ready and I could come pick it up. By then I was walking 70 miles away.

Julie went with me to pick up the pilot car. She followed me in the Highlander when I drove the rental car to return it. After returning the rental car, I got in the driver's seat of the Highlander. As soon as I backed the vehicle up, I noticed the problem had not been resolved.

The next morning I called and spoke with the manager at the transmission shop and told him that the presenting problem still existed. He informed me that the work was under warranty and told me to bring the SUV back.

This trial was getting to be quite costly, along with the expense of sending Wendi home with her father and the cost of getting her back to the walk. It was not a surprise that two women in Kansas felt led to send us a sizable donation out of the blue—enough to cover the unexpected expenses.

I called Julie to let her know about the car having to go back in the shop. Since I no longer had a rental car, Julie said we could use her car. She drove to Mesa the next morning and picked me up at Bobby and Vernice's house. We drove an hour and half before I was back to where I left off walking.

Each evening Julie drove me back to Mesa where I spent the nights with Vernice and Elizabeth. It was nice to be embraced by Wendi's family. Vernice, a nurse, worked the night shift. I had dinner with the two women before she took off for her shift at the hospital. Elizabeth and I watched television and every night and at precisely 9:00 we ate Fudgesicles. I still miss my 9:00 Fudgesicle!

After two weeks away from the walk, Wendi flew back to Phoenix while her father stayed in Ohio to be with his critically ill mother. The same day Wendi arrived back, I got a call from the transmission place and was told the problem had finally been detected and resolved and we could pick up the Highlander. Vernice drove me to the shop to get the SUV and I drove to the airport to get Wendi. When I put the car in reverse it jerked even worse than it did before.

I called Peter who had paid over $5,000 for a rebuilt transmission. Because the transmission place was a branch of a national chain, Peter suggested we take the vehicle to another one of their locations along our route. Peter began making calls to the corporate office.

Tucson

We made it to Tucson and Wendi was able to obtain housing at a Ramada Inn on the path where I was walking. The first night in town there was a rainstorm. That night someone broke the window on the driver's side of the Highlander and stole our GPS, my camera, Walker T.'s bag of personal belongings, a bag of apples, and one walkie-talkie.

We didn't notice this until the next morning. After filing a police report, Wendi placed some calls to local garages. It was Sunday and it was still raining. One place after another was closed so Wendi got recordings or answering services. Finally she got a real person. He was a Godsend. The gentleman came to the hotel, in the rain, hauled our SUV to his home, and put it in his garage to keep it out of the rain. He told us he would fix the vehicle on Monday.

We took a bus to the airport and rented a car.

Wendi took me out to walk 10 miles on Monday before we drove to pick up the SUV. The mechanic gave us a discounted rate which was covered by our insurance. Once again, we had a trial but God sent an angel!

The Thing *That Happened on Interstate 10*

As I walked along Interstate 10 in Arizona, I was either on a service road or right on the freeway. There were big signs along the interstate for hundreds of miles that advertised The Thing. Well we walked right up to one of those signs in Benson. It was posted at the actual site of The Thing. We took the little tour behind the gift shop to see what this Thing was all about. It actually looked like some kind of mummified something or other.

I walked away from the tourist attraction and headed eastbound on Interstate 10. Wendi followed along behind me with her emergency lights flashing, and a pilot light on top of the SUV. She stayed about two- or three-tenths of mile behind me as I walked along the inside edge of the shoulder.

The next day, we were about 18 miles east of Benson, when Wendi called me on the walkie-talkie to ask me to walk back to the car. I got to the car to find she had run over a bungee cord and it was lodged in the tire. I tried to tug the cord loose but it wouldn't budge. I called AAA. We were towed to a repair shop in Wilcox where the bungee cord was removed and the tire was repaired. The repairman told us he had never, in over 20 years of working on

319

cars, seen a bungee cord lodged in a tire like that. This was THE THING that we experienced in Arizona.

DANIEL, OUR BROTHER

Our trials in Arizona came to an end as we walked in to San Simon. We met a couple who were overseers of a little church in the small community. They allowed us to stay in the basement of the church while we finished walking the state.

Sunday morning we met Pastor Clyde and his wife, Glenda, and I was invited to share my testimony. They had a young man, Daniel, staying with them. He was a youth pastor walking from the West Coast to Nashville to plant a church. Daniel also shared his vision and mission with the congregation.

Pastor Clyde and Glenda invited us to stay at their 10,000-acre ranch which was about 20 miles east in New Mexico. By Tuesday we were walking in New Mexico and their home became our home for the rest of the week. By the end of our stay, we got to experience what real ranching was all about. One evening we rode in the back of a pickup truck with Glenda, as Clyde drove the vehicle about a mile on the bumpy desert terrain in search of a calf that had become separated from his mother.

Later in the week, as we pressed forward toward Las Cruces, Daniel walked with me. We agreed to team up and walk together while Wendi went home to Ohio to see Molly perform the leading role in her high school play.

I took Wendi to the Airport in El Paso after a 10-mile walk on Thursday. Daniel continued to walk so he would be ahead of me and we could do a leap-frog kind of spotting the next day.

Daniel said he and his team would cover our lodging for the time Wendi was home. He told me his team had been working on it all day. By the time I picked him up it was after 7:00 p.m., and I was tired from walking 10 miles in the heat and driving to El Paso and back. I asked Daniel if lodging had been arranged for the night.

"Not yet!" he answered.

I drove around Las Cruces aimlessly while he made calls. An hour and half later, I pulled up to a Best Western and sat there for 20 minutes while Daniel talked on the phone. Finally out of exhaustion and desperation, I went inside to see about a room. I explained the situation to the manager and I was able to get a room for a discounted rate.

When I got back to the vehicle with the keys, Daniel was upset with me because he believed his team would have arranged for us to stay there. By the time we got to our room it was going on 10:00 p.m. I had nothing to say.

I could see that Daniel and I were not getting off to a good start on this partnership, so the next morning we knelt down and prayed for the unity of our hearts.

Because Daniel and I were both walking and Daniel said that he too was connecting every step, he dropped me off where I had left off and he drove the SUV eight miles ahead where he had left off the day before. When I made it to the vehicle, I drove to pick him up. The next day, he dropped me off again, where I left off, and we repeated the routine from the day before. This was how we worked it out as a team.

Daniel's team did not come through for us with lodging. A friend of mine from Colorado arranged for a place for us for the second night. On the third night, Daniel introduced me to couch surfing. This is an online service only available to members. You can join by going to couchsurfing.com and filling out an application. You can both offer services and give services. To offer services, you give a profile and let members know where and when you are available to offer lodging to travelers. To receive service, you let your needs be known online and wait for a response or check listings in the area you are interested in surfing and inquire about lodging.

The first place we stayed was with Mary who was about 10 years my junior and 10 years Daniel's senior. She was pleasant and very accommodating. She showed me to the guest room and Daniel was suited in a spare room with an air mattress.

Our first evening there, Daniel fixed a spaghetti dinner, Mary prepared a salad, and I provided strawberry shortcake for dessert. We stayed there a couple of nights and we enjoyed visiting with Mary and her friends and neighbors in the evenings.

The second place we stayed was with three college boys who were renting a house together. They offered us two sofas in their living room. We each put our sleeping bag on a sofa and crashed for the night. The guys fixed burritos for us for breakfast. I bought veggies, buns, and Italian sausage, and the guys grilled them for us for dinner. Again, it was a great experience!

Daniel made arrangements for us to stay in the basement of a Calvary Chapel Church for the weekend.

We walked into the city on Saturday. From Las Cruces, I headed south toward El Paso and Daniel headed northeast toward Amarillo. Monday morning I dropped Daniel off to walk and I drove to El Paso to get Wendi from the airport.

She spotted me for about eight miles then I rode with her about 20 miles north to check on Daniel. He was still walking and had no place to stay so we brought him back to Las Cruces where the three of us stayed with the college boys again.

Wendi was able to secure lodging for us at a hotel in Las Cruces, for the next two nights, so each day we dropped Daniel off, then Wendi drove me south so I could get 10 miles in before we would go find Daniel.

Finally, we had to move our home base to El Paso and Daniel was on his own.

We would check on him now and then. A week later we heard that he had made it to Tennessee. We were not sure how he moved that fast. Eventually we got word that he hitch-hiked over 500 miles. I guess his mission was not about the walking—it was about his pilgrimage.

Meanwhile, I was still walking and walking and walking, in the heat of May in the desert, ten miles a day, six days a week.

NOTHING SMALL IN TEXAS

We took the SUV to a transmission place in El Paso, the same company that had worked on it in Mesa. We contacted Peter and asked him to talk with the manager. Peter gave the manager a credit card number and told him to check the vehicle. Peter also said he would appreciate it if the original problem would be fixed and reminded the man that the transmission was under warranty. The manager at this shop said he had to have the go-ahead from the corporate office before he could do the work.

Meanwhile our pilot car was tied up in a garage again. This was costing us lots of money and time. We got a rental car so I could keep walking.

◊ ◊ ◊

The day I walked through El Paso, two local TV reporters and a newspaper reporter tracked me down for interviews. It was hot. Wendi was running errands and looking for a place for us to stay for the night. When I was finishing the sixth mile, she contacted me and told me she was on the way to check on me. I informed her that I was very hot and needed to get out of the sun. I asked her to pick up lunch for us at What a Burger, where we had been given coupons for free burgers. By the time she got to me, I was overheated. I sat down in the car, drank some cold soda, and passed out. I had experienced a heat stroke. It was the second heat stroke I had in seven years. I also had one in 2004 in Maine.

I had only walked seven miles but I had to quit for the day.

I was back to walking the next day and was able to cover a full 10 miles. Each day I walked 10 miles farther away from El Paso along the southern border of our country.

One evening, a week or so later, we drove into Sierra Blanca for dinner after searching our GPS for local restaurants. Only two were listed and we drove to the first only to find that it had gone out of business, so we drove to the second listing, Michael's. When the GPS announced that we had arrived at Michael's, we looked around and the only restaurant in sight was Curly's. We walked into Curly's and were told that Michael's was down the road, but we concluded we were right where we were supposed to be.

After visiting with some of the locals, we were sure that it was no mistake that we had been led to Curly's that evening. This was a little hole-in-the-wall kind of place, where the owner was also the waitress and cook. We ordered our dinner and were amazed at the size of the portions. I remembered being told years earlier, "There is nothing small in Texas!" Not only were the potions large but delicious too!

Wendi left in search of lodging possibilities for the next week, while I stayed back and visited with the folks in the restaurant.

Maui, one of the locals, took on the position of the local public-relations person. He went out into the community to let the folks know who we were, why we were in town, what we were doing, and that we would be staying there for the next week. He returned to the restaurant with a financial blessing for us from one of the judges in town. Apparently, this small town of less than 1,000 was the county seat.

Wendi was able to secure lodging at two different motels in town and Denise, a woman we had met at Curly's, opened her home for the rest of the week.

Within a few days I was walking through the town. I was greeted by a small welcoming committee which included a newspaper reporter. The crowd congregated in front of Curly's and clapped, hooted, and hollered as I hobbled toward the restaurant.

We visited a local church on Sunday morning and Denise arranged for me to speak at the town park that evening.

It was not long before we were miles and miles away from Sierra Blanca, making our way along Interstate 10 in the blazing desert heat, when I received a call from Peter and Helen. They informed me that someone had tried to use Peter's credit card in El Paso. The person tried to get over $3,000. When that did not go through, there was an attempt for a little over $2,000. With that being rejected, there was a third attempt, that time for around $1,000. Peter had filed a complaint with the Better Business Bureau and was trying to get through to the corporate office. He suggested I keep walking for the time being.

By the time Peter was able to talk with someone at the corporate office, I was walking over 70 miles from El Paso, just east of Van Horn. Peter was advised by the representative from corporate to take the car to one of their transmission shops in Austin.

We drove an hour and half back to El Paso, picked up the SUV, and dropped off the rental car. Wendi had plans to fly out of

Austin a week later. She would be in Ohio for a total of six weeks to see her oldest daughter perform at the community theater and attend Molly's honors banquets and graduation. I would be flying to Ohio for the last six days of her time home and we had plans to fly back together. So we decided to drive the SUV, as it was, until then.

The next week I took Wendi to the airport in Austin before I delivered the Highlander to the suggested transmission shop. I had a coupon for a hotel room for $29 per night. I got a cab to the hotel and got a room for a week. I had no one to spot me at that time so I planned to stay put while the car was in the garage. Meanwhile, I made calls in an attempt to find someone to spot me while Wendi was away.

The motel actually turned out to be rather nice for the price. It was surrounded by business offices and some upscale hotels. The rooms were large and clean. There was a coin laundry on the second floor. And it was about three blocks from a convenience store. Even though I did not have a car, I was within walking distance from everything I needed.

A week passed. I called the transmission place to find that vehicle had not yet been worked on. The manager said he was waiting for the corporate office to give the go-ahead. I still had not found someone to spot me on the walk so I stayed put in the hotel.

The following Monday, I sat down at my laptop which I had placed on the small table in the motel room and I began writing this book. The story just flowed from my fingers. I am not a writer, not any more than I am a walker, so this was as miraculous as the walk. During the week I wrote most of the first five chapters and an outline for the rest of the book. God was showing me that He was going to be the Author. All I had to do was pray, turn it over to Him, then sit down and write.

Going into the third week, I still had no word on the Highlander and still did not have a spotter so I stayed, prayed, and wrote. Toward the end of the week I heard from my pastor friend, Linda, from the west coast. She told me, Lottie, a woman in her church felt called to help me out on the walk. She was going to put her on a bus in San Bernardino the following Wednesday evening and she would be arriving in El Paso on Thursday about 4:30 p.m. She was scheduled to be with me for eleven days, which included two Sundays, but I would have her for a total of nine walking days.

"Praise be to God!" was all I could say.

I was getting cabin fever, to say the least, and I was wondering how I was going to make it back to South Beach by December 31st. I knew I would make it! I had faith that I heard God's voice, but I was wondering *how?* The year would be more than half over by the time I flew back from my Ohio visit, and I would not yet have walked even 1,000 of the 2,600 miles! I could not wait to see this miraculous endeavor come to fruition!

The next Wednesday, with the Highlander still in the transmission shop, yet to be worked on, I had a rental car delivered to my room and I loaded it up for a long trip to El Paso to pick up Lottie at the bus station.

No, nothing is small in Texas! We experienced *big* car problems, long delays, and lengthy trips. But the blessings were *big* too!

LOTTIE

On my way to El Paso on Thursday morning, I stopped in Balmorhea, which was the next town I walked into after I picked Lottie up at the bus station. I saw there were cars at the Methodist church so I stopped in to see if anyone knew of a place we could stay over the next few days. The pastor of the church informed me that the mayor of the small town owned a hotel on the main drag and he was sure she would be glad to accommodate me and Lottie.

I stopped in and talked with the mayor and she gave me the keys to a room on the second floor, showed me a work room in the building where there was a refrigerator and microwave that were made available for our use. She said we could have the room through Monday morning. There was one stipulation: no pets! Walker T. was not permitted to stay in the room.

I got to the bus station in El Paso about 4:30, soon after Lottie arrived. After I picked her up, I had some difficulty getting back on Interstate 10. I didn't see the on ramp and actually ended up driving the wrong direction on a one-way road. Once I finally found the ramp it was smooth sailing to Balmorhea, where we spent the night.

I walked 10 miles on Thursday and 10 miles on Saturday. It was getting really hot by noon, so we attempted to beat the heat by getting off to an earlier start each morning. I walked as fast as I could so I could get out of the sun by one o'clock each day. Then we had to find a shady place to hang out with Walker T. until dark. We took him to the park so he could run and get some exercise. After sunset, I left the little guy in the car until morning. He didn't seem to like the situation, but he was a good sport about it.

Sunday we attended the Methodist church. We tucked Walker T. in his kennel, in a shaded area in the bushes in the front of the building. The pastor announced our presence in the service and asked if there was anyone present who could house us for the next week. After church a young couple came to us and offered to host us for the next several days. They had two young children who loved playing with Walker T.

Sometimes I was not able to get 10 miles in before the intense heat of the early afternoon, so I would go back out in the evenings to finish the miles. Monday evening as I was walking on a service road along Interstate 10, I got a phone call from Wendi. Her Grandma Miller passed away while Wendi was attending an honors banquet for Molly. My heart hurt for Wendi and her family and I felt sad I wasn't able to be there. I planted the next cross in memory of Jean Miller, mother, grandmother, great grandmother, aunt, great aunt, and friend. She would be greatly missed.

Lottie, Walker T., and I spent that night and the next few nights with our little host family, a beautiful Hispanic woman, her husband, her two little girls, and her grandmother. It was so nice to be embraced by this family since both Lottie and I were homesick. They cooked for us and we cooked for them. We attended church with them the following Sunday.

By the end of the week we were walking in Fort Stockton. I tried to get a good deal on a room and was about ready to give up when I walked into the Motel 6. The manager gave us a discounted rate so that is where our home base was for the rest of Lottie's time on the walk.

On Sunday we attended the Fort Stockton Christian Center for the worship service. The pastor let me share my testimony and the church took up a love-offering to help cover our lodging expenses. I also had a need for someone to take care of Walker T. while I flew home for six days. The pastor announced this need also. As I was about to get in the Highlander after the service, a young mother pulled up beside me. She said that as she was leaving the church, both of her girls began to cry because they were sure they were the ones who should offer to keep Walker T.

I was able to cover 90 miles while Lottie was spotting me and I so greatly appreciated her willingness to spend hours and hours in the extreme heat of the desert in late May of 2010. Her service to this walk was vital for me making it back to South Beach, Miami, by December 31st.

I finally got word that the SUV was repaired just a few days before I was to leave to go to Ohio. I asked the manager at the shop if I could leave the vehicle until I returned from my trip. After all, the Highlander had already been in his shop for five weeks! What was another week?

I walked to about 15 miles east of Fort Stockton before I took Lottie to Pecos to catch a bus back to San Bernardino.

I drove the rental car to the airport in Austin and caught a plane to Ohio. It was a short and busy six days home. The first of the six days was spent traveling to the airport, flying home, and traveling from the Cleveland airport to my daughter's house. I spent a couple of days in Cleveland with my daughter, son-in-law, and granddaughter before I drove to Canton, where I got a few things in order. I attended Molly's graduation with Wendi then I traveled to visit my friend Jerry who lives about an hour southeast of Canton.

For the past several years, Jerry has been a constant in my life. Not only did she bless the walk financially, she kept us in prayer and would call every week or so to check in with us. Her home was a place of refuge for me. Jerry and I spent hours sharing about God, listening to worship music, and chilling out.

I got back to Canton in time to have a quick visit with Wendi's family before it was time to head back to the walk. Wendi and I flew back to Austin from Cleveland. We picked up the SUV to find that our car problem had finally been corrected. We spent the night in a hotel and the next morning we drove to the Motel 6 in Fort Stockton which would be our home base for the next few days. I had gotten to know the manager when Lottie and I stayed there before I left to go to Ohio. She offered the same discounted rate and gave us an additional complimentary night by forfeiting her own night's stay.

We picked up Walker T. Now our team was complete. Only 1,700 miles to go!

THE HILLY REGION

It was great to be back on the walk. I felt supernatural strength, walking as many as 17 miles a day in the hot sun as we worked our way across the Big Bend desert region. We passed through the small towns of Bakersfield, Sheffield, Ozona, and Sonora. The people were wonderful and accommodating. Wendi had no problem finding lodging and donations came just enough to provide sufficient food and water and to keep gas in the pilot car.

By the end of June, we had made it to Junction, Texas, which was about halfway across the state. The landscape had become greener and I experienced a more strenuous walk as we were leaving the desert and entering the hilly region of the state.

As I walked through the town we met one friendly person after another. A newspaper reporter caught up with me to take a picture. The mayor, Larry, came out to talk with us and began to shower us with blessings. He asked us what our needs were and began to meet every one of them. He took one of our brochures, handed it to his secretary, and asked her to make copies for us. He invited us to attend a women's conference that was taking place at the Methodist church that weekend, which happened to be his home church. He looked down at Walker T., in all of his fur, and asked if he could take the little guy to get a summer haircut.

Wendi and I were excited to attend the women's conference. It started on a Friday with a dinner. I walked 12 miles before we rushed back to our motel room, cleaned up, and headed to the conference.

On Saturday, we got up before dawn and I walked 10 miles before 11:30 so we could attend the luncheon and all of the afternoon sessions. We enjoyed the fellowship with all of the wonderful women who were there from all over the county.

Sunday we attended the church and Mayor Larry and his wife invited us to their home to have lunch with them and their daughter Melanie. The family blessed us financially and promised they would pray for us as we continued our journey across the country.

Instead of walking into San Antonio, we crossed north of the city on Highway 46. On July 7th, 2010, I planted cross #9,000 at the Gathering Place in Springbranch, Texas.

By July 9th, my fifty-sixth birthday, we had made it to just west of New Braunfels. I walked in a downpour all day. This was so refreshing after so many days in the sun with high humidity. Thank God for rain!

As we were walking toward the city, I walked into a convenience store to use the restroom. I was greeted by Miki, one of the most pleasant attendants I have ever met. She had seen an article about the walk in the local paper and was happy to meet us. She invited us to stay in her home for the weekend.

Miki and her husband, Rocky, were so accommodating. It was nice to be with a family again. We were able to wash our dirty laundry and catch up with computer work. We were treated to wonderful home-cooked meals, one of which was a surprise birthday meal with pecan pie for dessert.

Our friend, Madeleine, who we had met in Bandon, Oregon, sent $50 to spend on a birthday celebration. I was hoping to go up to San Marco and go on a tube ride behind the state college, but Rocky gave us some good tips on tubing the Guadalupe River right near their home at a horseshoe in the river.

By Monday, July 12th, the weather had cleared up. I walked 10 miles in the sun before Wendi and I headed to the horseshoe in the Guadalupe River for an afternoon of tubing. It was the first time for Wendi. I had been one other time. We really did not know what to do. We rented two tubes, I put on an old, beat-up prosthesis, and we headed for the river.

Wendi got in the water first and held my hand as I walked in the water over slippery rocks and got on to my tube. Off we went. We noticed that other people in groups had their tubes roped together. We just tried to stay together. This worked for about 10 minutes.

Then I got swept away in a fast current and was separated from Wendi. The water swiftly carried me down the river and through some rapids. I grabbed a branch and began looking for Wendi. She was quite a ways behind me. I watched her get swept up onto a flat bed of rocks. She got off of her tube and carried it across the bed and threw her body across the tube, belly down.

I yelled, "Nooo!" as I watched her approach the rapids that had swept me downstream. I grabbed her hand as she floated past me. We held on to each other's tube as we came to the end of the horseshoe.

"Whew! That was stressful!" I exclaimed as we climbed the bank.

"Yeah, let's do it again! This time with a rope!" she replied.

And we did. The second time was much more enjoyable.

The tube rental was only $10 each so we had enough left over for some delicious German cuisine. Even though I missed my family, this was the ninth birthday I had spent on this journey. I had a wonderful fifty-sixth birthday celebration. Actually the best gift was when my four-year-old granddaughter called me on July 9th and sang *Happy Birthday.*

By Wednesday I was walking along Interstate 10. I got a phone call from Lisa, who lived west of New Braunfels. She had just found one of the crosses at the end of her driveway. She invited us to a Bible study at her home and said that she and her husband, Jim, would love to have us stay with them. I thanked Lisa for the invitation but I told her I had planted the cross over a week ago and we were already 60 miles away. I told her Wendi was trying to secure lodging near our route.

That evening Wendi told me she was not able to find lodging for the night. She had been to over a dozen places and made several calls which resulted in places for Thursday and Friday, but we did not have a place to go that night.

I told Wendi about the call I had received earlier. We both knew I needed to call Lisa back and ask her if it was too late to take her up on the invitation. She was glad to keep the offer open and couldn't wait to meet us.

We had a blessed time with the couple and I believe we made a connection for life. They were out of town that weekend but offered their home to us in the event we had no other place to stay. It turned out that we were not able to secure lodging for Saturday and Sunday and took them up on the offer. The two returned home Sunday evening and the four of us had a wonderful time of fellowship.

CALIFORNIA CONNECTIONS

Connection for a Foot

I felt God's hand of protection and provision as I entered the greater metropolitan area of Houston. I had covered over 1,500 miles on my prosthetic foot and it was completely worn out. I was also in great need of liners. I had great faith that God had it covered.

Wendi contacted Freedom Innovations in Irvine, California, from where I had two previous feet donated. She talked with Meghan who was glad to be able to help us once again. She instructed Wendi to contact a prosthesis provider in Houston and see if there was someone willing to attach the foot. She asked Wendi to provide her with an address once the appointment was made.

By then, I had less than 1,500 miles to go so the donation would get me through to the end.

Meanwhile, Wendi had been conversing with Ruth, a sister of our friends Judy and Darletta who lived in California. Ruth, who lives in an eastern suburb of Houston, was anxiously waiting for us to stay with her and her husband, Jerry.

Ruth has a grandson who happens to be an amputee. She gave Wendi the name of his prosthesis provider, Houston Amputee and Prosthetic Clinic. Wendi made a call to find the business had several locations. She asked for the number to the office closest to where were staying. She was referred to Leslie, the spokesperson for Limbs of Love, a nonprofit organization associated with the Houston clinic.

Leslie was excited about the mission and became a temporary PR person for Faith Walk Ministries. She made an appointment with a prosthetist to attach the new foot. She also ordered liners that were presented to me at no cost. She arranged for the local television station to cover the fitting at the clinic and another cameraman to meet me on the road. She also arranged for a newspaper reporter to catch up with us on the walk.

I was having trouble deciding which route to take as I was mapping my way through the eastside of Houston. I spent a lot of time praying over maps and asking God to direct my steps. I still did not have the answer when I approached the intersection where I needed to make a decision.

The TV reporter contacted Wendi and asked her which way I would be walking. I still wasn't sure so I decided I would take the safer route. She passed this on to the reporter who was on his way to interview me.

When I got to the intersection, I could see that it was a much safer walk with a wide shoulder if I made my intended turn. The road ahead had no shoulder. I would have to walk in rough uneven ground with very high weeds. It looked very dark and spooky. I was pleased with my decision. I turned to cross the street, but immediately God let me know I had to continue forward. I called Wendi on the walkie-talkie and told her I was going forward and asked her to inform the reporter about the change.

About a half mile down the road, the cameraman arrived. After the interview, Wendi told me that a woman approached her and inquired about our walk and asked why I would take that particular route. Wendi explained to her that I had planned to make a turn but God let me know I had to head down that road instead. The woman shared that the area needed prayer. She added that I had just walked by a business owned by a man who had murdered her brother. The stranger thanked us for including this path in our prayer walk.

Connection for a Home

We stayed with Ruth and Jerry for the next 11 days. Both of them were good cooks. Jerry blessed us with homemade beef and vegetable soup the night we arrived, and made spaghetti for us later in the week. Ruth made a big pot of fresh green beans with ham, potatoes, and onions. Good country cookin'!

Jerry asked us to attend his monthly American Legion meeting where I was given an opportunity to give a short testimony. It was an honor to speak to this group and to thank them for their service to our nation.

One evening, Jerry took us on a little sightseeing tour and the couple took us to Galveston on Sunday afternoon. I took my shoes off at the car so I could stick my foot in the Gulf of Mexico. The sidewalk was so hot I had to walk fast to keep from burning my foot. The sand was almost as hot, and the water was as warm as bath water.

It was hard to move on after such a long stay and making such a connection.

We had yet another California connection. Donna Watkins from Santa Clarita, California, happened to have a brother, Dr. Gary Mennie, who lived near Beaumont. He and his wife, Pam, their two sons, Donavan and Dominic, and Pam's mom, Charlene, were our host family for a long four-day weekend as we were wrapping up our walk across Texas.

We felt like we already knew this family before we even met them because we had become such good friends with the Watkins. The Mennies embraced us like family, with love and hospitality. They took us to a country club for dinner and on an outing to an alligator refuge where we tasted 'gator for the first time. We enjoyed cooling off in the family's pool after a hot day on the road. We went to church with them on Sunday and I shared my testimony. Afterward, the family took us out for brunch. Later that evening they showed us pictures of a recent mission trip they had been on.

We have kept in touch with the Mennies and they continued to help us in various ways, including a connection in Louisiana that led to a connection in Florida. As with the Watkins, I believe the Mennies are friends for life.

CALL TO VIDOR

I have to start this chapter with, "God is so good!" because this is something Pastor Sheila loves to hear me say!

As I was walking east of Vidor, Texas, Wendi was up ahead of me in the car. When I got to the car, I noticed a sign right next to the vehicle that read SERENITY OAKS RETREAT CENTER with a phone number. I pointed to the sign and told Wendi I believed that would be our next home. I had no idea we were actually right in front of the center—I thought it was just a sign advertising the center.

Wendi was right on it. She had confirmation and was making the call. Pastor Sheila answered the phone and did not hesitate to offer lodging. She told us to stop in the office after I finished walking. I had nine more miles to go; we were just getting started for the day.

About 1:00 that afternoon, we walked into the office and met Pastor Sheila in person. She and her husband, Pastor Jerry, are the founders of the small retreat. She escorted us to a trailer nestled in the woods right next to the chapel and gave us a key for the door. She told us we were welcome to stay as long as we liked.

The trailer was used for retreats and there was a stack of cots in the back room. Pastor Sheila had set up two of them for Wendi and me. It was great to have a kitchen and to have some quiet time away from people. Please do not get me wrong. We absolutely love people, especially our host families, but once in a while, it felt good to retreat after a day's walk. God knows this and He provided these places for us every now and again.

I became instant friends with the pastors. I shared with them some of the visions God had given me for a retreat center. They smiled and listened then Sheila showed me a drawing of my vision. God had given them the same vision. I felt God tugging at my heart to connect with the two and to make plans to go back to the retreat after the walk was completed and to help them build and move forward in the vision.

I told them that I was offered a position at the Amputee and Prosthetic Center when the walk was over. One of their branches happened to be in Beaumont which is only 30 minutes from the retreat center. I had been praying about this opportunity. I went on to share that I saw a real need for a place for differently-abled people, especially newly amputated individuals to retreat and be encouraged. She felt confirmation and we have a dream of this becoming a reality at Serenity Oaks Retreat Center. I could see pieces of a divine puzzle coming together.

Pastor Sheila invited Wendi and me to attend a Warrior Chicks Women's Conference at the Four Square Church in Vidor. We really needed the spiritual food, and it was enriching and good! I was invited to come back and speak at the center the following Sunday.

MAKING HISTORY

One of our California connections was still reaping a harvest in Louisiana. Donna Watkins' sister-in-law, Pam (the wife of Donna's brother Gary), connected us with her cousin Terry Wood in De-Quincy, Louisiana. Terry, her husband Mike, and their daughter, Tyler, were our first host family after we crossed the state line.

Right after Terry received a call from Pam she made nachos and burritos and brought lunch to us on the road. She introduced herself and told us she and her family were looking forward to our stay. Again, it was like an extension of the family we had already embraced along our journey and we felt right at home with the Wood family.

The Wood's followed us to church on Sunday when I went back to speak in Vidor. And to our surprise, the Mennie family came to the service. We were so glad to see them; it was like a family reunion. It meant the world to us that they came to hear me speak.

We got to experience some home-cooked Louisiana Cajun food. Miss Terry fixed us about every specialty dish known to that part of our country. The U.P. of Michigan may have the hardest working people, Minnesota may have the most lakes and biggest mosquitoes on the perimeter, Montana may have the highest mountains, and Texas may have the biggest of everything, but Louisiana has Cajun food—my favorite eats! And our eating frenzy had just begun!

Mike enjoyed hearing about the walk and he and Terry were both concerned that I may be stopped at the Huey P. Long Bridge in Louisiana. It is a bridge that prohibits bicycles and pedestrians. Both Wendi and I began to pray about the situation. We posted our concerns on my blog. We asked for people to pray that God would make a way for me to connect every step through Louisiana. I had met a lot of bicyclists and walkers who were crossing the southern portion of the country and every one of them had to take a ride over that bridge. To my knowledge no one had ever been given permission to walk the bridge, which prevented anyone from ever connecting every step when crossing the southern portion of the country.

I called the Louisiana State Highway Patrol office in Baton Rouge and explained to the patrolman that I had walked over 9,000 miles, connecting every step around the perimeter and I asked for a police escort over the bridge. I was told that they had never given a police escort to a pedestrian over that bridge but he would see what he could do.

All I could do was keep walking in that direction and trust God.

I was walking an average of 14 miles a day as I pressed on. By September 1st, we were halfway across the state. Terry Wood called the mayor of Opelousas and told him we would be walking through the city. She gave Wendi the mayor's phone number. When Wendi called the mayor's office she was told that arrangements had been made for us to stay at the Bellevue Baptist Church. The groundskeeper, Steve, met us at the building and helped us move in for a weeklong stay. We followed him to an old Sunday school room that was available. He set up cots and even put a TV in the room.

Each day after I walked, we enjoyed visiting with Steve, a gentleman who was going through some tough times. We ministered to him and he ministered to us. One evening Steve fixed us a home-cooked meal of catfish, etouffee, and salad. He topped the meal off with sweet potato pie. I couldn't believe how delicious it was!

As we shared with Steve about the walk and about my call to Vidor after the walk, he showed great interest in helping with the retreat center. We exchanged phone numbers and I hope to see him again in Vidor.

I continued to have contact with the Highway Patrol in Baton Rouge but was not getting an answer. I actually had Wendi drive me to another bridge to see if it could be an alternative. It was posted nonpedestrian.

341

On September 9th at about 3:00 in the afternoon, Wendi got a phone call from a Highway Patrolman and was asked when I would actually need an escort. She informed the patrolman that I would be willing to walk the bridge anytime of the day. He asked when I would actually be at the bridge. She said 10:30 the next morning. He said he and three other patrolmen would be there.

The next day, history was made. I was given a police escort over the Huey P. Long Bridge on East 190 in Baton Rouge. I was informed that I was the first person to ever be given permission to cross the Mississippi River in Louisiana on bicycle or foot for any purpose or cause. It happened to be the seventy-fifth anniversary of Huey P. Long's death. Try to tell me, God isn't large and in charge!

I walked off the bridge having completed 9,473 miles around the perimeter of the United States and, because of that escort, I had connected every step. I had less than 1,000 miles to go and about three and a half months to complete the task. There was a news reporter present to document the event.

After the escort, I got in the car and asked Wendi to take me to a donut shop so I could get some donuts to take to the State Highway Patrol office. She set the GPS to find the closest donut shop and off we went. The GPS seemed to be taking us in a roundabout way.

I walked into the shop and told the cashier that I wanted to purchase donuts for the patrolmen in appreciation for their giving me the escort. She informed me that she was about to close and they were going to have to throw the donuts out so she gave me seven boxes of donuts to take to the patrolmen and she did not charge for them. What a blessing!

When I got back in the car I noticed the GPS was set for a pedestrian, instead of an automobile. That is why it took us

20 minutes to go eight miles, which just happened to put us at the donut shop when they were about to close—which resulted in the blessing of seven dozen donuts to be given to the patrolmen. It was a God thing! We could not have afforded seven dozen donuts.

I balanced the boxes of donuts as I walked into the State Highway Patrol Office. Wendi wanted to take a picture of me delivering the donuts but none of the officers wanted to be in the photo.

"Don't you want the donuts?" I asked.

"Oh yeah, we want the donuts! We just don't want to be in a picture *with* the donuts!" One of the patrolmen answered, as the rest his coworkers chuckled.

HOUSE CHURCH

A few days later, on Friday, I was walking on Hollywood Street in Baton Rouge, and a kind Christian brother, Ken Ward, stopped along the road to check on me. He told us he had seen the story about the bridge walk in the newspaper. He informed me that I was walking in a very dangerous neighborhood and asked if he could pray for us. I was thrilled to have this dear, sweet man praying for us.

Ken asked if we needed anything. I told him we needed lodging and he said he would work on that and get back to us. Later he called and invited us to stay the weekend with him and his wife, Carolyn.

The next morning Mia, from *Central Speaks Newspaper*, met with us as we were heading away from Baton Rouge. She took some pictures and invited us to stop by her house to freshen up before the interview. Afterward, she and her husband, Dave, took us out to eat and she invited me to speak to the youth at the Methodist church on Sunday evening.

After the interview we went back to the Wards. The youngest two of the couple's six daughters came over for a visit. Both girls, Bekah and Jordan, were very strong in their walk with God and a blessing to be around.

On Sunday, we went to House Church with the Wards. This seemed like the closest thing to the early church I had encountered thus far. It turned out the pastor of a fairly large fellowship that was actually growing quite rapidly went out on a limb as the Lord led him, and announced he was called to take a different approach to leading the church. He told the congregation he wanted to do away with all of the impersonal hoopla and focus more on personal growth than filling a building. He divided the church into small groups—House Churches.

He asked some who were more mature in their faith to be overseers of the small groups and to lead them in worship, Word, and fellowship. He believed this would give the church a more family-like setting where intimate relationships would develop and the members would be able to hold each other to a greater degree of accountability. The small groups would all gather together corporately every couple of months. This dear pastor lost some members but there has been tremendous spiritual growth in those who stayed.

Each person brought a covered dish to share. We feasted. We worshiped. We were fed. And we grew. I desire more of this kind of fellowship. This is what I believe church is…this is what the Bible says the church is…the people, not the building!

CAMP VICTOR

By the middle of September we crossed the state line into Mississippi, the thirtieth state on the prayer walk around the nation.

We had a wonderful week on the walk. The weather was pleasant and the scenery beautiful. We covered 63 miles in Mississippi. I walked over 50 of the miles right along the Gulf of Mexico. The beach was beautiful in spite of all that was being said about the oil spill. There were tents set up along the beach, for the BP workers and other volunteers, to provide shelter from the sun when they took breaks from combing the white sand for globs of oil residue. By then, they were finding very little debris from the spill.

We were being hosted by Camp Victor in Ocean Springs, Mississippi. It is a warehouse that has been turned into a place of lodging, dining, and recreation for volunteers. The building was sectioned off into a large dining area with a kitchen, a community area with several couches, a TV, a ping pong table, and tables and chairs to play games and work on puzzles. There were several restrooms, shower rooms, and laundry facilities. There were large dormitories, as well as double rooms, for sleeping quarters. Wendi and I were each blessed with a private room.

Volunteers from all over the world have stayed there while working on projects such as clean up after the BP oil spill, rebuilding after Hurricane Katrina, and other catastrophic disasters.

The walls both inside and out were covered with wholesome graffiti painted by volunteers from various churches, colleges, universities, high schools, Red Cross, Habitat for Humanity, Americorp, and various other volunteer groups. T-shirts, work pants, shoes, work boots, and now one of my prosthetic feet hang from the ceilings throughout the building. Faith Walk Ministries left our mark with one of Wendi's t-shirts, Walker T.'s paw print, and Wendi's artwork.

There were several groups from Americorp residing at Camp Victor while we were there. We enjoyed visiting with the folks in the evenings and hearing about their experiences as they travel from place to place providing disaster relief.

This place was right up my alley. I love to see people living together and working together in one accord for the good of the people, the church! This is how it all began, "All the believers were united in heart and mind. And all the believers met together in one place and they shared everything they had....all the while praising God and enjoying the good will of all the people. And each day the Lord added to their fellowship those who were being saved" (Acts 2:44, 47 NLT).

Walker T. was made king for the week. He hopped from one volunteer to another with each patting his head, scratching his back, or inviting him up to sit on a lap. I think Camp Victor is one of Walker T.'s top 10 places to stay!

EXHAUSTED IN ALABAMA

It took less than two weeks to walk across the southern shores of Mississippi and we were in Alabama before we knew it. I believe we only had about 70 miles to make it to Florida, once we crossed the Mississippi/Alabama state line.

I was getting so excited. I had only been home six days that year, when I flew home at the end of May. I missed my daughter and granddaughter and I had been praying God would make a way for me to be home for Christmas. With just hundreds of miles between me and the goal, it was looking promising.

Once in Alabama, it only took three days to get through Mobile. I had studied the map and it looked like it was going to be a straight shot on Highway 90 all the way to the Florida state line. Boy, was I surprised when I came to a tunnel at the east side of the city. I rerouted north on Telegraph Road to cross a bridge at Alt 90 in Prichard.

The bridge was not that difficult to cross but when I came down off the ramp I was in a marshy area. About a tenth of a mile after crossing the bridge, there was no shoulder and swamp grass about eight inches high along the side of the road. About 10 steps into the grass I came across a dead alligator and immediately after that I stepped over a dead water moccasin. I screamed as I looked ahead and saw that soon I would be walking in grass up to my knees. With heavy traffic, I could not step onto the road. I had to stay in the grass. This was a test. And I almost did not pass it.

"I can't do this!" I called to Wendi over the walkie-talkie.

"You have to, Carol, now come on!" she replied.

"I can't. I just stepped over a dead alligator and a dead water moccasin and now the grass is so high I can't even see what I'm about to step on!" I cried.

"They're dead!" she shouted. "They can't hurt you!"

"I'll drive through the grass and make a path for you! Now come on, you have to do this!" she attempted to encourage.

I sobbed as I not so courageously followed the tire tracks of the Highlander. I did not like this one bit. I repeated Philippians 4:13 over and over again as I treaded through knee-high swamp grass: "I can do all things through Christ, who strengthens me."

A mile or so down the way, the road was wider with a little shoulder, so I did not have to be right *in* the swamp grass any longer. Praise God!

Wendi had secured a campsite at a state park just north of Mobile. By the time we got to the campground, I was both physically and emotionally exhausted. We quickly set up the tent just as it was getting dark.

We were about to go out to find a place to eat, when a young man, Josh, walked up to our vehicle and was excited to announce he had made a decision to follow God and told us his mother was a Sunday school teacher. He had noticed the magnet on our car and was happy that we were Christians. He pointed out to us that the SUV's exhaust system had a serious leak. While examining the situation, he also discovered that we had a bubble in one of our tires. We shared with Josh that we had been praying for God to send a mechanic to help us because several things were going wrong with the car including a short in one of our headlights.

"You have one!" he said. He smiled and told us that his dad was an auto mechanic and would be back to the campground soon. Josh planned to help his dad change the tire, fix the headlight, and take care of the exhaust leak.

We went on to get something to eat. By the time we returned to the site, the camp was quiet and we went to bed for the night hoping we would meet Josh's parents the next day.

In the morning, we met Josh's parents Dave and Darlene. Dave examined the vehicle and told us it needed a catalytic converter. He told us he would check with his boss about ordering the part for us at cost. Dave put our spare tire on the Highlander. It was apparent that we needed four new tires.

Dave's boss was willing to order the part for us and Dave said he would let us know when the part was in. Darlene invited us to attend church with them on Sunday at Saint Francis Methodist Church at Taylor Park in Mobile. We agreed to meet them there.

We were getting close to the Florida state line and Wendi had arranged for us to move to Lazy Acres Campground which was closer to where I was walking. In the meantime, we kept in touch with Dave and Darlene.

On Sunday morning, we drove back to Mobile for church. I shared at the adult Sunday school class then with the children, during the ten o'clock hour. Afterward, I was asked to share for the church service at 11:00. This was a very small congregation but they gave abundantly to help this ministry.

I made phone calls to many of the people who told us to call if we needed anything at all. I shared about our needing new tires, a front headlight, and a catalytic converter. The estimated expense was over $1,500.

The exhaust leak was getting worse every day. Wendi and I were both experiencing headaches and we were concerned about how Walker T. was doing.

We walked into Florida on a Tuesday. Just before we crossed the state line, we met Tim, the Orkin man. He was having lunch at the Country Store. Wendi told him about the walk as they were engaging in some friendly conversation in her quest to find a post office. Tim was all about serving the Lord and after buying our lunch, he asked if there was anything we needed. Wendi told him we needed lodging and he happened to have a couple of complimentary rooms he had not used. Tim arranged for us to stay at the Comfort Inn in Pensacola for the next two nights.

People began to come through with donations for repairs. We were able to find four tires that were barely used for $150. Dave fixed the short in our headlight and we continued to trust for the exhaust problem to be resolved.

In pursuit of a campsite, Wendi met Jackie, who was in her yard near a campground. She told Wendi that her husband was in charge while the owner was away.

"I wouldn't stay there!" she said, pointing in the direction of the campground.

Jackie and her husband, Freddy, had a camper trailer set up on a concrete slab in a fenced area. They no longer used it since their house had been built. She smiled and pointed to the camper and said we could stay there as long as we needed.

Jackie brought seafood chowder to us one day and had us over for a fish fry on another occasion. We exchanged life stories and became instant friends. The couple had five dogs and just loved Walker T. We made arrangements for them to watch Walker T. when we traveled to Ohio for Christmas. It was exciting to know we would see these new friends, again.

One morning Wendi dropped me off at the side of the road after a bathroom break, when our friends Jean and Jeff from the Upper Peninsula of Michigan pulled off the road to surprise us. They drove over 1,300 miles to spend some time with us on the walk. I enjoyed their company and especially enjoyed walking with Jean.

I am still blown away with the fact they even found us. Like I mentioned, I had just been driven to a McDonald's for a restroom break. If they had come 10 seconds earlier, they wouldn't have seen me. It was God's perfect timing, perfect positioning, and perfect plan!

Wendi had heard from Dave. The part had come in for the exhaust. She had to travel back to Mobile the next day to get the car repaired, which meant she would have to leave me for several hours or I would lose a day of walking. God had a better plan—he sent these angel friends over 1,300 miles to help us keep on keepin' on with the walk. Jeff spotted us and Jean walked with me while Wendi made the trip to Mobile.

It took Wendi all day to make the trip. It was about a two-hour drive to Mobile. She arrived at the dealer to find they had ordered the wrong part. So she returned the part and headed back in hopes of finding a mechanic down the road. By the time she got to the tunnel, traffic was bumper to bumper and it took over an hour to get through.

God was in the tunnel! Remember, the exhaust leak was so bad we were getting headaches while driving in normal traffic.

Wendi kept praying the whole time she was in the tunnel as she felt herself begin to drift off to sleep several times, "God, please keep me awake! God, please keep me awake! God, please keep me awake!" He did! He kept Wendi awake and Walker T. too.

Jean walked with me for the next few days. The couple took us out for dinner a couple of times and helped with the many expenses for car repairs. They stayed with a friend of theirs who lived near Pensacola while we camped in Freddy and Jackie's trailer.

Boo Boos

We moved right along the Florida panhandle, staying in one campground after another.

One evening Wendi and I walked to the shower rooms and, at this particular campground, there was not a shower room with several shower stalls. Instead, there were individual units each entering from the outdoors. I went in one room and Wendi went in a unit a few doors down. I sat on a bench in the shower and placed my prosthetic leg outside the stall.

After I had finished bathing, I dried off and carefully attempted to transfer from the wet bench to a dry bench outside the stall. My real foot slipped and I fell hard hitting my head on the concrete shower wall. I hit so hard my glasses fell off my face and slid across the floor. My real leg hit my prosthesis and knocked it out of reach. Not sure if I had broken any bones and a bit shook up, I sat for a few minutes and examined my arms and legs. My arms were banged up especially my right forearm and elbow. My tailbone was hurting, in fact, I was hurting all over.

I crawled across the room and got my glasses and my prosthetic leg then crawled back to the other side and climbed up on the dry bench where I literally put myself together.

I posted the incident on Facebook and several people suggested I take it easy the next couple of days. I knew the freak accident was resistance and I was not happy about that, so I got up the next morning and pressed forward to cover 10 miles—in spite of the aches and pains and the devil who was trying to trip me up!

Pressing forward, it was not long after that incident when I found myself surrounded by six medium-sized dogs, each had its lips curled back with its teeth showing and each was viciously growling at me. Not knowing what to do, I stood paralyzed and spoke softly to the canines. The owner came out of her mobile home and called to the dogs but to no avail. I told her that I was concerned the dogs may bite me. She assured me that I did the right thing by standing still and talking to them. The brood viciously stared at me and growled more and more as the owner approached. She was able to herd the pack away from me but before she got them to the house they all returned to once again encircled me. Before the woman could get to me again, one of the dogs bit the back of my leg.

I showed the owner the wound, she just shrugged her shoulders, and herded the pack to the mobile home.

When Wendi caught up with me and saw the injury, she thought we should contact the authorities and maybe I should be checked out at the emergency room. I sensed it was just a distraction. I did not want to make any waves in that rural community, so I chose to pray over the wound and keep walking.

I have to admit my faith was a little shaken. I had trusted God would keep me safe on this trip. I trusted He would not let me get bit by a wolf, mountain lion, or poisonous snake or spider. I was a little shaky in my faith but I chose to move forth in faith rather than fear. After all, I only had minor wounds from the dog bite.

I remembered back to a time in Montana when I looked over in the woods and saw a wolf staring back at me. The wolf stalked me for a while but soon went on his way. I remembered another time when a mountain lion walked in the woods beside me but after a while took off ahead and crossed the road right in front of me. God showed me time and time again that He was keeping me safe. And He did send a very large Native American angel with a message that *I would finish this walk.*

I remembered Warren and pressed forward in great faith that I would finish this walk in one piece. Well, at least, in no more than two pieces.

Not long after that, I accidentally slammed my hand in the car door which badly bruised my fingers, causing me to eventually lose two finger nails.

For a while there, I was wondering if Satan was having a discussion with God about me. Yes, I imagined the devil standing up to God with a statement like, "Consider Carol, she is moving forward with this prayer walk because you are blessing her along the way and providing her with safety and meeting all of her needs. Take your hedge of protection off her and see how faithful she will be!" This thought humbled me. I thanked God that He believed in me enough that He could remove his hedge of protection and trust I would persevere.

ANGELS ON THE ROAD

The weather was beautiful, in the mid-seventies the day we walked through Florida's capital, Tallahassee. The people were friendly. Several folks stopped to check on us and we enjoyed the southern hospitality.

One Friday morning I began praising God that our car was finally running well and I was making strides in the walk—less than 500 miles to go! It looked like we were going to be able to take a break and go home for Christmas.

When I walked up to the pilot car, Wendi informed me that the brakes were rubbing. I had noticed a sound in the back of the car but I thought maybe something had gotten stuck in the brakes from all of the off-road driving Wendi was required to do to spot me on the road.

I examined the tires and it was obvious there was something wrong. At first I said, "Can't wait to see how God works this one out!" Then I became discouraged as I got sucked into the enemy's lies about having to cancel our trip home because of more car expenses and down time, but I soon concluded that God was still *large* and in charge!

We headed toward Perry, Florida, to the first auto garage we came upon. It was a place that had just opened. The owners had not yet put their sign out. But Wendi noticed the garage doors were open and pulled onto the lot with great expectation. Mike, the owner wasted no time diagnosing the problem. He told us that he had 23 years of experience working on cars and had never seen a situation like ours. We had front and rear brakes replaced within the past several months but for some reason, our left rear brake pad somehow disappeared—it was just gone!

Mike made a few phone calls then reported he had both good news and bad news. The good news was he could get the parts. The bad news was that it would not be before 4:30. *Another day down!* I thought. He must have read my mind because he told me his wife would take me back so I could continue to walk. Wendi planned to ride her bike and join me out on the walk for a while, then ride back to the garage to pick up the Highlander before returning to get me.

His wife Melanie shared with me, as she drove me back to where I had left off, that her 11-year-old son, Bradley was born with a stump and was a right-leg amputee. She said he was quite the little football player once he convinced his coach to let him play on the team. We discussed the possibility of Bradley walking with me for a stretch.

After I was dropped off, I walked toward the garage while Wendi rode her bike 14 miles to catch up with me. She carried Walker T. in the basket. After we met, she and T. joined me for three miles, then with only two more miles to walk before it got dark, I instructed Wendi to ride back to the garage, wait for the repair, then come pick me up. On the way back to the garage, she got a flat tire and had to get off and push the bike with Walker T. in the basket—he had exerted himself to his limit and needed a break.

She phoned to tell me about the flat. I told her to hold up at a nearby rest area and I would phone for a ride. I called the garage and Mike said he would come and get us. As I was getting off the phone, a pickup truck with two men in it pulled up and the driver asked if I needed a ride. I told them about the walk, the situation, and told them that there was help on the way. The two men, Mark and his son, Drew, said they would be happy to help out. I called Mike and caught him before he left the shop, to let him know that we had a ride.

I got into the truck and as we headed back toward Perry, we found Wendi still pushing her bike toward the rest area. The two kind gentlemen stopped the truck. As Drew loaded the bike in the back, Mark motioned for Wendi and the dog to get in the back seat. We rode with these two angels to the garage where another angel had just completed replacing the brake pad at no charge. Mark gave us a sizable donation and told us where to go have dinner—on him!

I asked Mike and Melanie if they believed in angels! They said they did! I told them that I do too, and I believed that on that day we were surrounded by them.

The next day, Saturday, when I made it close to where the garage was located, Wendi drove ahead and brought Mike and Melanie's son, Bradley, back to walk with me. The two of us walked to the garage and planted cross #9,996 by a sign Mike and Melanie had just placed in front of their business.

The next day, I planted cross #10,000 in Perry, Florida. The day after that, we attended church with Mark's wife, and Drew and his girlfriend. Afterward, Mark and his family took us out for lunch. I told them that I planted cross #10,000, two doors down from the restaurant.

The next day a newspaper reporter came out to take a picture of Mark holding the 10,000th cross, which Mark claimed. He placed that cross in his small museum right next to Spider Man's costume. Yes, the real thing! The super hero I serve is the only true Super Hero, so I was glad to see the cross in front of the costume.

We were blessed with a campsite right on the Gulf of Mexico the following weekend. On Monday morning we decided to have breakfast at a local restaurant as we headed back to where I would be walking that day. We somehow got off the path and ended up at a lovely restaurant.

We told the waitress about the walk and asked for directions to get back on our path. She told us she was sad she did not know about the walk because she would have loved to put us up in one of their cottages. I thanked her and told her that we were trusting God to be able to go home for Christmas, and if we did go home, we would need lodging on our way back. She smiled, put the date in her book, and said she would see us on December 27th. I thanked her and told her Wendi would call and confirm the date if we did indeed get to go home.

GIVING THANKS

God may have lifted our hedge of protection for a short while, but He guarded our lives and continued to bless us with the means to make it through every trial. I believe if we stay faithful to our call even through the trials and tribulation, God will always bless us for our efforts.

After all, when you have a child who does their best even when things get tough, you can't seem to do enough for that child, to show them how much you appreciate their obedience and good behavior. God loves us even more than we are capable of loving our children. He wants to bless us even more than we are able to bless them. As our faith increases so do our blessings. God has proven this to me over and over and over again on this walk of faith.

God continued to shower us with one blessing after another as we walked the west coast of Florida. He was preparing a way for us to have a safe trip home for Christmas and for all of our needs to be met for that trip. God promises to give us the desires of our hearts if we delight in him (Psalm 37:4).

On Thanksgiving Day in 2010, we got up early and headed out to Tampa where I had left off walking the previous day. I walked through Tampa. The only people I saw that day were the city's homeless and less fortunate citizens. They all seemed to be in good spirits. Several of them informed me of the different feedings that were taking place throughout the city. A couple of them asked if I had a place to eat dinner that day.

I talked with folks along the way. And I thanked God for the day, for my health, for my family, for Wendi and her family, for my friends, and for all of the many blessings God bestows upon us each day. I missed my family, but I could not think of one thing I would rather do that Thanksgiving morning than be true to the call on my life.

I got 7 miles in before noon and we headed to our host family in Saint Petersburg. Our host, Ginny Do, happened to be the sister of Terry Wood, who is the cousin of Pamela Mennie, the wife of Dr. Mennie, the brother of Donna Watkins back in Santa Clarita, California—another God connection!

Ginny and her husband John fixed us a feast for the holiday meal.

Ginny and John showered us with blessings while we were their guests. Ginny made arrangements for me to speak at a church that meets in a barbershop. This was similar to the House Church experience back in Louisiana.

God is in the bar, God is in the campground, God is at the card table, God is in the house, and God is in the barbershop. Yes, God is at the ballgame, God is at the funeral, God is in the storm, and God is in the valley as well as on the mountain top. God is anywhere you seek Him and He is waiting for you to knock *so He can open the door*, to seek *so He can show you the way*, and to ask *so He can give you what you need* (Luke 11:9).

COMING IN

Preparation for a Trip Home

We were showered with one blessing after another as we headed down the Gulf Coast. Wendi spent hours on the phone arranging housing for the rest of the year and she was excited to share with me that we had been given lodging for December 28th through the 30th at a nice hotel in Miami. Another hotel gave us a generous discounted rate on a room for December 31st and January 1st. Every hotel and motel in Miami was booked for the holidays, yet God made a way for us to have five nights of luxurious lodging.

We were scheduled to go on a celebration cruise with nine friends leaving out of Miami on January 2nd on the *Norwegian Pearl*. The cruise line upgraded our cabins and gave me a VIP status which would benefit the entire group.

We were given lodging in one hotel after another as we headed down the coast. I was making great strides in the walk. The car was running better than it ever had and I felt confident it would be mechanically sound to make a trip to Ohio and back. It had become evident that we were going to be able to go home for Christmas.

The blessings continued. As Wendi was about to make all of the arrangements for our lodging for the trip home, she got an email from the manager of a hotel in Tallahassee. He apologized for not being able to help us when we walked through the city and wanted to know if there was any way he could help us now. Wendi and I shook our heads in amazement of the timing of this email. Tallahassee is about a day's drive from the Everglades. Wendi made arrangements for this to be our first provision for lodging for our trip home.

Deb, my advance person from 2002, lives in Fort Lauderdale and goes home for Christmas every year. She planned to ride home with us and help with the expenses of the trip. We had been given gift cards for gas and restaurants, enough to cover the rest.

Host Family

We love all of our host families and many of them are life-long friends. I am sure the last host family we stayed with on this trip is one of those families.

Wendi had received a call from David who was the friend of a woman we met in Apple Valley. She had told him about the walk and that we would be taking the Tamiami Trail through the Everglades. He told Wendi to call him when we got close to Marco Island and he and the church there would see to it we were provided for during the completion of the walk.

When we were about a two-hour drive from the island, Wendi called David and he made arrangements with his pastor for me to speak at a Wednesday night service. We were warmly received by the congregation and Kathy, a member of the church, talked with us after the service, about making her home our home base as we completed the walk.

God opened this door for us on Marco Island, one of the most beautiful places on the face of the earth, with one of the most beautiful, humble families I had ever met—Rich, Kathy, Kaitlyn, and Joshua. Rich worked at an Indian reservation in the Everglades and Kathy home-schooled Kaitlyn and Joshua.

We already had housing arrangements for the week, so we made plans to move in with Rich and Kathy the following Monday. By then I was walking close to Naples, minutes from Marco Island.

By the time I reached Naples, I began seeing signs for Miami. My adrenaline was flowing. I was *coming in*! I was on the home stretch!

Within a few miles, I began to walk with swamp on one side of the road and a canal on the other. The first time I came upon a live alligator, I turned around to motion Wendi to drive forward in the pilot car. She was nowhere in sight. I tried to reach her on the walkie-talkie and she apparently couldn't hear me. I was concerned about how the alligator was going to react to my presence, and desperate for the pilot car as a place to escape from the wildlife. I crossed the road and prayed I would not see another 'gator. This situation was as my 5-year-old granddaughter would say "not comfy!"

Wendi had pulled off the road to take a picture. When she finally got to me, I was pretty shook up and I babbled about seeing the alligator and her not being anywhere in sight.

"Don't you ever leave me out of sight while I am walking in this swamp!" I ordered. "And there is no room for argument—anyone would agree with me on this!" I continued.

She chuckled and said, "Okay, I won't let you out of my sight! I promise!" Later we both laughed at my stern orders while I was in that shook-up state.

Not knowing much about the wildlife in the Everglades, I continued to experience some anxiety about walking in the swampy jungle. Kathy, who had lived in that part of the country for many years, volunteered to escort me through the worst stretch. I was delighted!

Early each morning, Kathy prepared lunches for Wendi and me and for herself, Kaitlyn, and Joshua. With lessons assigned for the day, we all piled into the Highlander and headed for the wilderness.

Alligators sunned themselves on the banks of the canal, some of them over 12-feet-long. I counted over 100. Most of the time they would plop in the canal and disappear as they sank in the water but there were a couple occasions when very large 'gators would jump in the water and swim toward us. Kathy informed me that this was very out of character for them, as she guided me to the other side of the road. I was glad to have Kathy with me.

We carried walking sticks to ward off snakes. I had seen several dead water moccasins as I was walking into the Everglades.

One day the children joined us and Kathy and the kids walked up to a live cottonmouth. I was walking behind the family and was spared the encounter.

Wendi stayed close by in the pilot car and Walker T. was left back at the house. We did not want to take any chances of the little fellow being a snack for a hungry 'gator.

In the evenings we enjoyed dinners with the family and a couple of nights we watched movies with the kids. I usually fell asleep before the movie was over.

One night Rich and Kathy made us a seafood buffet. I had been to some seafood buffets on this walk, but never a homemade seafood buffet. This happened to be the best ever. We had stone crab, shrimp, and fish that Rich caught from his dock. Their home was right on the water.

Christmas with Family

After we got within 40 (39.9 to be exact) miles of South Beach, Miami, Florida, we began our trip to Ohio to celebrate Christmas with our families.

We drove to Fort Lauderdale to get Deb before we headed to Tallahassee to enjoy our miraculous complimentary room. The next morning we left Walker T. with Jackie and Freddy and continued driving north to Louisville, Kentucky, where we got an economy room for the night.

On the third day of our trip, December 18th, we dropped Deb off at her sister's home in Chillicothe, Ohio, then we drove to Columbus where I picked up my granddaughter. We had found a great deal on a Drury Inn in a coupon book and I gave my five-year-old granddaughter a mini-vacation for her fifth birthday. On the 20th we attended a Christmas party for Wendi's mom's side of the family in Canton.

The 21st and 22nd I visited my friend Jerry in Amsterdam. The 23rd we attended a Christmas party on Wendi's dad's side of the family in Canton. We drove to Columbus to spend Christmas eve with my daughter, son-in-law, and granddaughter. We picked up Deb on Christmas day and drove until late evening. We spent the night in Louisville, Kentucky with our friends, Sherry and Tina. On the 26th, we stayed with our friend, Cecelia, in Attalla, Alabama. On the 27th we picked up Walker T. from the Florida panhandle and drove down to our complimentary room on the gulf. The next morning we drove Deb to her apartment in Fort Lauderdale before returning to the walk.

It was a very hectic and rushed trip to Ohio and back, but it was such a blessing to see our families. I believe I needed to have that time with my daughter and granddaughter because I had really missed them and my missing them would have clouded the experience of victoriously *coming in* to Miami.

Coming In

I had developed a severe chest cold and was running a fever, so the walk was difficult, to say the least. Having traveled on the 28th, I didn't return to the walk until almost dusk and only got 3.9 miles in before I had to quit, which left 36 miles to cover over the next three days.

My friend Jerry, who had walked so many miles with me on the east coast, joined me the next morning as I headed toward the goal. It was great to have Jerry by my side again. He was with me when I started this journey so it seemed fitting to have him with me for the end.

On the last day of the walk, Jerry and I covered eight miles together early in the day. We had plans to meet a group of people that evening to finish the walk I had started nine years earlier.

As we were heading across the Venetian Way, we had to cross a series of bridges. On one of those bridges, we saw a very large lizard (about four feet long) get hit by a car. The creature raised its head and stared at us. It was struck over and over again before it stopped thrashing and lay lifeless on the road. If the reptile had not been killed, our paths would have crossed. Jerry and I looked at each other and shook our heads. We felt this was symbolic of the completion of the mission. The *serpent* was defeated and no longer has authority over this country.

We walked silently as we headed for the location where we would stop until later that evening. I reflected on how my life had changed on this journey. I thought about the person I was nine years earlier as I took the first steps up the coast. I hardly even recognized that person anymore. So much had happened to me, around me, and within me on this pilgrimage.

I didn't realize it at the time, but when I began this journey I was much more judgmental, controlling, self-righteous, demanding, insensitive, and egotistical than I was walking back into Miami. I was still a work in progress but much more pliable.

God had done a healing on me in so many ways. I had lost around 40 pounds and my health had tremendously improved, as well as my stamina. When I began the walk, I was on three different blood pressure medications, a statin, and a diuretic, just to manage my hypertension. I was now only taking one blood pressure medication. At the beginning, it took eight to twelve hours and all the energy I could muster to walk 10 miles, with nothing left at the end of the day. Now a 10-mile day was like a stroll in the park to me and I could accomplish it easily in five or six hours, with plenty of energy left to do whatever I wanted for the rest of the day. So, physically, God had healed me in many ways and was continuing to heal me daily!

I thought I had worked through many issues from my past and had gotten rid of baggage from failed relationships. But I realized, as I walked toward the goal, I had barely begun to shed that stuff when I began this walk heading north out of Miami. I felt 100 pounds lighter, emotionally, as I walked back into the city.

On this journey, I learned what prejudice was about from walking beside the afflicted. I learned what judgment was about by being judged and seeing hatred displayed by people holding signs that said GOD HATES GAYS and GOD HATES BABY KILLERS condemning them to hell—all of this supposedly done in the name of our loving God.

I was surprised when I was asked if I was one of *those Christians* who hate people. I had to take a real good look at my heart and bow before God in repentance for anything I had done that may cause someone to think such a thing about me or my walk.

I had to pray long and hard about how to word the rest of this story. I am trusting God's Holy Spirit to direct my fingers as I type this.

One day when I was walking, I thought about failed relationships with men and women, friends and partners, family and colleagues. I was struggling with thoughts about poor choices I had made. I thought about the loneliness I felt when I sought out those relationships and the loneliness I felt in them. I thought about how I was struggling with relationships on many levels when I began this pilgrimage. I praised God, in the awareness that I, a single woman, hundreds of miles away from family and most of my friends, spending hours alone on the side of the road, was not lonely anymore. I was never alone—I found that ultimate companionship with my Creator, my Savior, and my Comforter.

God let me know that day that man had damaged me but He had healed me. God has called me to be the church (along with every other believer) and the church is the bride of Christ. I am content and complete in that alone. This is my call, this is the courtship that fills my soul, and this is the matrimony I most joyfully await, Jesus the bridegroom, coming for His bride, the church. I am very excited to know one day I will be a part of the bride of the King of Kings. I hope to see you there!

I have friends in all walks of life. I have friends in various levels of growth and maturity in their walks and I have friends with different titles and some have been given labels. I feel no need to judge anyone in their personal walk or choices. My personal belief, after this nine-year journey, is that each person has their own walk before God and each will stand before Him one day in judgment, to be held accountable for what they have been convicted.

Each of our walks with God is unique. One person may feel convicted when they drink alcohol; another may have total peace about having a glass of wine. One may feel convicted about hoarding treasures in the attic; another may have no struggle with that at all. Each of us has our own journey. What may be a stumbling block for one may actually be an opportunity for another. Some eat meat; others are vegetarians. Some play cards and games with dice; others feel convicted at a card table.

The Apostle Paul speaks about these things in the book of Romans. He speaks against judgment in chapter 2, verse 1: "But you are just as bad, and you have no excuse! When you say they are wicked and should be punished, you are condemning yourself, for you do these very same things" (NLT).

In Romans chapter 14, verse 1, Paul addresses the dangers of criticism: "Accept Christians who are weak in faith, and don't argue with them about what they think is right or wrong" (NLT).

God convicts each of us differently as He sees fit. I believe we should all let go and let God!

It was the Holy Spirit's voice who spoke truth and life into me. Not one word of hate, judgment, or ridicule has ever drawn me closer to God; in fact, there was a time in my life when hate, judgment, and ridicule caused me to stumble in my faith, walk away from the church, and try to hide from God.

I struggled with my identity most of my life. I was given labels, I labeled myself and others. God has called me to a new place with Him. He has stripped me of labels, titles, and the sense of false security that comes from identifying with this group or that.

No! I am not one of those Christians who hate people! I love all people and the God I serve loves all people! God represents love! God is love! "For God loved the world so much that he gave his one and only Son, so that *everyone* who believes in Him will not perish but have eternal life. God sent His Son into the world not to judge the world, but to save the world through Him. There is no judgment against anyone who believes in Him. But anyone who does not believe in Him has already been judged for not believing in God's one and only Son," Jesus Christ, as recorded by John in chapter 3, verses 16–18, in the New Living Translation.

◊ ◊ ◊

For me, it was a whole lot easier coming out, as this or that or something else, than it was to *come in*, to the person God has called me to be.

I encourage all to be true to themselves and to God. If you love God and are living a life that is pleasing to Him, who is anyone to judge? If you put any relationship, activity, or possession before God, there may be a problem—but if God is first in your life, He will direct your path and let you know what is right or wrong in your individual walk with Him.

On December 31, 2010, I was joined by 21 people from five different states and from various walks of life, to walk with me to South Point Park as I completed the prayer walk around the United States—a nine-year journey of walking through 32 states and covering 10,466 miles. Everyone who walked those last few miles had one thing in common. We all loved God and we all had a heart to serve Him to the best of our abilities. We were each on our own spiritual journey, yet walked in one accord to complete this journey which I believe was not mine, but a mission for God's people to reclaim this land for Him, and for the Godly principles on which it was founded.

We sang *God Bless America* as we walked toward the park. The wind picked up as we headed toward the spot where I would cross the path I started in 2002. We pressed forward and lifted our arms in praise as we fought against the wind and stepped onto the edge of the beach. We crossed the finish line with cross #10,466, which represents the number of miles walked around the nation.

I wept as we held hands and prayed and sang *Silent Night*. We sang *Amazing Grace* as we walked away from the park.

The next day, New Year's Day, 2011, at three o'clock in the afternoon, I met with a group that included several folks who were physically challenged, including my dad and my God-given, spiritual mother, Naomi Harvey. I had saved this last mile for those who were not physically able to make the city walk the night before. This was the miracle mile—the victory march. Fifteen people were present as we traveled through the park on a walkway that could easily accommodate the wheelchairs, walkers, and scooters. We made our way to the eddy next to the pier, where I knelt down and etched #10,467 and the symbol of the cross in the sand, right where I had planted the very first cross exactly 9 years before.

Again it was a group of friends and family from all walks of life from several different states gathering in one accord to celebrate this historical and miraculous event. The United States of America had been walked and prayed for. I felt extremely humbled and honored to be chosen by God to connect every step around this nation.

I walked away knowing that I was no longer *that kid, trouble, the mistake.* With my head bowed humbly before God, I walked away from there knowing I was His child—in 1954 He created me in my mother's womb for His pleasure, and He does not make mistakes!

God has simply called me to be His child, His joy, and to continually walk in the *State of Grace.*

End of story!

September 15, 2010

Cross Mile #9,462

Hi,

Just writing to let u know we found your cross when we had a flat. Read ur message and wanted to let you know that the cross will be passed forward. It was found Sunday, September 12th, west of Louisiana. Thanx for ur dedication and the efforts u do to inspire others. Have a blessed day, and may God keep u blessed in ur walk in prayer.

Michelle

Five days later:

September 20, 2010

Cross #9,462

A friend of mine just handed me this cross. It really touched me. As I sit here and write this email my life has fallen apart and I don't know how to fix it. I am afraid to live or try any more... but then I look at this and what u are doing and I think u are amazing. I am gonna hold on to this for a while because it gives me hope and I wake up and don't want to die today... thank you and God Bless.

Angela

Bayou Sorrel, Louisiana

December 6, 2010

To Whom It May Concern:

I'm a little late in sending this letter, but I have been wide open for the last 8 months at work. One of my four grandsons and I were out riding our 4-wheeler one Saturday a month ago when he said look PaPa, there's a cross in the ditch. I stopped and picked it up and began to read the note. I was taken back that someone with such a disability would have the courage and perseverance to attempt such an adventure. The most rewarding part to my soul was the fact that this individual is making a stand for our Lord and Savior and is spreading the gospel and God's love in such a powerful way. It also gave me the opportunity to share with my grandson (who is a Christian)

370

that someone has such courage to walk the perimeter of our great country and share the gospel.

May God Bless you and may you and your family have a blessed Christmas.

Merry Christmas!

In the Name of Our Lord & Savior,

Dennis

WHAT NEXT?

O N JANUARY 2ND, WE SET sail with nine friends to enjoy a celebration on the *Norwegian Pearl* on a western Caribbean cruise. The group included myself and Wendi; Cherie and Sandy from San Leandro, California; Mary from Apple Valley, California; Moe and Delores from Salton City, California; Naomi from Washington; Vickie from Oregon; Deb from Fort Lauderdale, Florida; and Wendi's mother Debbie from Ohio.

I was exhausted at the beginning of the cruise but by the middle of the week, I was soaking up the sun, enjoying the exotic islands and chilling out with my friends. It was exciting to see Wendi having so much time and fun with her mother, who she had not seen much over the previous eight years.

After the cruise we spent about a week in Florida with Wendi's mom then we headed to Georgia where our dear friends, Suzanne, her mother Dorothy (who we have come to know as Sugadotti), who live in Smyrna, and our friend Cecelia from Attalla, Alabama, arranged for us to have a getaway up at Big Canoe Resort. They own a time-share and chose to share their time with Wendi and me for retreat and relaxation before heading back to Ohio. This was most definitely the best gift we could have received. We were exhausted from the walk and the celebration and the thought of "what next?" was overwhelming.

There we were five women living together in a three bedroom condo for five days and four nights. The five of us gathered together in one accord with all things in common. We broke bread, we prayed, we sang, we laughed, we rested, and we all shared in the chores which made them seem effortless. I have never experienced such harmony in my life.

Suzanne, a massage therapist, gave massages to everyone; I, having studied reflexology, was blessed to do a foot washing and foot massage for each of my four friends. Wendi braided Suzanne and Sugadotti's hair. Cecelia was not able to join us until the last night, her arrival made the group complete— "hoo-hoo" and the Yahweh Sisterhood was formed—just spend a couple minutes with Sugadotti and you will understand what the "hoo-hoo" is all about! A beautiful 90-year-old southern belle with enough love to go around, Sugadotti will "hoo-hoo" you to dinner, "hoo-hoo" a hello or a good-bye, and "hoo-hoo" everything in between!

After this mountain-top experience, Wendi and I returned to Canton to see what God had next for us.

My work was cut out for me with the timely completion of this book.

Now with the walk walked and the book written—I'm going to Disney World!

Seriously, I am going to Disney World with my daughter, son-in-law, and granddaughter.

After some time with Mickey, Minnie, Donald, Cinderella, Sleeping Beauty, Belle and the Beast, it is back to reality in traveling the country with speaking engagements through October of this year. Then I plan to travel to Vidor, Texas—to help Pastors Sheila and Jerry build Serenity Oaks Retreat Center.

Wendi is making up for lost time with her family and helping her oldest daughter with wedding plans. She is also my publicist—that should keep her busy for awhile.

Walker T. misses being on the road but he doesn't seem to mind the life of a couch potato. Look for *his* book to be published soon.

THANK YOU

Wendi Love Miller, for your obedience to the call on your life and for being a constant, by my side for seven and a half years. Your companionship and covenant with me and God is a blessing beyond words. I will always be grateful to you and I will always love you, my dear sweet sister, friend, companion, my Aaron, my Ruth, my Jonathan, and my answer to prayer for a partner in ministry.

Walker T., for your loyal companionship, for walking over 3,000 miles with me, for comforting the challenged, hurt, and lonely people along the way!

Jessica Sims Fant, Rose Moore, Suzanne Doyle, Koz St. Christopher, and Joni Webster for proofing portions of the manuscript.

This was not my walk. It was God's walk; I am just a vessel. This walk would not have taken place, if it were not for the hundreds of people who helped along the way.

To all of you who were there when we started the walk at South Beach, Miami, Florida.

Selah Ministries, Terry Ousley, The Voices of St. John's MCC, Deanna Jaworski, Marsha Stevens, Balm Ministries, Jeanie Cunningham, Christopher Hoffman, D.J. Lee, Kadie O, Sherry Stanton, Randy Meadows, Sherry Roby, Joe Warner, Obed, Danny Riddle, Marcus Young, Orbit, Judy Cassidy, Kevin Jacobson, Angel Blacker, and Carolyn Marshall for contributing to the *Walk by Faith* CDs, Vols. I and II, and for the benefit concerts.

Open Door Community Church, for sending us off, for prayer and financial support and always keeping your door open, even when it looked like it was about to close!

Deb Tanner, for being the advance person in 2002, for your prayer support, and for arranging housing, transportation and speaking engagements for the completion of the walk.

Jerry Wright, for all of the miles you walked with me and for all of the help with lodging, meals, and financial support, most of all, for your prayers!

Laurie and Mike Stewart, for putting up with my absence, embracing me when I was home, and for always working it out for me to have plenty of time with my beautiful granddaughter when I was home on breaks.

Bronwyn Stewart, for all the many phone chats and for all of the time we spent together when I was home. You are the best granddaughter ever!

Dad, for being there when I started the walk and for being there when I completed it.

Terry Vignos, for taking such good care of the girls while Wendi was on this mission.

Courtney Vignos, for being so brave when your mom was called to this walk, for all of your sacrifices, and for doing a great job of handling things back on the home front.

Molly Vignos, for drawing on God for your strength in your mom's absence and the beautiful job on the book cover.

Jenny, Shawn, Lucy, and Riley Shaw, for providing a home and family for me, on my return home, and Jenny for all of your hours of editing this book.

Miller family, for extending your love to me and Bronwyn.

Merrithew family and Faith in Christ Ministries, for sponsoring Walker T. since the winter of 2005.

Walt and Patti Wynbelt, for keeping us on the road, for all of the care packages, for monthly contributions and other financial blessings, but most of all, for being a wonderful sister and brother to both Wendi and me and for being an aunt and uncle to Walker T.

Casa de Christo, for monthly support and for all of the times I have been given an opportunity to share my testimony with the congregation.

Cecelia Benefield, for your constant prayers and financial support—you provided for a good portion of our needs for the last three years of the walk.

Jerry Cole, for all of the financial support, many phone calls, and for providing a haven of rest when I was home.

K. St. Christopher and J. Webster, for monthly financial support, most of all, for providing a room and office over the past six years.

R.J. Miller, for Cavalier #1 and such a good deal on Cavalier #2, for financial blessings, gas cards, and for always being there when I need a friend.

Bo Masters and Arnitha McAfee, for providing me with a flight home when my daughter had surgery in 2005, for providing the money to purchase Cavalier #2, and for being our friends.

377

MaryJim Wages, for providing me with a flight home when my daughter experienced her hearing loss.

DeAnna Bennett, for your sizable contribution, for eye glasses, car repairs, meals, clothes, Bibles, hotel rooms, fun, laughter, and everything else you did for us.

DeAnn Stout and Carol Slavek, for your generous support and all of your prayers.

All of the friends, family members, acquaintances, churches, and businesses who helped us along the way—too many to mention—thank you for your friendship, your prayers, and your support. All of you were a *big* part in our completing the Walk.

Pastor Todd and Cornerstone Church for the financial and prayer support and for the great send off in 2007.

DownEast Christian Church for the ongoing prayer support and financial blessings.

Jeff and Jean Nordine, for the great newspaper articles, your surprise visits, help with the final proofing, and for the constant encouragement and support.

Dr. Robert Gsellman, for providing me with such good medical care and extending professional courtesy to Wendi for the past eight years.

Dr. David Sterna, for providing Wendi with eye exams and contacts lenses while she was serving as my pilot car driver for the past several years.

Jimmy Barfield and Myrtle Beach Brace and Limb, for providing two of the legs I used to walk this walk.

Alexander L. Lyons, Jimmy Barfield, and Lyons Inc. Prosthetics and Orthotics for providing a liner, foot, and pin system.

Promis Prosthetic and Orthotic Services, for providing three of my legs, eight liners, and several wool socks. I thank you and God for the miraculous fittings.

InMOTION Magazine, and Brandi Erisman, for the great story in the July-August 2003—Volume 13, Issue 4 of *InMOTION* Magazine.

Achilles Prosthetics and Orthotics, for providing a pin system while I was walking the California coast.

Limbs of Love, Houston, Texas, for the liner and installation of a foot and for arranging for the news coverage.

Freedom Innovation in Irvine, California, for providing three prosthetic feet. I literally walked this walk in your feet!

Ohio Willowood, for providing such quick service when I needed information about my pin system and for delivering parts to Achilles Prosthetics!

Fox news, Fox Family and Friends, CBS, NBC, ABC, and all of the local TV channels and the hundreds of newspapers for the news coverage throughout the country!

All of the inns, motels, hotels, campgrounds, resorts, and retreats for providing lodging!

All of the restaurants and grocery stores that provided food for us!

Churches, schools, and organizations, for allowing me to speak and for supporting this walk!

To all who took part in making the 10,467 crosses and tags!

To all of the mechanics, and garages that provided auto care for the pilot cars!

To the beauticians who provided haircuts, hair coloring, manicures, and pedicures!

To all who provided veterinary care, food, and other necessities for Walker T.!

To all who provided T-shirts, magnets, recreation, and other gifts!

Thank you, Dorothy Doyle (Sugadotti) and the Yahweh Sisterhood, Suzanne Doyle, Cecelia Benefield, and Wendi Miller for a mountain-top experience that I will never forget!

All who were there when I completed the walk!

Norwegian Cruise Lines, for the upgrade and for the VIP treatment on the *Norwegian Pearl*, sailing January 2nd, 2011.

Norman Boyd, for making this printing possible.

Naomi Harvey, Vicky Dunn, Mary MacLucas, Deb Tanner, Debbie Kraft, Cherie Brumfield, Sandy Stevenson, Moe Mezori, Dolores Burley for celebrating with us on the *Norwegian Pearl*.

Most of all, I want to thank:

God my Father, for choosing me to walk this walk and for carrying me every step of the way;

Jesus Christ my Lord, for paying the price on the cross for the redemption of my sin;

Holy Spirit for being my guide and my comforter.

In memory of people near and dear to us, who passed away while we were on this journey:

My mother, Betty Cruise

My grandmother, Charlotte (Sharlie) Cruise

My aunt, Joanne Popa

My aunt, Marie Smith

Wendi's grandfather, C.I. Miller

Wendi's grandmother, Jean Miller

Wendi's grandmother, Ruth Hall

Wendi's aunt, Gail Davis

Wendi's great aunt, Bonnie Miller

Wendi's cousin, Pam Caplea

Wendi's cousin, Laura Hoagland

Our dear friends:

Torie Merrithew

Dee Steffani

Betty Pettigrew

and who could forget Poot

Crosses were planted in memory of our loved ones as we walked this prayer walk around the nation,

I WROTE THIS POEM to my grandmother many years ago. I ran across it as I was writing this book. Sharlie has been deceased for over five years now and I am still growing from her love. When I read the poem now, I see that God used my grandmother as His vessel to carry me through trying times. Because of His love, her love remains with me in a different Light.

SHARLIE

Grandmother I hope you know and see
All that you have been to me.

Of all the people I have known,
It was through your love I have grown.

You loved me from the very start
At my birth you took me in your heart

CROSS WALK

And as I began to learn and grow
Your love for me would softly glow

I so young and you so wise
I gazed at you through crying eyes.

I always knew with you, I could be me
Yet with others I dare not be

For much was asked of one so small
A little one, who tried to be all to all

To be all that was expected of me
Being others but seldom me

You wiped away my many tears
Never knowing all my untold fears

Yet you knew there were many, you saw the sign
So you channeled your love from your soul to mine

When you would come to visit me at my home
You left with me a message I would never be alone

I have captured your love way deep in my soul
And to follow your path remains my goal

I knew your love so dear and sweet
And through your love, I felt complete

Complete enough to carry my fears
Until I could face them in future years

With others I felt ugly and not too smart
I had tattered clothes and a broken heart

What Next?

Yet with you, Grandmother, I can say
You saw me perfect in every way

I dread to think where I would be now
If you had not been there to show me how

You taught me to not say "never"
For you knew the path I was on was not forever

In my life you've been a guiding light
And in all ways, your way seemed so right

Take care of self is what you would display
And it does not matter what others will say

I followed you the best I could
Through that confusing mixed-up childhood

I blocked out so much of those childhood pains
Your words of wisdom is what remains

Throughout my life you've been like a dove
Guiding me with unconditional love

Accepting who I am as me
And encouraging me to be all I can be

You taught me to do my best
And face life's challenges as a might quest

For you knew from each experience I would grow
And if I would stay strong it would surely show

I've learned real well from what you have shown
And I cherish your heritage as my own

CROSS WALK

In your life I feel as though I belong
Without your love I would have been so alone

I know my Creator answers prayer
When I prayed for love you were there

To nurture and to give me hope
And with your love I was able to cope

There is something I know deep within
One day you will not be there to raise my chin

It hurts real deep and breaks my heart
To know one day we must part

If you arrive first at God's golden gates of love
Please shine down from up above

So I will know and feel
that what we shared remains here still

Bodies part yet love remains firm
To guide through all we have learned

In spirit we will always be one
Thanks to our Creator and His universal Son

Forever, Grandmother, I love you!